Underwood's Interference Practice

UNDERWOOD'S
Interference Practice

BY
HOMER C. UNDERWOOD
DETROIT, MICH.

Published by
PATENT LAW PUBLISHING COMPANY
408 Buhl Block
DETROIT, MICH.

T
Un 265i
1920

PREFACE.

In the preparation of this work I have sought to confine the text to matters which pertain particularly to Interferences and to cover all the important points which have been the subject of controversy in the past twenty years and which have not been rendered entirely obsolete by changes in the Rules of Practice in that period Many old cases are considered, but they are such as are believed might have a bearing upon the construction of present rules I have considered that brevity in the statements of points of law would be more useful than extended argument It is assumed that those who use the book are familiar with the subject in general and all they need in the conduct of a case is a reminder of the points which may be made and a citation of authorities relating thereto Without such reminder one may overlook important points of evidence which might be presented A busy lawyer can not stop to read a volume on evidence before, or at the time of taking testimony, hence evidence is herein treated in a limited sense, relating to those matters which are most likely to arise in taking testimony in an Interference.

I send this book forth, hoping that it may aid in a more accurate presentation of causes and in developing a more uniform practice

Your obedient servant,
HOMER C UNDERWOOD

Detroit, Michigan

TABLE OF CASES.

XIX

INTERFERENCES.

1. Origin of Interferences. An interference is a statutory proceeding, arising solely under the authority of Sec 4904, and means a dispute on the question of priority of invention It is a contest between rival applicants for a patent, or a contest between one or more applicants for a patent, and the owner of one or more outstanding letters patent *Western Electric Mfg Co. v. Chicago Electric Co.*, 14 Fed 691

2 Interference Statute. Sec. 4904, R S. U. S "Whenever an application is made for a patent which, in the opinion of the Commissioner, would interfere with any pending application, or with any unexpired patent. he shall give notice thereof to the applicants or applicant and patentee, as the case may be, and shall direct the Primary Examiner to proceed to determine the question of priority of invention. And the Commissioner may issue a patent to the party who is adjudged the prior inventor. unless the adverse party appeals from the decision of the Primary Examiner, or the Board of Examiners-in-Chief, as the case may be, within such time, not less than twenty days, as the Commissioner shall prescribe "

3. The Declaration of Interference. A brief but general summary of the Patent Office proceedings in Interference cases will be found in *Westinghouse v Hein*, 159 Fed. 936-939, in which Judge Sanborn said "When an application for a patent is filed, an officer known as a Primary Examiner decides whether the application on its face shows patentable invention, Rules 95. 96 No appeal lies from his decision Rule 124 Patentability being affirmed, it may occur that the application dis-

1

closes the same invention as another application on file or as a patent already issued If so, interference exists, and the patent officers are then required, according to the practice and rules of the office, to set on foot an interference proceeding, in order to determine which of the hostile claimants first discovered the invention. This proceeding is carried on before the Examiner of Interferences, and is a proceeding inter partes and results either in a decision awarding priority to one, and denying it to the other, or for some particular reason denying priority to either

"This question of priority of invention, meaning priority in time, has become the important and almost sole question for consideration in an interference proceeding. Other questions may arise in the Patent Office, such as whether one or both parties has the right to make the claim, whether he has really disclosed in his drawings the invention claimed, whether he is the real inventor, whether he is guilty of laches or estopped to claim priority, whether his devise is operative, whether both claim the same invention so as to actually show interference. By the course of practice in the Patent Office, however, an interference proceeding is confined to the question of priority in time, other questions being raised by motion before the Primary Examiner The Examiner of Interferences may also call the attention of the Commissioner to facts showing that no interference exists, or that the declaration of interference was irregular, and the Commissioner may then suspend the interference proceedings and remand the case to the Primary Examiner for consideration of the question so raised Rule 126 It may also appear in the interference proceedings that while both applications disclose patentability and interference, and one is clearly prior in time, yet that neither party is entitled to a judgment of priority against the other, because it would operate inequitably against the other. This happened in *Bechman v. Wood,*

2

15 App D C. 484, where Wood first discovered a broad invention, but made only a narrow claim, and the junior applicant, Bechman, claimed a specific device in the same field, and also claimed the broad invention. Wood was adjudged to be not entitled to the broad claim because this would defeat Bechman's special apparatus, and Bechman was not entitled to it because he was not the first inventor, but in the ordinary case an award of priority follows as a matter of course

"While the question whether the interference was properly declared, or any interference in facts exists, can not be directly raised in the interference proceeding, it may by a motion to dissolve the interference It is the practice to present to the Examiner of Interferences a motion to transmit the motion to dissolve to the Primary Examiner, together with the motion to dissolve. If the latter motion is in proper form he transmits it to the Primary Examiner, and he may at the same time proceed with the interference, Rule 123 When the Primary Examiner has decided the motion, an appeal may be taken to the Commissioner but no further appeal is permitted, the motion being regarded as an interlocutory proceeding *U S ex rel Lowry v Allen*, 203 U S 476, 27 Sup Ct 141, 51 L Ed 281. If the motion to dissolve is denied, the Examiner of Interferences, in the usual case, renders judgment awarding priority of invention to one of the contestants and also fixes the limit of appeal from such judgment If no appeal is taken letters patent are issued to the successful party, and the Primary Examiner notifies the other party that his claims stand finally rejected Sec 4904, Rev St U S. Comp St 1901, p 3389. Rule 132 If the defeated party desires to appeal he may do so within the time limited The appeal first goes to the Examiners-in-Chief (Sec 4909, U. S. Comp St 1901, p 3390), then to the Commissioner in person (Sec 4910, U S Comp St 1901, p 3391), and from his decision to the Court of Appeals of

3

the District of Columbia (Act Feb. 9, 1893, c. 74, 27 Stat. 476, Sec. 9, U. S. Comp. Statutes, 1901, p. 3391)."

(Note :— Since the above decision the rules of practice have been amended as to jurisdiction of officers who pass upon motions to dissolve.)

4. Declaration of Interference Is Within the Discretion of the Commissioner. Sec. 4904 commits to the judgment of the Commissioner the effect of an application upon a pending one as to whether it interferes with such pending application; something more, therefore than the effect of two applications, something more than the mere assertion of a claim. The assertion must be, in the opinion of the Commissioner, an interference with another, and it is this other that is first in regard, not to be questioned except at the instance of the Commissioner by an exercise of judgment upon the circumstances. *Ewing, Commissioner v. U. S. ex rel. Fowler Car Co.*, 238 O. G. 983, 244 U. S. 1.

5. Earlier Application Excluded in Case of Doubt. When there is doubt as to whether the earlier application discloses the invention in a later continuous application involved in interference, the earlier application will be excluded. *Munro v. Alexander*, 106 O. G. 1000.

Mechanical Equivalent. An interference should be declared between a patent and an application where a claim of the application is the same as the claim of the patent with the exception of one element which is a mechanical equivalent of a like element of the patented claim. *Read v. Scott*, 14 Gour. 2-4.

6. What Should Be Made Counts—Only Claims Patentably Different. Where the claims are not patentably distinct, an issue consisting of a single count will be sufficient to determine the question of priority, and the parties should be notified that if priority of invention is awarded against them their claims which do not contain patentable subject matter over the issue, will be rejected. *Votey v. Wuest v. Doman*, 111 O. G. 1627.

4

7. No Interference When. A party is not entitled to an interference if his claim when broadly construed is unpatentable, since a claim must be patentable before it can be put into interference In *ex parte Riddle,* 145 O. G 1021, Riddle asked to be put into interference with certain claims of patentees Dement and Hull and insisted that the claims were patentable because patent had been granted thereon, but it was held that when read upon the Riddle structure it could not be allowed because he would have no right to make the claim and in this respect the case was distinguished from that of *In re Orcutt,* 141 O G 567

No interference will be declared when it is apparent from the outset that no patent can issue on an application, since a party is not entitled to an interference except as to an allowable application *Crane,* 106 O. G. 999 In an early (1898) and important decision it was held that an interference should not be declared where one of the applications contained no allowed claims *Hammond v Hart,* 83 O. G 743

No Interference on Rejected Claims. No interference will be declared on claims which have been rejected. *Holland,* 99 O G 2548, 1902 C D 199, *Duker,* 115 O. G 803, *In re Neill,* 82 O G 749, 11 App. D C 582.

8. Prior Application—Reference to in Declaration. If the application is clearly a division of, or a continuation of an earlier application, the Primary Examiner should so state. If there is doubt upon this question, no reference should be made to an earlier application, the matter being left for determination upon motion to shift the burden of proof (See Burden of Proof) *Jackson v. Patten,* 150 O G 265, *Roulet & Nicholson v Adams,* 114 O G 1827

9. Preliminaries to Declaration of Interference. Before a declaration of interference all preliminaries must be settled by the Primary Examiner, and the issue must be clearly defined, the invention which is to form the subject of the controversy must be decided to be patentable, and the claims of the respective parties must be put in such condition that they will not require alteration after the interference shall have been finally decided, unless the testimony adduced upon the trial shall necessitate or justify such change. Rule 95.

10. One of the Applications Should Be Ready for Allowance. Before an interference between two pending applications is declared, one of the pending applications should be placed in condition for allowance. *Spoon*, 97 O. G. 176, 1901, C. D. 188.

11. Claims Not Forming a Part of the Controversy Need Not Be Considered. When one of the interfering applications is in condition for allowance, if there be any claims in the other application which are not to form part of the controversy, or never could form part of a controversy, it is not necessary that they should be considered before declaring the interference. *Spoon*, 97 O. G. 176, 1901 C. D. 188.

12. Effect of Putting a Claim in Interference. Putting a claim in interference is an allowance of the claim. *Luger v. Browning*, 100 O. G. 231, 1902 C. D. 230; *Reece v. Fenwick*, 14 Gour. 3-7. In the foregoing cases there had been no allowance of the claims of one of the parties prior to the declaration of interference. If any question is raised on such state of the record it should be by motion to dissolve upon the ground of irregularity in declaring the interference. In an earlier case (1898) of *Hammond v. Hart*, 83 O. G. 743, it was held that where one of the applications contained no allowed claims the interference should not have been declared.

10. Claim Suggested by the Examiner. Rule 96. The Examiner has the right and it is his duty under Rule 96 to suggest claims. The purpose of the practice of suggesting claims is not for the purpose of avoiding interferences between applications because of some differences in the form of claims, but merely by suggestion to

6

bring the parties together upon an issue which shall be as nearly as possible the same as the claim of the parties so as to reduce to the minimum the chances for motions and controversies during the progress of the interference based upon differences between the claims. *Thompson*, 98 O. G. 227, 1902 C. D. 6, *Myers v Brown*, 112 O. G. 2093.

Rule 96 provides the conditions under which the Examiner may suggest claims to applicants and when claims are suggested thereunder the applicant should make the claims in the precise words suggested if they are applicable to his structure, but at all events should vary therefrom as slightly as possible. *Braucht v. Murdock*, 13 Gour 66. If the applicant fails to make the claims suggested within the time specified, such failure or refusal shall be taken, without further action, as a disclaimer of the invention covered by the claim. (Rule 96) Where one party claims only a part of a combination claimed by another, such combination claim should not be suggested *Mercer*, 193 O. G. 1017 (1913); *Handenschild v Huych*, 164 O. G. 515 (1911). The Examiner may suggest the claims of a patent and unless such claims are made by the applicant, his claims may be rejected and the correctness of the ruling may then be questioned on appeal. *Card v Card*, 112 O. G. 499 (1904) Avoiding the languages of patented claims to avoid an interference will not be permitted where the inventions are the same. *Card v Card, supra* The Examiner should not suggest claims to other applicants who disclose the process but claim only the apparatus for carrying out the process *Werener*, 139 O. G. 197 (1909) A party may not argue the patentability of suggested claims before the interference is declared *Sutton v Steele*, 107 O. G. 541 A party to whom claims are suggested can either make them, refuse to make them, or make them under protest, after which he may make a motion to dissolve, but if he refuses to make them the Commissioner will not review the ques-

7

tion under his supervisory authority. *Samboni*, 20 Gour. 22-14; *Eichelberger & Hibner v. Dillon*, 129 O. G. 3161. Where an applicant is entitled to an interference with a party who is already involved in a different interference on different subject matter, his application should not be held until final termination of the first interference, but the Examiner should request jurisdiction of the application involved in the first interference for the purpose of declaring a new interference. *Brakey*, 156 O. G. 797 (1910); *Moore v. Hewitt v. Potter*, 115 O. G. 509 (1905). Since under Rule 96 the Examiner may fix the time within which a party shall make suggested claims, if the applicant is unable to make them within the time specified, he may, upon proper showing, have the time extended. *Hellmund*, 141 O. G. 565 (1909).

PARTIES TO INTERFERENCES.

14. Arrangement of Parties. It is the duty of the Examiner under Rule 97 to arrange the parties to an interference in the inverse chronological order in which they filed the applications directly involved in the interference. *Roulet & Nicholson v. Adams*, 114 O. G. 1827 (1905); *Jackson v. Patten*, 150 O. G. 265 (1910); *Steel & Steel v. Meyers*, 205 O. G. 1021 (1914).

Who Are Proper Parties. Only those who can make claim to all the counts should be made parties, and if there is another party who can make some of the counts, but not all of them, a new interference should be declared between his application or patent and the other applications containing like claims. *Dow v. Benson*, 107 O. G. 1378 (1903). An assignee may prosecute an interference where the assignor refuses to prosecute the same. Such right of an assignee may be determined upon motion. *Adams*, 119 O. G. 650 (1905); *Lottridge v. Eustice*, 121 O. G. 689 (1906). An exclusive licensee will not be permitted to intervene so long as the licensor is in good faith prosecuting the same. *The National Railways*

8

Materials Co, 129 O G 481 (1907) Judgment may be rendered against such parties as fail to overcome, in their preliminary statements, the prima facie case made by the party first filing *Swaren v Sandage, etc*, 17 Gour. 34-1 (Apr, 1905).

15. **New Parties** may be added to an interference, but that does not extend the time of the original parties for making a motion to dissolve to 30 days from the date such new party is added *Townsend v Ehret etc*, 137 O G. 1484 (1908) It is too late to add new parties after decision on priority has been rendered by the Examiners in Chief and the Commissioner, *Corey & Baker v Trout*, 99 O. G 2547; 1902 C. D 195 One who does not claim all the counts can not be added as a new party, but where it appears that an applicant can make part of the counts the Examiner should request jurisdiction for the purpose of declaring a new interference with the parties who make the same counts. *Dow v. Benson*, 107 O G. 1378 (1903) Where it is found on motion to dissolve that one of the parties has no right to make the claims, the interference should be dissolved as to him and continued as to the other parties *Marwell v Byron v Henry*, 98 O G 1968, 1902 C. D 67.

16 **A Sole Applicant May Be Placed in Interference With Himself and Another as Joint Applicants.** *Gilbert v Gilbert & Lindley*, 160 O G. 775 (1910). A sole applicant can not claim the benefit of an earlier application filed by himself and another. *Haskell v Miner v Ball*, 109 O G 2710 A joint application can not be changed to a sole application by motion Sole inventors and joint inventors are distinct entities *Gassau & Marklein v. Odell*, 190 O. G. 1028 (1913)

17 **Notice to Parties.** Rule 153 provides that in contested cases, reasonable notice of all motions and copies of motion papers and affidavits must be served, as provided in Rule 154 Proof of service must be made before a motion will be entertained by the office

9

Motions will not be heard in the absence of either party, except upon default after due notice.

What amounts to reasonable or due notice has been defined by the decision which will be hereinafter set forth

Rule 154 provides for the giving of due notice to the opposing party of the taking of testimony, as to the time when and the place where testimony will be taken, of the cause or matter in which they will be used, the names and residences of the witnesses to be examined, that the notice shall be such as to give the opposing party or his attorney full opportunity to be present and cross-examine the witnesses If witnesses are examined who are not named in the notice and the opposing party fails to object to the examination of such witnesses, or cross-examine them, he waives his right to object to such examination for want of notice. The notice shall be such as to give the party reasonable opportunity to travel to the place where the testimony is to be taken, or to the place where the motion is to be heard.

18. **Notice of Taking Testimony**, which contains the names and addresses of certain witnesses and contains the added statement "and perhaps others," is not good except as to the witnesses named *Potter v Ochs*, 95 O G. 1049, 1901 C D 39; *Tripp v Wolf v Jones*, 108 O G 563. Notice by telegram on Saturday to take testimony on Tuesday, which did not give the names and addresses of witnesses, but followed on Monday with a formal notice of the taking of testimony of R, "and perhaps others," was not sufficient, and testimony was struck out *Rice v Frick*, 160 O G 1040 (1910) Notice may be waived by conduct of attorney who might otherwise successfully urge objections to the notice *Munster v Ashworth*, 128 O G 2085 (1906). Objection to the insufficiency of notice should be urged at the earliest opportunity, or it will be deemed to have been waived.

10

Naulty v Cutler, 126 O G. 389 (1906). In computing time a notice served on Saturday will be deemed to have been served on Monday at the same hour, for counsel can not be compelled to travel on Sunday, even if no objection to Sunday travel is raised *Goodfellow v Jolly*, 111 O. G 1940 Time to communicate with client should be given counsel, in determining whether reasonable time is given *Goodfellow v Jolly*, 111 O G 1940 Notice served in Chicago to take testimony in Erie, Pa., less than two days thereafter, is not reasonable notice *Tripp v. Wolf v. Jones*. 108 O. G 563.

19. Service of Notice. The notice of taking testimony or any motion, must be served upon the attorney of record, if there be one, or, if there be no attorney of record, upon the adverse party. A stipulation in writing, signed by the attorneys and filed in the cause, dispenses with the necessity of notice

20. How Served. There are five ways of serving notices 1, by delivering a copy of the notice to the adverse party or his attorney; 2, by leaving a copy at his usual place of business and with some one in his employment, 3, when he has no usual place of business, then by leaving a copy at his residence; 4, by registered mail, and 5, by express

21. Notice of Motions, Petitions, Etc. Notice to an attorney of a party is notice to him whether he has actual notice or not *White v Hewitt & Nolen*, 115 O G 1847 (1905). A motion will not be entertained when no notice was served on opposing party. *Hansen,* 117 O G. 2632 (1905). Like notice must also be given where a motion is renewed *Dyson v Land, etc ,* 133 O. G. 1679 (1908). Notice of petition must be given. *Robin v Muller & Bonnett,* 107 O G 2527 (1903) Where a party is represented by more than one attorney of record, a notice signed by one of them is sufficient *Heyne, Hayward & McCarthy v DeVilbiss,* 125 O. G. 669 (1906) It is within the discretion of the Examiner of Interferences to dis-

11

pense with notice of a motion to extend time for filing preliminary statement *Keeler v Bailey v. Davis,* 14 Gour 82-1 (Dec, 1902), *Quick v McGee,* 107 O. G. 1376 Copies of affidavits must be served five days before the hearing unless they are reply affidavits, in which case they should be served before the hearing *Brown v Stroud,* 122 O G 2688 In all cases where service is required by the rules, proof of service must be made under Rule 154 *Allen, Commissioner,* 127 O. G 2398 (1907); *Lipe v Miller,* 105 O G. 1532 (1903).

22. Sufficiency of Notice. A notice delivered by private messenger on Saturday afternoon to the office of counsel, notwithstanding Saturday afternoon is a legal holiday in Washington, is good, where counsel is given ample time to prepare for the hearing, and it appearing also that counsel actually received the notice on Monday afternoon *Goodfellow v Jolly,* 115 O. G 1064. Where the attorneys for both parties resided in the same city and notice to take testimony was served at 10 a m to take testimony at 2 p m of the same day, it appearing that the attorneys for both parties appeared, it was held that the testimony should not be stricken out, notwithstanding the objection in the record of insufficient notice and a refusal to cross-examine *Roberts v. Webster,* 115 O. G. 2135 (1905). A notice given in New York City on June 22, that testimony would be taken in Troy, N. Y, on June 24, was held insufficient *Randerson v Hanna & Hanna,* 173 O G 586 (1911). An affidavit opposing a motion to dissolve, served four days before the hearing was held insufficient notice *Thieme v Bowen,* 21 Gour 70-13 (Aug, 1909).

ISSUES.

23 The Issues. The issues in an interference are the counts—the claim or claims

The Issue Must Remain Fixed. It is necessary to orderly procedure that the issues remain fixed throughout the

interference proceeding To permit a party to change
the issue by adding new matter, would lead to the great-
est confusion. *Brill & Adams v. Uebelocher,* 99 O G.
2966, 1902 C D 220

24 Construction of Issue—Terms in Claims Should Be
Given Their Ordinary Meaning. The reasonable presumption is that an inventor intends to protect his invention
broadly, and the scope of the claims should not be restricted beyond the fair and ordinary meaning of the
words, except for the purpose of saving them from invalidity *Andrews v. Nilson,* 123 O G. 1667, *Eschinger v Drummond, etc,* 121 O G. 1348

25. Claims Broadly Construed. (See Exception, Sec.
35.)

While the applications are pending in the Patent Office, the claims will be construed as broadly as the ordinary meaning thereof will permit. *Junge v Harrington,*
131 O G 691, *Miel v Young,* 128 O. G 2532, 29 App
D C 481, *Barber v. Transue,* 19 Gour. 34-6; *Kirby v.
Clements,* 216 O G. 1319, 44 App D. C 12

Issue Construed as Broadly as Disclosures Warrant. A
limited construction should not be forced upon a broad
claim in order to free a party who had asserted such
claim upon the supposition that he was the first in the
field, from the exigencies of the situation into which he
was forced by the subsequent appearance of another
parthy who created the broad subject matter of invention of an earlier date *Viele v. Cummings,* 19 Gour 2-6,
Monte v. Dunkley, 245 O. G 278

26. Estoppel to Urge Limitations Upon Issue. A party
who first presents claims should not be later heard to
urge limitations upon the terms thereof which might
readily have been expressed therein, had it been intended that they should be so restricted *Junge v Harrington,* 131 O G. 691, *Paul v Hess,* 113 O. G 847, *Leonard v Horton,* 189 O G. 781, 40 App D C 22

13

27. Language of the Issue Should Not Be Given a Forced Meaning. Nor should it be given a meaning founded upon specific differences in the devices of the parties which are not set forth in the issue *Lemp v Randall & Bates,* 123 O G 349, *Phillips v Sensenich,* 132 O G 677 (1907)

28. Construction Where Applicant Copies Claims of a '
Patent. Where the claims of a patent are copied for the purpose of provoking an interference, the claims are construed in the light of the specifications of the patent. *Bourn v Hill,* 123 O. G. 1284, 27 App. D C 291; *Funk v Whitely,* 117 O. G. 280, 25 App. D C. 313, *Engel v Sinclair et al,* 152 O G 489, 34 App D. C. 212, *Curtis v de Ferranti, etc,* 171 O G. 215, *General Electric Co v Steinberger,* 214 Fed. 781, 206 O. G 1161.

29. Are Construed in the Light of the Application of the Party First Making Them *Sobey v Holschlaw,* 126 O G 3041, 28 App. D C 65; *Tracy v Leslie,* 14 App. D C 126, *Ruete v Elwell,* 15 App. D C. 21; *Neuberth v. Lizotte,* 141 O. G 1165, 32 App D C 329, *Western Electric Co v Martin,* 182 O. G 723, 39 App D C 147.

30. All Elements of the Claims Must Be Assumed to Be Material *Jones v Wolff,* 17 Gour 52-8, *Collom v Thurman,* 131 O. G 839, *Streat v Freckelton.* 87 O G 695, *Wilson & Forest v Ellis.* 211 O G 286, 42 App D C 552; *Bijur v Rushmore,* 246 O G 301, 46 App D C 395

31. Different Inventions of Different Parties Defined by the Same Claims. When the same language is used by different parties to define different inventions, it is clear that the language of the claims must be ambiguous or indefinite, and should be amended to clearly distinguish the inventions before issue of patents thereon *Alfree v. Sarver,* 122 O. G 2391; *Podelsak v McInnerney,* 120 O G. 2127, 26 App. D C 399

32. Construction in New Art. A limited construction will not be put upon terms of a claim where it appears

14

that the art is comparatively new and the terms used have not acquired a fixed and definite meaning therein *Lindmark v Hodgkinson*, 137 O. G. 228, 31 App D. C 612.

33 **Necessity of Considering Prior Art** Where the meaning of the claims of an interference are clear and they read upon both parties, it is not error to refuse to consider the effect of the prior art *Creveling v Jepson*, 256 O G 226, 47 App D C 597

34. **Vague and Indefinite Counts.** If the claims are so vague and indefinite as to be susceptible of various meanings, the interference should be dissolved, or the claims amended (Sec 31). *Briggs v Lillie, etc*, 116 O G. 871 (1904)

35. **Exception to Broad Interpretation.** Where there is a clear difference in the structures making the claims wholly without point when applied to one, the claims should be given a reasonable interpretation, consistent with the specification in which they originated to the end that the real inventor may prevail *Murphy v Cooper*, 228 O G. 1458, 45 App D C 307. They cannot be construed so as to ignore limitations which give them life *Gammeter v Lister*, 253 O G 259

Whether a Party Has the Right to Make the Claim—Construction. A claim should be given the broadest meaning consistent with its terms; but it cannot be enlarged beyond the plain import thereof as set forth in the specification on which it is based *Sinclair v Engel*, 147 O G 769, 1909, 152 O. G 489, 34 App D C 212

Different Parties Use Different Terms to Describe Same Structure. It is immaterial that the parties use different terms to describe the same structure *Pratt v De Ferranti, etc*, 148 O G 569

THE PRELIMINARY STATEMENT

36. **Filing of Preliminary Statement** After the issues of an interference have been fixed, the next step required

15

of a party is to file a preliminary statement. The office fixes the time within which the parties shall file their statements. What a preliminary statement shall contain is set forth in detail in Rule 110. The statement should be prepared with great care for it is very difficult to obtain leave to amend. The rule itself contains a caution to the practitioner that the statement should be carefully prepared and that the parties will be strictly held in their proofs to the dates set up therein. If a party prove any date earlier than alleged in his preliminary statement, such proof will be held to establish the date alleged and none other. The statement must be sealed up before filing (to be opened only by the Examiner of Interferences as provided in Rule 111), and the name of the party filing it, the title of the case, and the subject matter of the invention indicated on the envelope. The envelope should contain nothing but this statement.

Reasons for Requiring a Preliminary Statement. The Preliminary statement is made in ignorance of the dates claimed by the opposing party, and this is required for the purpose of avoiding the temptation to fraud. If a party could make his statement after knowing the date of invention claimed by his opponent, there would be strong temptation to fraud and perjury. *Davis v. Ocumpaugh v. Garrett*, 104 O. G. 2440 (1903); *Woodward v. Kennedy*, 104 O. G. 1393 (1903).

37. What Statement Must Contain. The allegations of the statement must conform to Rule 110, hence a statement that the inventor reduced the invention to practice by constructing the devise, without any allegation as to its successful use, is insufficient. Ordinarily an invention is not reduced to practice by merely constructing the devise. The fact, if it be a fact, that the invention is of such nature that no test of its practicability is required, will appear on final hearing, but a party may not be excused from alleging the use which he has made of his devise, merely because he believes he is not required

16

to prove use *Klocke v Buth,* 189 O G 779, 1913 C D
85; *Williams v Foyer & Kurz,* 142 O G 1114 (1909)
Loose and careless assertions tend to discredit the statement *Miles v Todd,* 112 O G 1479   The allegations
must be clear and complete *Shoemaker v Sintz,* 123
O G 2974 (1906)   Inconsistent allegations will not be
accepted. *Robinson v Copeland,* 112 O G 501, 24 App.
D C 68, *Guett v Trengoning,* 114 O. G 544

38. **Who May Sign Statement.** The inventor is of
course the proper party to sign the preliminary statement, but if he refuses to do so, an assignee may sign and
file the statement. *Reynolds v Bean,* 100 O G 1763,
1902 C D. 307, *Lottridge v. Eustice,* 121 O G 689
(1906)   Upon a proper showing an assignee of only a
part interest may file under Rule 131   *Lotterhand v
Cornwall,* 148 O. G. 1344 (1909).

39. **Motions for Extension of Time for Filing—How
Made** This motion should be made in accordance with
Rule 104   The motion should state the reasons for asking the extension   It must be verified, a copy served on
the other party or parties or their attorneys, together
with a notice of the time of hearing of such motion and a
proof of service of a copy of the motion and notice of
hearing should be filed with the motion. The granting
of the motion is within the discretion of the examiner.
Bailey v Davis, 102 O G 819 (1903); *Ohmer v Neth
& Tamplin,* 118 O G 1686 (1905), 123 O G 998 (1906),
27 App D. C 319   The motion should state a definite
time of extension asked for, or it will be refused *Keech
v. Birmingham,* 191 O G 2825

40. **Time for Filing Statement.** Where a party is unable to prepare his preliminary statement within the time
fixed, it is his duty to present the facts to the office and
ask for an extension of time, before he is in default, or
as soon as possible *Fowler v Boyce, etc,* 107 O G. 543
(1903).

Filed After Expiration of Time. A preliminary statement filed nine days after time expired, was accepted, reasonable diligence in procuring the necessary data having been shown *Charlton v Sheldon,* 111 O G 2492.

41. **Circumstances Warranting Extension.** It is not possible to state any rule as to what circumstances will warrant an extension for each case must rest upon its own facts A party must at all times act in good faith; he must not be careless or negligent; he must exercise reasonable diligence in preparing his statement and he must not seek to take advantage of his opponent. *Doble v. Eckart v. Henry,* 110 O. G. 604 Where it appears from the showing made that a party his assignee, or his counsel, or all of them, have been negligent or careless in the matter of preparing and filing his preliminary statement. an extension of time will be denied *Anderson v Peck,* 133 O. G 229, 1908 C. D 66. *Hartley v Mills.* 110 O G 604

42. **New Counts Added—New Statement Should Be Filed.** Where new counts are added, additional preliminary statements applying to the new counts should be filed. *Halwood v McCormick,* 16 Gour. 84-9.

43. **A Preliminary Statement May Be Taken as a Substitute for an Affidavit Under Rule 75.** *Forsyth v Richards,* 115 O G. 1327

44. **Allegations as to Reduction to Practice.** If merely making the device is alleged it must be stated whether such device was successfully used *Klocke v Burk,* 189 O G. 779 (1913).

Allegations as to Time. "In the early spring of 1900 ' means not earlier at the utmost than March 1, 1900 *Richardo v Meisno,* 114 O G 1831

45. **Inspection of by Opposing Parties.** The rules provide that where preliminary statements are filed and approved, the opposing parties will be permitted to see and obtain copies of their opponents applications and all of the papers in the case and to make motions for dissolu-

18

tion within 30 days (Rule 122) *Whipple v Sharp*, 98 O G 226, 1902 C. D. 5.

46. Amendment of Preliminary Statement. A preliminary statement may be amended under Rule 113, which provides " In case of material error arising through inadvertence or mistake, the statement may be corrected on motion (see Rule 155), upon a satisfactory showing that the correction is essential to the ends of justice The motion to correct the statement must be made, if possible, before the taking of any testimony, and as soon as practicable after the discovery of the error "

Permission to Amend is Within the Discretion of the Commissioner (or the Examiner of Interferences in the first instance). The rule requiring preliminary statements is a salutary one, its obvious object being to elicit from each of the parties certain vital information before any party is informed as to the statement of any other Owing to the purpose of the rule, the exercise of the Commissioner's discretion in passing upon motions to amend such statements will not be disturbed unless it is plain that there has been an abuse of that discretion. *Thomas v Weintraub*, 177 O G 772, 38 App D C 281, *Brown v Dyson & Land*, 188 O. G. 809, 39 App D C. 415, *Hammond v Busch*, 115 O G 804, 24 App. D C 469; *Cross v Phillips*, 14 App. D C 228, 237, 238, *Neth & Tamplin v Ohmer* 123 O G 998 (1906), 27 App 319

It is within the discretion of the Examiner of Interferences to permit amendment *Karpenstein v Hertzberg*, 127 O G 2393 (1907) , *Klenk v Kruse*, 177 O G 1300 (1912) , *Cramer & Hodge v Carrier*, 177 O G. 769 (1912).

47. What the Motion Must Show. It is not sufficient to show merely that the original statement is incorrect, but it must also be shown that the error did not arise from lack of proper care and diligence in preparing the statement *Becker v Currier*, 104 O G 2439 (1903)

Not merely a statement that the error was due to inadvertence and mistake, but a showing of facts which will enable the office to judge that there was inadvertence or mistake and that amendment is essential to the ends of justice. *Brown v. Keeney*, 105 O. G. 260 (1903); *Brown v. Cutler v. Keelen*, 104 O. G. 1896. Where it is alleged that the mistake is due to not understanding the meaning of "reduction to practice," it was held that it was the party's duty to discover the meaning of the allegations which he made, or ascertain the meaning from his attorney. *Dunn v. Holliday*, 119 O. G. 1261 (1905). Where a party alleges that he stated the facts in his original statement as he believed them to be and subsequently discovered his error, it must also appear that he could not have discovered the facts sooner by careful and diligent search. *Hamilton v. Carroll, etc.*, 110 O. G. 2510. Where it is alleged that an assignee accepted the statement of an associate of the inventor, it must also be shown that he made diligent effort to ascertain the facts from others who would likely know the facts. *Hamilton v. Carroll, etc.*, 110 O. G. 2510. Where it is alleged that a party when preparing to take testimony learned of an earlier disclosure than that alleged in his statement, there must also be shown a good reason for not discovering the fact sooner. *Fowler v. Boyce, etc.*, 108 O. G. 561. Where a party seeks to amend by showing the making of a model, he must show a satisfactory reason for omitting it from the original statement, and also a good excuse for delay in bringing the motion. *Fullager v. Jungren*, 114 O. G. 1550. Where forgetfulness is alleged it must be shown what effort was made to refresh the affiant's recollection originally or what steps were taken to fix definitely the dates alleged. *Friestedt v. Harold*, 116 O. G. 594 (1905). It must not only appear that there was error in the original statement, but that such error could not have been avoided by the exercise of reasonable care in the preparation of the statement. *Neth & Tamplin v.*

Ohmer, 116 O. G 874 (1905). A party must not only show diligence in discovering the facts, but also diligence in bringing the motion to amend. *Hock v Hopkins,* 21 Gour. 67 (Aug , 1909).

48. Insufficient Showing. A showing to support a motion to amend a preliminary statement must be such as to make it appear clearly that the error in the original statement could not have been avoided by the exercise of reasonable care in preparing it. A showing is insufficient to warrant amendment setting back the date of conception and reduction to practice, where the moving party files his motion after learning of his opponent's dates and he fails to set forth fully the reason he was unable to learn of and set forth the earlier dates in the first instance *Neth & Templin v Ohmer,* 116 O G 874 (1905) Since a party must show due diligence in presenting the motion, a showing that the delay was occasioned by negotiations for settlement is not a sufficient excuse for such delay *Bradley v Midgett,* 150 O. G 1042, 1910 C. D 24 A showing is insufficient when it is not made to appear that due diligence was exercised to ascertain the true facts alleged to have been erroneously stated, or omitted. *Hock v. Hopkins,* 21 Gour 67 (Aug , 1909) Showings are also insufficient in the following instances: Where one seeks to carry his dates back of his opponent's dates, but no good reason is shown why the correct dates were not discovered and alleged originally *Freistedt v Harold,* 116 O. G 594 (1905) Where the motion is upon the ground of newly discovered evidence from a proposed witness and it does not appear why the facts were not discovered before *McHarg v Schmidt & Mayland,* 105 O. G. 263 (1903) Where the ground was newly discovered evidence and it is alleged that a search for certain evidence in the past was not successful, but no satisfactory explanation is given why the search could not have been completed in time for the original statement instead of after learning his

21

opponent's dates. *Hoyt v. Sanders v. Hawthorne*, 119 O. G. 1260 (1905). Where it was alleged that a mistake was made by the inventor as to what was meant by "reduction to practice," but there was no explanation of what the mistake was, or how it arose, and the dates he desires to allege are not given. *Fowler v. Boyce, etc.*, 107 O. G. 544 (1903). Where it is not shown that the party informed his attorneys of all the facts, and it is not shown that he used the utmost diligence in trying to find the alleged new evidence before making his preliminary statement. *Seeberger v. Russell*, 107 O. G. 2528 (1903). Where a party discovers the error in his original statement and makes no effort for a long time to discover the true facts and does not use diligence in presenting his motion to amend. *Atkins v. Paul v. Johnson*, 94 O. G. 1785, 1901 C. D. 35. Where a party in making his preliminary statement was aware of the facts, but not of the force and effect thereof. *Thomas v. Trissell*, 1901 C. D. 200, 97 O. G. 1598; *Franklin & Norton v. Cooley*, 1901 C. D. 49, 95 O. G. 2063; where the facts alleged show that the error was one of law and not of fact. *Dalgren v. Crocker*, 98 O. G. 2586, 1902 C. D. 107; *Miller v. Wallace*, 131 O. G. 1689 (1903); *Bonsall v. Gilmore*, 16 Gour. 82-3; *Fowler v. Boyce. etc.*, 108 O. G. 561. Where a party makes up his preliminary statement from memory and after looking up the records discovers that he made a mistake. *King v. Hansen*, 101 O. G. 1129, 1902 C. D. 378. Where a party states that the utmost diligence was exercised in making the discovery of the new facts, without stating what means were employed and the reasons why the same means could not have been earlier employed. *Beamen v. Brooks*, 100 O. G. 685, 1902 C. D. 267. Where there is no reason shown why the question could not have been considered in the first amendment. *Borg v. Strauss*, 130 O. G. 2719 (1907). Where there is no showing that proper care was exercised in preparing the original statement and no expla-

22

nation as to how the original mistake occurred, or why it was not sooner discovered *Johnson v Erckson, etc.*, 131 O G 2419 (1907) A motion based on acts performed abroad will not be considered as any reason for amendment. *Emmet v Fullager*, 114 O G 1551. A failure to appreciate the scope of the claims is an error of law and is no ground for amendment. *Ryder v White*, 145 O G 763 (1909) Where on account of the press of business a party fails to investigate letters and records *Somerville v. Larmuth*, 190 O G 1028 (1913). Where the motion is based on statements made to a prior attorney of record and no affidavit from that attorney is filed. *Rechnitzer v Bernegan*, 193 O G 512 (1913) Where the error is alleged to have been due to a misunderstanding of a telephone conversation *Hamtish & Moriarity v Congdon v Kelsea*, 106 O. G. 542 (1903). Where the showing indicates carelessness and negligence in preparing the original statement *Basch v Hammond*, 15 Gour. 34-4 (May, 1903) Where the error occurred by reason of the attorney being engaged in other pressing work. *Jones v Linn*, 110 O. G. 1430.

49. Amendments Have Been Permitted. Amendments have been permitted under the following circumstances:

Where the notice of declaration was not clear. *Hoeker v Farr*, 193 O G 220 (1913). Where there was doubt as to a certain part of a machine involved, and no testimony had been taken. *Carroll v Stahlberg*, 111 O G. 1937 Where the affidavit of the inventor was corroborated by another and it was shown that due care and diligence was exercised in the preparation of the original statement, and that a bona fide mistake was made *Butterworth v Boral, etc*, 13 Gour 2-1 (Jan, 1901) Where a party acted with diligence in discovering the mistake and moved to amend before any testimony had been taken, and was diligent in preparing the original statement, and that the amendment would not injure the other party. *Silver v Eustis*, 14 Gour. 4-8 (Jan, 1902).

23

Where there was a bona fide mistake due merely to a clerical error, and there had been no unreasonable delay. *Hamilton v. Ide v. Lowenthal.* 14 Gour. 4-9 (Feb., 1902). Where there was a bona fide misapprehension as to the sense in which the word "model" was used. *Day v. Adt v. Hardy,* 125 O. G. 2765 (1906). Where the failure to recall the early disclosure was due to illness. *Paul v. Chapin,* 187 O. G. 831. Where the grounds of amendment were based on records in the Patent Office. *Cramer & Hodge v. Carrier,* 177 O. G. 769 (1912). Where there was no attempt made to change the dates and it was shown that it would not injure the opposing party. *Williams v. Liberman,* 100 O. G. 1331, 1902 C. D. 295. Where a party showed prior diligence in making his original statement and also made his motion to amend before any testimony had been taken and there would be no additional burden or expense thrown upon the opposing party. *McDermott v. Hildreth,* 98 O. G. 1282, 1902 C. D. 43. Where no testimony had been taken and the amendment would not carry the date of reduction to practice back of his opponent's, and a reasonable excuse is presented for delay in presenting the amendment. *Gules v. Berrigan,* 100 O. G. 232, 1902 C. D. 232. Where the ground was an accidental discovery of a publication referring to the invention, and this publication was not discovered when the original statement was filed, although a careful search had been made. *Davis v. Ocumpaugh v. Garrett,* 104 O. G. 2440 (1903).

The Examiner of Interferences May Require Amendment. *Allyn & Turner v. Ames,* 21 Gour. 66-6 (Sept., 1909).

50. Amendment After Taking Testimony. After testimony has been taken, an amendment to set back dates set forth in preliminary statement is open to suspicion and will be received only upon a clear showing of mistake, and the moving party must be free from negligence, and must show the utmost diligence in seeking to correct the

24

mistake *McDermott v Hildreth*, 98 O G. 1282, 1902 C.
D 43, *Pope v Mims v McLean*, 104 O G. 2147 (1903);
Henderson v Noakes, 1892 C D 114, 59 O G 1431,
Bliss v. Cleverling, 112 O G 499 Changing the date of
reduction to practice will not be permitted where there is
no showing of the utmost diligence in preparing the
original statement *Lockwood v. Schmidt*, 100 O G 453,
1902 C D 253, *Parker v Lewis*, 110 O. G. 305. A claim
that the party making the statement did not understand
the terms used, is not sufficient *Parker v Lewis*, 110 O
G 305 That a party did not read all of the counts is
no excuse *Smith v Ingram*, 131 O G 2420 (1907) A
showing that a party made an investigation as to certain
facts before making his original statement, but which
failed to show that he exhausted every reasonable means
of obtaining the desired information, is not sufficient to
warrant amendment *Floyd v Rohlfing*, 133 O. G 992
(1908) A motion based on testimony taken in a case
must point out the particular parts of the testimony
upon which he relies to sustain his motion. *Floyd v
Rohlfing*, 133 O G 992. Where the opposing party had
not completed the taking of his testimony and the motion was based upon an accidental discovery of an exhibit which was dated at an earlier date than that set
forth in the preliminary statement, and other affidavits
were filed by parties who stated that they saw the exhibit
on the date alleged and it further appearing that the
moving party had made diligent search for all of his
drawings previous to making his original statement,
amendment was permitted *Brenning v. Ridgely*, 19 Gour
65-2 (Aug 5, 1907). A party may not give notice of
intention to amend and then delay in presenting his motion until his opponent has completed taking his testimony *Green v Farley*, 132 O. G 235 (1907) Where
a party discovers a mistake in his preliminary statement,
he must act promptly to correct it, and if there is any
delay, he must show a satisfactory excuse for the delay

25

Kent v. Wilson, etc, 137 O. G. 1943; *Anderson v. Nilson*, 105 O G 2059 (1903) A notice of intention to move to amend, given during the taking of testimony, must be exact and explicit as to what amendment is to be made. *Kent v Wilson, etc*, 137 O. G. 1943 Where a party doubted the accuracy of his original statement at the time he made it, but made no thorough search for the true facts, amendment was denied *Whitall v. Gillespie v Blaw*, 171 O G 744 (1911). The fact that a party did not fully appreciate the effect certain evidence would have upon the issue, but knew of the existence of the evidence at the time he made his original statement, would not entitle him to amend *Thomas v Trissel*, 97 O. G 1598, 1901 C D. 200 Where a party discovers a mistake in his preliminary statement and thereafter permits his opponent to take and file his testimony without giving notice to amend, the motion will be denied. *Mills v. Torrence*, 98 O G 416, 1902 C. D 17. In passing upon a motion to amend the Examiner of Interferences will not try the question of whether the allegations in the motion are true or false, before granting or denying the motion. *Mills v Torrence*, 98 O. G. 416. To warrant amendment after the testimony has been taken, the ground being newly discovered evidence, it must clearly appear that the evidence could not have been discovered at the time of the filing of the original statement *Fordyce v Tuisey*, 102 O. G. 821 (1903). Where a party seeks to carry his date of conception back ten years, basing his motion upon testimony taken in his own behalf, the motion will be denied in the absence of any sufficient reasons why the facts were not discovered at the time his original statement was filed. *Woodward v Kennedy*, 104 O. G 1393 (1903) Even where the testimony shows clearly that a mistake was made in the preliminary statement, the amendment will not be permitted in the absence of a showing of due care in making the original statement. *Woodward v Kennedy*, 104 O G

26

1393 Where a party had been notified that his statement was indefinite, but no motion to amend was filed until eight months later and after his opponent had taken his testimony, and no satisfactory excuse given for the delay, he was not entitled to amend *Dixon v McElroy,* 127 O G 2393 (1907)

51. Motions to Amend When Reviewable. Consideration of motions to amend may be postponed until final hearing in which case the decision of the Examiner of Interferences is reviewable by the examiners in chief *Gammeter v Thropp,* 190 O G 266 (1913), *Forsberg v Bradbury,* 177 O G 239 (1912)

AMENDMENT OF ISSUE.

52. Adding—Counts—Rule 109. After an interference has been declared, it often becomes important to add new counts to an interference This may be done at any time within thirty days after the preliminary statements of the parties have been filed and approved One who desires to add new counts should make a motion to amend in accordance with Rule 109 and Rule 153, the latter rule applying to giving notice of the motion to the opposing parties, service of copies and proof of service. The procedure should follow Rule 124 as amended May 7, 1914, which though applying to motions to dissolve, has been held to be applicable and the proper practice on motions to add counts *Townsend v. Copeland v Robinson,* 126 O G 1355 (1907).

The motion to amend the application should contain the claim or claims which the moving party believes should be made the basis of interference between himself and the other parties It should contain a statement that it is believed the claims are patentable and should be made an issue in the interference, and it should be pointed out specifically wherein the claims which it is desired to add are applicable to the structure of each of the parties, and must not be conditional or with a proviso

27

Ames, Jr., v. Ryan, 238 O. G. 1639 (1917); *Wheeler v. Palmros,* 133 O. G. 230 (1908).

The purpose of Rule 109 is to enable a party to claim a patentable invention which he shows and describes, but *has not claimed,* and which the opposing party *has* claimed. *Perrussel v. Wickmann,* 99 O. G. 2970, 1902 C. D. 228. A further purpose of the rule is that an interference may be made to completely cover the patentable invention which is common to the applications involved. *Reece v. Fenwick,* 97 O. G. 188, 1901 C. D. 143. And to avoid a second interference. *Townsend v. Copeland v. Robinson,* 126 O. G. 1355 (1907).

Since it is the purpose of Rule 109 to give a party to an interference full opportunity to put in issue matter which he may think patentable or common to the interference applications, but which was not included in the interference as originally declared, if he fails to take advantage of this rule while the interference is pending, he is estopped thereafter from presenting broader claims. *In re Capen,* 214 O. G. 685, 43 App. D. C. 342; *Capen,* 214 O. G. 683 (1914); *Sutton, Steele & Steele,* 121 O. G. 1012 (1906).

53. An Appeal May Be Taken from the decision of the Law Examiner refusing a motion to amend, to the Examiners in Chief in the first instance, but the appeal must be *inter partes.* Rule 124. Since the amendment of Rules 109 and 124, May 7, 1914, when a motion to amend is made, if found in proper form, it will be transmitted by the Commissioner to the Law Examiner and if the Law Examiner renders an adverse decision, he shall fix a limit of appeal, not less than twenty days, for appeal to the Examiners in Chief, and if the appeal is not taken within the time fixed by the Law Examiner it will not be heard except by permission of the Commissioner. In *Townsend v. Copeland v. Robinson,* 126 O. G. 1355 (1907), it was held that the reasons which led to the change in Rule 124, set forth in *Newcomb v. Thompson*

28

(122 O. G 3012), apply with nearly the same force to motions under Rule 109, hence it was held that the proper practice was to follow the procedure under Rule 124 The reason for allowing such appeal is that a final adverse decision rendered on such motion would obviously constitute ground for refusing such claims presented after the conclusion of the interference *Mortimer v Thomas v. Brownson*, 192 O G. 215 (1913).

54 When Motion Must Be Made. Rule 109 provides that a motion to amend may be made at any time within thirty days after the preliminary statements of the parties have been received and approved However, for various reasons, motions have been presented long after the thirty days' limit therein stated, hence there have been many rulings applying to the particular facts presented.

55. Reopening Interference to Amend Issue. After the expiration of the time allowed for bringing motions, and after a decision of the Law Examiner on a motion to dissolve has become final, the interference will not be reopened to amend the issues, especially where there is no valid excuse shown for delay in bringing the motion Ignorance of the provisions of Rule 109 is no excuse *Kimball v. Sharples*, 21 Gour. 68-10 (Aug , 1909) , *Davis v Zellers*, 167 O. G 513 (1911) But it would seem that upon proper showing an interference might be reopened

56. Amendments Have Been Allowed Long After Thirty Day Limit. Where a party was able to make satisfactory explanation for the delay in bringing the motion, as was the case in *Becker v Otis*, 127 O G. 1267, amendment was permitted after the thirty day limit. But where the motion was made after testimony was taken, alleging as the reason for the delay the fact that the Examiners in Chief, on appeal on priority, found that the moving party had no right to make the claims, which was contrary to the ruling made by the Primary Examiner and the Examiner of Interferences, the motion

29

was properly refused as there was no excuse for the delay of six months after the decision of the Examiners in Chief. (Distinguishing *Becker v. Otis*, 127 O. G. 1267; *Hanan & Gates v. Marshall*, 21 Gour. 54-16 (June, 1909).

57. Where the Necessity for Amendment Did Not Arise Until After a Decision on Motion to Dissolve, it was held that the motion to amend should be transmitted for the reasons given in *Becker v. Otis*, 127 O. G. 1267; *Williams v. Gibbon*, 20 Gour. 82-4 (Nov., 1908). New counts will not be admitted after partial dissolution where proofs as to the same may be presented in connection with the counts remaining. *Scott v. Emmett & Hewlett*, 119 O. G. 2233 (1905).

58. Adding Counts After Taking Testimony. Where testimony has been taken, the Examiner should not suggest new counts before judgment on priority. *Freeman v. Parks*, 117 O. G. 276 (1905); *Potter v. VanCleck v. Thompson*, 95 O. G. 2484, 1901 C. D. 53; *Newell v. Hubbard*, 15 Gour. 82-3 (Dec., 1903). After decision on priority it is too late to amend by adding new counts. *Safert v. Meyer*, 109 O. G. 1885.

59. Amendment Substituting Patentable for Unpatentable Counts. It has been held in *Churchward v. Douglas v. Cutler*, 106 O. G. 2016 (1903), that where some of the counts of the issue are unpatentable and one of the parties proposes amended claims as substitutes for them, they should be considered by the Primary Examiner, and if found patentable he should suggest them to the other party and fix a time limit within which such other party may make them, and if he fails to make them within the time, such failure should have the same effect as suggested claims under Rule 96. It was also observed that at the time Rule 109 was adopted the practice of suggesting claims had not been inaugurated and that the practice outlined in this case is not provided for in Rule 109 (Note: Rule 109 has since been amended). If new patentable counts are proposed after the original counts have been held unpatentable, on the evidence taken, the interference may be redeclared and a motion under Rule 157, to use the testimony previously taken, would be in order *Brooks v Foote v Wenk*, 108 O G 287 The foregoing decisions are given for the purpose of assisting the practitioner in interpreting Rule 109 as now in force.

60. Adding New Counts by Stipulation. New counts may be added to an interference by motion signed by all the parties to the interference, if the Law Examiner holds the proposed counts to be patentable, though there are no rules providing for such practice. *Reese v. Fenwick*, 99 O G 669, 1902 C. D. 145, *Norman v Krimmelbein*, 115 O. G 249

61. Proposed Counts Must Be Patentable. The Law Examiner should decide whether the proposed counts are patentable If so, they should be included in the interference, and if not, he should make a specific ruling to that effect, giving his reasons therefor, and the amendment should be refused admission, and the party whose motion is denied may then appeal to the Examiners in Chief. *Reece v Fenwick*, 14 Gour 3-7 (Feb, 1902), *Hillard v. Fisher*, 101 O G 2290, 1902 C. D 448; *O'Connor v Vanderbilt*, 102 O G 1782 (1903).

62. Proposed Counts Must Be Such That All Parties Can Make Them and Patentably Different From Those Already in the Interference. *O'Connor v Vanderbilt*, 102 O G 1782 (1903); *Hollifield v Cummings*, 154 O. G. 1107 (1910), *Moore v Hewett v Potter*, 115 O G. 509; *Hicks v. Costello*, 103 O G 1163 (1903), *Townsend v Copeland v Robinson*, 124 O. G 623 (1906)

63. Questions Considered on Motions to Amend. A motion to amend raises the question of the patentability of the proposed counts, the right of the parties to make them and all grounds raised in opposition to the motion, but the same questions will not be again considered on a

31

motion to dissolve. Rule 109. *Dunlap v. Creveling v. Rector*, 21 Gour. 67-8 (Sept., 1909); *Lotterhand v. Cornwall*, 154 O. G. 515 (1910).

64. After a Motion Has Been Transmitted, additional claims not set out in the original motion, will not necessarily be considered by the Examiner. *Mattice v. Langworthy*, 132 O. G. 678 (1907).

DISSOLUTION.

65. Dissolution of Interference—Rule 122. Rule 122 sets forth three separate and distinct grounds for dissolving interferences.

1. That there has been such informality in declaring the same as will preclude a proper determination of the question of priority of invention.

2. On the ground that the claims of the issue are not patentable.

3. That a party has no right to make the claim.

It has been held that the three grounds for dissolution mentioned in Rule 122, relate respectively to very different matters and should not be confused, one with the other. *Kaczander v. Hodges & Hodges*, 118 O. G. 836; *Woodward v. Newton*, 86 O. G. 490; *Owen v. Richardson*, 111 O. G. 1037 (1904).

66. Motion to Dissolve—In General. It should be borne in mind in considering the older decisions relating to motions to dissolve, that the rules were amended May 7, 1914, transferring from the Primary Examiner to the Law Examiner jurisdiction of motions to dissolve. 202 O. G. 634.

Motions to dissolve must set forth definitely the grounds, upon which motion is based and a failure to be specific and accurate often results in denial of the motion. If the ground is, that the issue is not patentable, then the motion must clearly set forth why it is not patentable. It must state how the patents cited anticipate the issue, that is, whether each patent anticipates the issue, or if not, how they are to be combined to show anticipation of the issue. If there is more than one count in the issue, it must be shown to what count the anticipating patents apply and how they apply. *Rountree v Sloan,* 189 O G 1281 (1913); *Keyes & Kraus v. Yunck,* 182 O G 248 (1912, *Vanderveld v Smith,* 159 O. G. 490 (1910), *Heyne, etc v DeVilbiss,* 125 O G 669 (1906); *Burleigh v Elliott,* 197 O G. 240 (1913).

A party may base his motion upon all the grounds mentioned in Rule 122 and the Primary Examiner (Law Examiner) is required to decide the motion upon all the grounds and fix a limit of appeal as to those grounds upon which an appeal may be taken *Hopfelt v. Read,* 106 O G 767 (1903), *Oldham & Padbury v Peck et al,* 99 O G 670, 1902 C D 148, *Read v Scott,* 14 Gour. 3-5 (Jan, 1902); *Hinkley v Baker,* 97 O. G. 2742, 1901 C. D. 236, *Owen v Richardson, Jr,* 111 O. G. 1037

The several grounds mentioned in Rule 122 have separate, distinct and well defined meanings, and the motion should not state the facts in such way that the Examiner will not be able to determine what facts are relied upon to support each separate ground for dissolving the interference The Examiner is required to decide the motion upon each ground alleged and therefore it is important that the motion should state what facts furnish the reason for dissolving the interference upon ground 1, what facts furnish the reason for dissolving the interference upon ground 2, and what facts furnish the reason for dissolving the interference upon ground 3. *Woodward v Newton,* 86 O. G. 490; *Vreeland v. Fessenden, etc,* 117 O G. 2633 (1905) and same case, 119 O G 1259 (1905) *Dunker v Reist,* 119 O. G. 1925 (1905), *Thulen v. Young & Townsend,* 118 O G 2251 (1905); *Klepetke v Becker,* 120 O. G. 658 (1905), *Owens v Richardson,* 111 O G 1037 (1903)

We have seen by the foregoing decisions that the motion must be definite and certain as to how the facts apply to each ground stated in the motion, but the question often arises as to what is and what is not definite. Where there was more than one count in the interference and the moving party failed to specify whether his motion was directed to all or only a part of the counts in issue, and there was no specific statement as to which element of the claims are not supported by the original disclosure, it was held that the motion should not be transmitted. *Lizotte v. Neuberth*, 124 O. G. 1842 (1906). Where the motion was on the ground of unpatentability in view of eight references, of which it is stated "each of the counts is met by each of the patents singly or in combination, "it was held that the allegations were in the alternative and indefinite. *Thullen v. Townsend*, 130 O. G. 1312 (1907). Where the allegation was that the issue is not patentable in view of certain references, but it was not stated how these references are to be applied, transmission of the motion was refused. *Phillips v. Scott*, 130 O. G. 1312 (1907). Where it was alleged that each of the counts of the issue is anticipated, or necessarily limited, it was held that the allegations are in the alternative and the motion therefore does not state which counts are to be urged as anticipated and which limited, nor does it show which patents are to be relied upon for anticipation and which for restriction. *Murphy v. Borland*, 132 O. G. 231. All the references must be put into the motion when filed. A moving party will not be permitted to cite certain references in his motion and then state that he will cite others more than five days before the hearing. The motion would be good as to the patents cited, but not as to any that might be thereafter cited. *Papendell v. Bunnell, etc.*, 131 O. G. 362 (1907).

67. **References Discovered After the Motion Has Been Filed or Transmitted.** If a party can make a proper showing that he has discovered since the filing of his motion, or since its transmission, a new and pertinent reference, and a further satisfactory showing that it could not have

34

been earlier discovered, he may, by giving due notice to his opponent, have such reference considered as a part of his motion. *Kurts v Jackson & Pierce*, 98 O. G 2568, 1902 C D 106, *Young v Lick*, 113 O G 547 But where no such showing is made a party will not be permitted to argue the pertinency of references not set out in his motion *Hilliard & Parsons v. Hewlett*, 19 Gour. 55-10 (April, 1907)

68 Only One Motion to Dissolve. A motion to dissolve may not be presented in piece meal by presenting a motion on one ground and if it is denied, present another motion upon a different ground The whole case must be presented in one motion *Richards v Kletzker & Goesel*, 98 O G 1709, 1902 C D 62, *Finch v Singleton*, 98 O G 1709, 1902 C. D 61, *Egly v Schultze*, 117 O G 276 (1905).

69. Motion to Extend Time for Filing Motion to Dissolve. The granting or refusing of a motion to extend time for filing motion to dissolve is within the discretion of the official before whom the motion is filed. *Egly v Schultze*, 117 O G 276 (1905).

70 Amendment of Motion. Amendment of a motion may be permitted and time given therefor, if it appears that a party is acting in good faith *Jones v Hulse v Melville*, 21 Gour. 86-15 (July, 1909).

Questions involving priority are not presented by motions to dissolve and the Examiner should not pass upon such questions *Clement v Brown v Stroud*, 126 O G 2189 (1907), *Wende v Horine*, 118 O G 1070 (1905)

71. Operativeness. On motion to dissolve on the ground of inoperativeness, it was held that the interference would be dissolved whether the structure of one or both of the parties is inoperative, but where a party files a motion before the Examiner of Interferences for permission to take testimony on the ground that his opponent's structure is inoperative, it is necessary for the moving party to show that the alleged ground of inopera-

35

tiveness does not apply to his own structure   This is because if the structures of both parties are inoperative, there is no question of priority presented. *Clement v Browne v Stroud*, 126 O G. 2189 (1907) ; *Bodwitch v. Todd*, 98 O. G. 792

72. Informality in Declaring the Interference. Where there were 132 counts in the interference, it was held that the great number of counts would of itself tend to preclude a proper determination of priority, and under the provisions of Rule 212, the interference should be transmitted to the Primary Examiner to determine whether the interference should not be dissolved and a reasonable number of counts substituted for those forming the issue *Ragena v Harris*, 150 O G. 266 (1909)

73. Defects in Oath. Where the oath filed with one of the applications was administered by the attorney for the applicant, the interference was dissolved. *Reigger v Barel*, 150 O G 826 (1909)   Where it was discovered during the taking of testimony that there was an informality in the oath of one of the parties and such party promptly filed a corrected oath, the motion was denied. *Jackson v Weber*, 18 Gour 84-13 (Nov., 1906).

74. Lack of Official Seal of officer who administered the oath may be cured by proof that the officer actually had authority to administer it. *Dukesmith v Covington v Turner*, 126 O G 348. The lack of such seal is an ex parte matter and not an irregularity warranting dissolution. *Auerbach & Gubing v Wiswell*, 108 O G. 289.

75. Supplemental Oath. Where a party has filed no preliminary statement, a motion to dissolve upon the ground that the claim should have been supported by a supplemental oath, should be transmitted for determination of whether a supplemental oath is necessary, and, if found necessary and is not furnished within a reasonable time, the interference should be dissolved *Gold v Dixon*, 194 O G. 1142, 1913 C. D. 217.

76. That the Issues Are Vague and Indefinite, are

36

proper questions to raise as constituting informality in declaring an interference *Field v Colman*, 131 O. G. 1686 (1907), *Anderson v Vrooman*, 123 O G 2975 (1906); *Dinkel v D'Oliver*, 113 O. G. 2507 (1903) An interference is irregularly declared where one of the applications does not disclose the subject matter of one of the counts *Gilbert-Stringer v. Johnson*, 102 O. G. 621, 1903 C D 20

77 **Abandonment.** Where an abandoned application is put in interference with another application, it may be dissolved as irregularly declared. *Coulson v. Callender & Callender*, 101 O. G 1607

78. **What Is Not Such Irregularity or Informality in Declaring the Interference as Will Preclude the Proper Determination of the Question of Priority of Invention.** Multiplicity of counts is not an irregularity, if the counts are separately patentable. *Narman v Krimelbein*, 118 O. G. 2251 (1905). That the Examiner has not notified the parties that the claims in issue are patentable *Luger v Browning*, 100 O G 231, 1902 C D 230 That a party has stated in his applications involved in the interferences that they are divisions of a prior patent granted to him; *Meyer v Sarfert*, 96 O G 1037; 1901 C. D 91. That a party has rejected claims and if they should be decided to be patentable, a new interference would be necessary *Truar v Robinson*, 13 Gour 82-2 (Dec., 1901). Where no irregularity was pointed out, and the issue was construed as broad enough to cover the inventions of both parties. *Gillespie v Dean*, 15 Gour. 83-7 (Nov, 1903). That the claims of the counts cover two species of invention *Atherton & Happ v. Cheney*. 111 O G. 1040 That the suggestion of claims was not authorized by the practice then in force. *Myers v Brown*, 112 O G 2093 The sending of a notice of interference to a patentee referring to his patent as an application *Gaely v Brand*, 16 Gour 50-4 That the suggestion of the claim in interference to the party by

37

the Examiner, was improper because said party had not
claimed substantially the same invention expressed in
said claim *Meden v Curtis*, 117 O G 1795 (1905)
That the Examiner improperly suggested claims under
Rule 96 Templin v Sergeant. 119 O. G. 961 (1905)
That the Examiner improperly issued a patent to the opponent of the moving party during the pendency of his
application (That is a matter the office can not remedy)
Dunher v Reist, 119 O G 1925 (1905). That the Examiner failed to include certain claims made by both
parties, where the claims not included are not patentably
different from those which were included. *Gally v Burton*, 120 O. G 325 (1905); *Earll v. Love*, 140 O G. 1209
(1909) Mere clerical errors which may be corrected by
a letter of the Primary Examiner calling attention to
them, does not warrant dissolution. *Gally v Burton*,
120 O G. 325 (1905) The fact that the issue involving
a parent case could as well have been included in the
interference involving a divisional application *Phillips
v Sensenich*, 122 O G 1047 (1906) That the counts of
the interference are not patentably different *Hawkins
v Young*, 21 Gour 34-3 (May 1909), *McKeen v Davis*,
21 Gour 84-7 (Aug, 1909) The fact that the Examiner formulated the claim suggested for the purpose of
interference, is not an informality in declaring the interference *Gold v Dixon*, 194 O G 1142 (1913).

Irregularities in the prosecution of an application
should not be confused with irregularities in declaring
the interference. *Colburn & Washburn v Hitchcock*,
145 O G 1022 (1909)

A party who requests a declaration is not in a position
to urge irregularity in declaring it *Wickers & Furlong
v Wannum*, 117 O G 1797 (1905).

Where a party makes suggested claims under protest,
it was held that while such facts might warrant a motion
by such party to dissolve on the ground that he had no
right to make the claims, the same facts, however, would

not sustain a motion to dissolve on the ground of informality and irregularity in declaring the interference. *Eichelberger & Hibner v. Dillon*, 129 O. G. 3161 (1907)

Where the Examiner includes in an interference counts which he has held not patentable, such inclusion is not an irregularity in declaring the interference, because the party had a right to appeal on the question of the patentability of those counts and they are properly retained in the interference, but if he fails to appeal within the time set therefor, the interference stands dissolved as to those counts In such case it is customary for the Examiner of Interferences, when the case is returned to him from the Law Examiner, to notify the parties that the interference is dissolved as to such counts. *Halwood v McCormick*, 16 Gour 84-7.

79. **Motion to Dissolve on the Ground That the Issue Is Not Patentable—Who May Question Patentability of the Issue.** A party whose claims are held not patentable can not question the patentability of the claim of his opponent *Soverign & Leuders v Lillie*, 185 O G 830 (1912).

80. **Who Has Jurisdiction to Determine Patentability.** A motion for dissolution was based on all grounds provided by the rules The motion was denied by the Primary Examiner A petition to the Commissioner was filed, asking that the Examiner of Interferences be directed to pass on the patentability of certain counts. The Commissioner held that the Examiner of Interferences had no jurisdiction to pass upon the questions which were sought to be placed before him, because they do not relate to the question of priority *Wood v Pfister*, 154 O. G. 837 (1910).

The question of the patentability of the issue should be raised by a motion to dissolve and will be determined by the Law Examiner (formerly by the Primary Examiner). The Court of Appeals, D C, has held that the question of the patentability of the issue is not a juris-

39

dictional one which must be considered by each of the tribunals called upon to pass on the question of priority of invention in an interference proceeding *Johnson v Mueser,* 29 App D C. 61, 145 O G 764 It is well settled that the patentability of the issue will be considered on final hearing only under the supervisory authority of the Commissioner and in a clear case *Dixon v Marsh, et al,* 127 O G. 1993; *Sobey v Holschlaw,* 126 O G 3041, 28 App D C 65, *Potter v McIntosch,* 127 O G. 1995, 28 App D. C 510; *Huber v Aiken,* 88 O. G 1525 Where an applicant sought to present the question of patentability on an appeal to the Commissioner from a judgment of priority, it was held that the interference should not be dissolved, though had the question been presented at the proper time by a motion to dissolve it would have been dissolved. *De Farranti v Lindmark,* 183 O. G 782 (1912).

81 **Nature of Right to Question Patentability.** A motion to dissolve on the ground of non-patentability is not a matter of right under any statute, but is a matter of procedure arising under the rules of practice, and the moving party appears in such motion merely as *amicus curea* Whether a certain count is patentable is a question between the applicant presenting it and the office, as is every claim presented in an application where there is no opposing party But following certain decisions indicating that it is of assistance to the office to have the opposing party argue the patentability of the issue, the rules were amended to provide for appeals on this question, inter partes. See *Appeal, Kelly v. Dempster,* 164 O G. 975 (1911); *Gold v Gold,* 150 O G. 570- 573, *Griffith v Dodyson,* 116 O G, 1731 (1905), *Lipe v Miller,* 109 O. G 1608, *Robbins v Titus,* 111 O G. 584, *Patterson v Heher,* 192 O G. 215 (1913).

82. **Effect on Moving Party.** Where an applicant moves to dissolve on the ground that the issue is not patentable, his opponent being a patentee, such applicant is

40

thereafter estopped from insisting upon the claims. *Weissenthanner v Goldstein*, 111 O. G. 810 (1904). A patentee may not urge non-patentability of his claims. *Fend v Miggett*, 223 O G 649 (1915).

83 When Motion Should Be Made. The motion to dissolve upon this ground should of course be made at the time and as provided by the rules, but such motions have been made at various stages of the proceedings Where the motion was made after the taking of testimony, it was held that the interference would not be suspended to consider the pertinency of a reference. To warrant such consideration the anticipation must be clearly apparent *Graham v Langhaar*, 177 O. G. 240 (1912). Where a party is an applicant and his opponent is a patentee and the applicant in response to a motion to show cause why judgment should not be rendered against him for failure to take testimony, no testimony having been taken, moves to dissolve on the ground that the issue is not patentable, the interference should not be dissolved, but judgment should be rendered. *Smith v Slocum*, 123 O G 1990, 1906 C. D 269

84. Character of Showing Required. Where the motion to dissolve alleges that the counts are not patentable in view of certain enumerated patents, if the moving party is of the opinion that each of the references is an anticipation of each of the claims, the motion should so state If not, the motion should enumerate the references in connection with the claims to which they will be applied in the argument If the contention of non-patentability is based upon the theory of aggregation, or double use, or substitution of equivalents it should appear in the motion, also the manner in which it is proposed to combine the references *Heyne, Hayward & McCarthy v DeVilbiss*, 125 O G 669 (1906). Ex parte affidavits will not support the motion, for the reason, that if the interference is dissolved, the claims must be rejected and the claims can not be rejected on ex parte

41

affidavits *Ellis v Boyce v. Burchenal,* 195 O G 273
(1913) , *Barratt v Swingelhurst,* 144 O G 818 (1909) ,
Ex parte Van Ausdel, 91 O. G. 1617 , *McKenzie v Gillespie, et al ,* 93 O. G. 2103.

Anticipating patents must be such as are not antedated
by the preliminary statement. *Forsyth v Richards,* 115
O. G 1327 (1905), but in *Martin v. Goodrum, etc.,* 130
O G. 1485 (1907), it was held that a motion setting up
such a patent as an anticipation should be transmitted
for the purpose of permitting the (Examiner) Law Examiner to consider the pertinency of the reference and
permit the filing of an affidavit alleging facts required by
Rule 75, outside those contained in the preliminary statement.

Patents granted on applications filed subsequent to the
date of invention alleged in the preliminary statement
of one of the parties, are not anticipating patents which
will support a motion to dissolve an interference upon
the ground of non-patentability *Raymond v Kitselman, et al ,* 134 O G 2243 (1908).

85. Appeal—When Not Permitted (See Appeal). No
appeal is permitted from a decision of the Law Examiner
affirming patentability of the issue. All interlocutory
matters, such as motions to dissolve, are regulated by the
Patent Office rules and a party has no statutory right to
appeal on any question except a judgment on priority
rendered in an interference, hence if he has a right to
appeal he must find that right in the Patent Office rules
The Primary Examiner is given authority to pass on
questions of patentability of the issue and neither the
statute nor the rules of the Patent Office permit appeals
from a decision rendered upon a motion for dissolution
affirming patentability of the issue (*Allen v Lowry,* 116
O G 2253) and it is only from decisions *adverse* to the
patentability of the claims that an appeal will lie (*Sobey
v Holschlaw,* 126 O G 304] 28 App. D C 65) As the
Primary Examiners are under the Commissioner, he

may, where it is clear that gross error has been committed in holding the issue patentable, exercise his supervisory authority and take jurisdiction of the question, but such will not be exercised where there is merely a difference of opinion on the part of the lower tribunals

86. How the Question of Patentability of the Issue May Come Before the Commissioner The Examiner of Interferences, in his decision, and likewise the Examiners in Chief on appeal, are confined to the question of priority, but if any other matter not relating to priority and which would amount to a statutory bar to the granting of a patent to either of the parties, shall come to their notice, they may direct the attention of the Commissioner to such matter under Rule 126, and the Commissioner may, before judgment on the question of priority, suspend the interference and remand the case to the Primary Examiner, for his consideration of the matters to which his attention has been directed, and from the decision of the Examiner an appeal may be taken. If the Commissioner does not remand the case, the Primary Examiner will, after judgment, consider any matter affecting the rights of either party to a patent which may have been called to his attention, unless the same shall have been previously disposed of by the Commissioner After the Primary Examiner has held the claims to be patentable and the Examiner of Interferences and the Examiners in Chief have omitted or declined to call the attention of the Commissioner to the non-patentability of the issue, or where the Commissioner has declined to review the decision of the Primary Examiner, after his attention has been called to the alleged non-patentability of the issue, the Court of Appeals will consider the patentability of the issue settled, except in an extraordinary case. *Sobey v Holschlaw,* 126 O. G 3041, 28 App D C 65, *Allen v Lowry,* 116 O G 2253 (1905)

87. No Right to Make the Claims Since the decision of the Court of Appeals, D C , in *Podelsack v McInner-*

ney, 26 App D C 399, the question of the right of a party to make the claims of the issue, has been uniformly held to be an ancillary question to be considered in determining the question of priority of invention and this question may be raised on final hearing and on appeal. As a result of this decision Rule 130 was promulgated, by the provisions of which, where the patentability of a claim to an opponent is material to the right of the party to a patent, said party may urge the non-patentability of the claim to his opponent at final hearing and on appeal, but he can not raise the question unless he shall have duly presented a motion under Rule 122 for dissolution upon that ground, or show good reason why such motion was not presented. It was therefore held in *McBerty v Shore & Shore*, 175 O G 843 (1911), that the Examiners in Chief properly awarded priority upon the ground that one of the parties had no right to make the claims Following further the development of the practice we find in *Cosper v Gold & Gold*. 151 O G 194, 34 App. D C 194, the Court of Appeals dismissed the appeal upon the ground that it was taken from a decision of the Commissioner dissolving the interference because Cosper had no right to make the claims of the issue, and under such circumstances it was not a final decision which could be appealed to that court Thereupon the Commissioner entered an award of priority based upon Cosper's lack of right to make the claims and from this decision Cosper appealed to the Court of Appeals, and it was held that under the practice established by the decision of *Podelsack v. McInnerney*, two questions arise in every interference case where the right of one of the parties to make the claims of the issue are presented on a motion to dissolve upon that ground, to wit the right to make the claims, and the priority of invention If the first shall be decided adversely to the claimant, the formal award of priority goes to his opponent as a matter of course. But in *Carlin v Goldberg*, 45 App. D. C

44

540, 236 O G 1222, 1917 C. D 128, it was held that no award of priority could be made on a motion to dissolve upon this ground, before proofs are taken, and it was pointed out that in *Cosper v Gold* the judgment was entered after the interference had been tried and the question of priority hinged upon the question as to whether Cosper had a right to make the claims Where there has been no hearing upon the question of priority, no award of priority can be made on motion to dissolve.

On motion to dissolve on the ground that a party has no right to make the claims, the sole question to be considered is whether the specification and drawings of the application are sufficient to justify the allowance of the claims in question *Seacombe v Burke,* 182 O. G 973 (1912)

A dissolution on the ground that a party has no right to make the claims, is merely a ruling that it was a mistake to declare the interference as to that party *Campbell v Dyson v Dunham,* 242 O. G 253 (1916).

Abandonment of the invention goes to the question of the right to make the claims. *Felsing v. Nelson,* 121 O. G 1347 (1906).

Where the issue was alleged to be substantially the same as that of a prior interference between the same parties, and the senior party had been defeated on the question of priority, it was held that the question presented was one involving the right of the senior party to make the claims. *Eschinger v. Drummond, etc,* 121 O G 1348 (1906)

Where the moving party alleges that he has no right to make the claims, the motion will be refused transmission, because if he is of the opinion that he has no right to make the claims, he should take action in accordance with the provisions of Rule 125, or he may take no action whatever in the interference and permit judgment to go by default. *Miller v. Perham,* 121 O G. 2667 (1906), *Kinney v Goodhue,* 123 O. G 1663 (1906),

45

Goodwin v Smith, 123 O. G. 998 (1906) But Commissioner Billings allowed the filing of motions under such circumstances. And where the claims were suggested under Rule 96, a different rule prevails, and a party may properly move to dissolve on the ground that he has no right to make the claims, but in such case he must state specifically the reasons upon which his motion is based. *Hermsdorf v Driggs v Schneider*, 133 O G 1189 (1908).

The facts which will support a motion to dissolve on the ground that a party has no right to make the claims, relate to the extent of disclosure, estoppel, operativeness, and the like, and if established will result in rejection of the claims to which they are applicable. *Booth, et al., v Hanan, et al.,* 123 O. G 319 (1906)

Alleging on motion to dissolve, facts which relate to priority does not present any question for consideration on such motion, and it will be refused transmission. *Dickinson v. Hildreth,* 122 O G 1397 (1906).

Recommendation by Examiners in Chief. If the Examiners in Chief in affirming a decision of the Law Examiner holding that a party has no right to make the claims, recommends that the other party also has no right to make the claims, such other party may appeal ex parte from such recommendation. *Woodbridge v Conrad*, 165 O G 241 (1911).

A party cannot be deprived of his right to make claims because his structure performs some function in addition to what is called for by the claims *Miel v Young,* 126 O G 2591 (1906), 29 App D C. 481

That a party is not entitled to the date of an earlier application because the claim was not made therein, and because there was included a disclaimer of it, relates to the right of the party to make the claims. *Dittgen v. Parmenter,* 99 O G 2966; 1902 C D 218

That a party's application did not disclose the invention until a certain amendment was filed therein, is a contention that he has no right to make the claims, and should be presented in a motion to dissolve and not in a motion to shift the burden of proof. *Tripp v. Wolff v. Jones,* 103 O G 2171 (1903).

The fact that an issue includes an element of a combination which one party does not disclose, is ground for dissolution on the ground that such party has no right to make the claim *Bodwitch v Todd,* 98 O. G. 792, 1902 C D 27

Inoperativeness should not be insisted upon in a motion to dissolve except in a clear case *Bodwitch v Todd,* 98 O G. 792

If a party's structure is capable of performing the function in question, it is immaterial whether or not his description refers to it *Western Electric Co. v Sperry Electric Co, 65 O G 597, Fenwick v Dixon & Dixon,* 15 Cour 71-23 (Sept , 1903)

88. Disclaimer—Rule 107. Rule 107 provides: An applicant involved in an interference may, with the written consent of the assignee, when there has been an assignment, before the date fixed for the filing of his preliminary statement (Rule 110), in order to avoid the continuance of the interference, disclaim under his own signature, attested by two witnesses, the invention of the particular matter in issue, and upon such disclaimer and cancellation of any claims involving such interfering matter, judgment shall be rendered against him, and a copy of the disclaimer shall be embodied in and form part of his specification (See Rule 182).

Were a disclaimer is filed, such disclaimer only extends to the particular claim or claims as to which the interference has been declared, and the judgment following does not effect the question of invention as to other claims, although they may contain other interfering matter *Reed v Concrete Machinery Co , et al ,* 239 Fed 869 (C. C A. 7th Cir. 1916). An assignee of entire interest may disclaim invention. *Moore & McKee v*

47

Bradley, etc., 180 O. G. 879 (1912). A judgment of priority may be avoided by disclaimer, or by filing an ap-priority may be avoided by disclaimer. or by filing an ap-only. *Fend v. Miggett*, 223 O. G. 649 (1915).

Disclaimer by Refusal to Make Claims Under Rule 96. If an applicant refuses to make claims suggested under Rule 96, he disclaims the interfering subject matter. *Ferris*, 114 O. G. 541.

Oral Disclaimer. If a party to an interference in answer to a question propounded to him in the taking of testimony, states that he does not claim to be the inventor of the subject matter in controversy, a judgment of priority can not be awarded to him. *Oliver v. Felbel*, 100 O. G. 2384; 1902 C. D. 565. A statement by an applicant to his assignee that he does not regard himself as the inventor of the subject matter claimed, is not sufficient to overcome his oath that he is the inventor thereof, especially where it appears that he is hostile to his assignee. *Gibbons v. Peller*, 127 O. G. 3643 (1907).

89. Miscellaneous Motions to Dissolve. The grounds for dissolving interferences are set forth in Rule 122, and a motion which does not state any of the grounds therein enumerated, is not a proper motion. *Keith v. George*. 16 Gour. 19-4. However, there have been many attempts of a miscellaneous character to dissolve interferences for grounds not mentioned in Rule 122, and which have been invariably refused transmission, illustrations of which are, that a party failed to file a supplemental oath, or that the oath is defective. The filing of an oath is an ex parte matter and not a ground for dissolution. *Graham v. Langhaar*, 164 O. G. 739 (1911); *Reitzel v. Harmatta*, 161 O. G. 1043 (1910); *Rowe v. Brinkmann*, 133 O. G. 515 (1908); *Emmet v. Fullager*, 130 O. G. 2719 (1907). Motions to dissolve upon the grounds of public use, and based upon ex parte affidavits, will not be transmitted. *Davis v. Swift*, 96 O. G. 2409; 1901 C. D. 134; *Shrum v. Baumgarten*, 104 O. G. 577 (1903); *Dunn v. Doug-*

lass, 184 O. G 804 (1912); *Barber v. Wood,* 128 O G.
2835 (1907) Nor where it is alleged that the structure
of one of the parties is greatly superior to that of the
other. *Kolb v Hemingway v Curtis,* 122 O G. 1397
(1906) Nor on the ground that a party is intending to
rely upon a certain machine in the production of his
testimony. *Barr v. Bugg,* 122 O G 2061 (1906). Nor
where the question raised is one involving the burden
of proof. *Townsend v. Ehret, etc,* 137 O G. 1484 (1908).
Nor where it is alleged that an affidavit filed under Rule
75 is false. *Schuler v Barnes, etc,* 140 O G 509 (1909)
Nor that a party has no right to make the claims because
of his delay in making them *Manly v Williams,* 21
Gour 85-11 (Aug, 1909), *Long v Flagg, etc,* 190 O
G 265 (1913) Nor that the claims were formulated by
the Examiner *Mixsell v Lovejoy,* 186 O G 294 (1912)
Nor upon the ground of intervening rights in the issu-
ance of a patent. *Perkins & Requa v Weeks,* 188 O G.
1052 (1913) Nor that the invention was made by a
third party *Welch v Auficro,* 219 O G 930 (1915).
Nor merely alleging abandonment of the invention by
reason of delay in renewing application. *Gehring &
Cadden v. Barry, etc,* 225 O G 371 (1914). Nor alleging prior knowledge and use as a bar *Murphy v.
Borland,* 132 O. G 231, and cases there cited Nor that
the issues are substantially the same as that of a prior
interference. *Sugden & Pidgin v Laganke, etc.,* 130 O
G. 1484 (1907) Nor an allegation by a sole inventor
that himself and another as joint inventors did not invent the device *Babcock v Pickard, etc,* 21 Gour 85-
13 (Nov, 1909), *Jarvis v Quincy,* 113 O. G 550 Nor
where the motion is based on affidavits as to inoperativeness *Horton v Leonard,* 155 O G. 305, *Keyes & Kraus
v Yunch,* 182 O G 248 (1912) Nor where the facts
set forth in the motion are based upon testimony taken
Ghallenberger v. Andrews, 100 O G 3013, 1902 C D
346; *Sullivan v Thompson,* 94 O. G. 585, 1902 C D.

6   49

21.   Nor that one of the parties is not an original inventor but derived his knowledge from another. *Corcy, etc., v. Blakey,* 115 O. G. 1328 (1905). Nor on the ground that a party desires to present claims of a broader nature, since proofs may be offered in the interference to cover any broader claims which the applicant may later present. *Phelps v. Wormley, etc.,* 118 O. G. 1069 (1905). Nor on the ground that the moving party is shown by the testimony in another interference to be the first inventor. *Newel v. Rose,* 119 O. G. 337 (1905) ; *Dorr v. Ames & Rearson,* 15 Gour. 35-6 (June, 1903). Nor where the question presented is one which may be determined on final hearing and which should be so determined. *Struble v. Young,* 121 O. G. 339; 1906 C. D. 95.

EVIDENCE.

90.   The subject of evidence as here treated has special reference to interference proceedings and such questions as are likely to arise in presenting proofs in such cases.

91.   **Burden of Proof.** Rule 116 provides that the several parties to interferences will be presumed to have made the inventions in the order in which they filed their completed applications for patents clearly illustrating and describing the invention; and the burden of proof shall rest upon the party who shall seek to establish a different state of facts.

92.   **What is the Filing Date.** The filing dates are the respective dates on which the applications were filed in the Patent Office. However, if the application is a true division of an earlier application, then the later application takes the filing date of the earlier application. This is only true where the earlier application clearly discloses the same invention. *Lowry v. Spoon,* 110 O. G. 858; *Meyer v. Sarfert,* 96 O. G. 1037; *Cain v. Park,* 86 O. G. 797, 14 App. D. C. 42; *Bundy v. Rumbarger,* 92 O. G. 2002; *Toledo Scale Co. v. Dunn,* 214 O. G.

1321, 43 App D C 377: *Curtis v Lindmark,* 171 O G 484 and 215, 37 App D. C 322

Earlier Application as Evidence. Even though the Primary Examiner fails to include an earlier application by one of the parties, in the declaration of interference, he is not deprived of the benefit of it, if it discloses the invention, since he may introduce it as a part of his evidence *Munro v Alexander,* 106 O. G. 1000 (1903), *Greenawalt v. Mark,* 111 O. G 2224, *Osborne v Armstrong,* 114 O. G. 2091.

93. Divisional Application—Evidence. The action of the Primary Examiner as to what is and what is not a division, is not controlling upon the Examiner of Interferences, since it is a matter relating to priority on which it is the peculiar province of the Examiner of Interferences to pass judgment, and where the Primary Examiner permitted an application to be amended by adding what in his opinion was not new matter, such ruling is subject to the independent judgment of the Examiner of Interferences *Robinson v. Copeland,* 102 O G 466 (1903)

94 Official Records as Evidence Subdivision (e) of Rule 154. provides that upon notice given to the opposite party before the closing of the testimony, any official record, and any special matter contained in a printed publication, if competent evidence and pertinent to the issue, may be used as evidence at the hearing This section relates to two classes of evidence, official records and printed publications

An official record is a record kept by an official, though usually it must be one required by law to be kept Thus in the State of New York, where death certificates are filed in the Health Department it was held that such certificates are "Official Records" within the meaning of Code Civil Procedure, Sec 959, providing that certain official records shall be presumptive evidence of their contents *Robinson v Supreme Commandery. Order of*

51

Golden Cross, 79 N. Y. Supp. 13, 16. Judgments, orders and decrees are properly proved by the minutes or calendar entries where the latter form the legal record thereof, but if the record consists of a judgment roll or some more formal writing, the latter if in existence, is the proper evidence It is not the purpose to here undertake to state the various classes of official records and how they may be introduced in evidence, but merely to call attention to the subject in a general way to illustrate the class of evidence that would come within the foregoing subdivision of Rule 154. For an extended discussion of the subject of Official Records as evidence, reference is made to Encyclopedia of Evidence,' Vol 10, page 716.

Testimony taken in another action is not rendered admissible by the introduction of the record in such action Encyclopedia of Evidence, Vol. 10, page 761 The Rules of Practice relating to the introduction of testimony taken in another interference, follow in a general way the rules of evidence in courts of law and recognize that such testimony is not an official record referred to in subsection (e) of Rule 154 Therefore special provision is made for introducing testimony taken in another interference Rule 157

An earlier application may become available as evidence, even though not involved in the interference, by introducing a certified copy thereof. To avoid any element of doubt there should also be introduced a certified copy of the filing date, or of the notice of allowance, if allowed In *Cain v. Park*, 14 App D C 42: 1899 C D 278. 86 O. G. 797, a certified copy of the application had been introduced in evidence and the Commissioner took judicial notice of his own records and found that the application was allowed and a pending application when the application in interference was filed In *Robinson v. Seclinger*, 116 O G 1735 (1905), 25 App D C. 237, the Examiners in Chief had taken judicial notice of the filing of a prior application (which had not been introduced in evidence) and the court held that it could not be expected to consider something which is not a record open to the public and which was in no form before the court as was the application which was taken judicial notice of in *Cain v Park, supra* It would seem, therefore, that while the office may take judicial knowledge of its own action upon an application and the date on which such action was taken, it is necessary to introduce a certified copy of the application to make it available as evidence

Any special matter contained in a printed publication may be used as evidence at the hearing if before closing the testimony notice is given to the opposite party as provided in subdivision (e) of Rule 154, of intention to so use the same A question may sometimes arise as to what is and what is not a printed publication In Walker on Patents, Sec 56, it is said "A printed publication is anything which is printed, and without any injunction of secrecy, is distributed to any part of the public in any country; and such publication may negative novelty Indeed, it seems reasonable that no actual distribution need occur, but that exposure of printed matter for sale is enough to constitute a printed publication But the mere existence of a printed thing is not a printed publication, though its deposit in a public library is A drawing, in a prior patent or printed publication, if its meaning is really undeniable, may negative novelty."

95. Continuous Application Takes Filing Date of Original Application. Where an application is a continuation of a prior application which became abandoned, the applicant is entitled to the filing date of the earlier application as to everything that it discloses, even though the later application may contain new matter not shown in the original application. *Tripler v Linde*, 101 O G. 2288, 1902 C. D 444; *Gilbert-Stringer v. Johnson*, 102

O. G 621 (1903), *Cain v Park*, 14 App. D. C. 42, 86 O. G. 797.

Identical Filing Dates. Where both applications are filed on the same day it is the practice of the office to throw the burden upon the one who was last to execute his application.

96. Burden as Between Applicant and Patentee Where through inadvertence an interference was not declared between two pending applications for the same invention until after a patent had been issued to the junior applicant, the patentee does not thereby gain any advantage with respect to the burden of proof, but is in the same situation he would have been had his patent not been granted *Evans v. Associated Automatic Sprinkler Co*, 241 Fed 252, 229 Fed 1007; *Cutler v Leonard*, 31 App D. C 297, 136 O. G. 438; *Andrews v Nilson*, 123 O G 1667 (1906), 27 App D C. 451.

If the patentee was the last to file he is properly the junior party *Furman v. Dean*, 114 O G 1552, *Miehle v Read*, 18 App D. C. 128, 96 O. G. 426; 1901 C. D. 396; *Paul v Hess*, 115 O G. 251, 24 App. D. C. 462

Patent Granted During Forfeiture of Application. Where a party permits his application to become forfeited, and while it is forfeited another files an application and secures a patent for the same invention which is put in interference with a renewal of the forfeited application, the burden of proof is upon the renewal applicant notwithstanding the earlier date of his first application *Lutz v Lewis*, 110 O G 2014. There is a distinction as to the burden of proof as between a patent granted while opposing party's case is pending and a patent granted while opposing party's case is forfeited. *Lowry v Spoon*, 110 O G 858

97. Proof Beyond a Reasonable Doubt—In What Cases. Where one party is a patentee and the other party filed his application after the issue of the patent, the burden is upon the applicant to prove beyond a reasonable doubt

54

that he reduced his invention to practice before the patent was gianted. *French v. Halcomb,* 26 App D C 307, 120 O. G. 1824 (1905), *Cherney v Clauss,* 25 App. D C 15, 116 O G 597 (1905); *Sendelbach v Gillette,* 109 O G. 276, 22 App D. C 168, *Talbot v Monell,* 23 App. D. C. 108, 109 O. G. 280, *Sharer v. McHenry,* 98 O G 585, 1902 C. D 503 (See also 98 O. G. 1486, 1902 C D 514, 103 O. G. 2174 and 1165)

Reasonable Doubt Defined. Effoits of courts to define what is meant by "reasonable doubt" have not iesulted in any established definition However the definition stated in Words & Phrases, Vol 7, page 5964, and supported by abundant authoities, is as follows

"Evidence is sufficient to remove a reasonable doubt when it convinces the judgment of an ordinarily prudent man of the truth of a pioposition with such force that he would voluntarily act upon that conviction, without hesitation, in his own most important affairs." *Stout v. State,* 90 Ind 1, 12, *Jaiiell v State,* 58 Ind 293, 296, *Aniold v State,* 23 Ind 170, *Troop v. State,* 92 Ind. 13-16; *Haiis v State,* 58 N. E 75, 77, 155 Ind. 265; *Williams v. U S.* 69 S W. 871, 874, *Miles v. United States,* 103 U S 304, 309, 26 L Ed 481; *United States v Allis,* 73 Fed 165, 167; *United States v Kenney,* 90 Fed. 257, 262, *United States v. Youtsey,* 91 Fed 864, 868, *United States v Fitzgeiald,* 91 Fed 374, 376, *United States v Wright,* 16 Fed 112, 114, *United States v Niemeyer,* 94 Fed. 147. 149, *United States v Politzer,* 59 Fed 273, 279, *Gannon v People,* 127 Ill 507; *People v Hughes,* 137 N Y 29, *Ryan v State,* 83 Wis 486, *Butler v State,* 92 Ga 601

98. Shifting the Burden of Proof. It often becomes a matter of controversy as to which party has the burden of proof and this usually arises out of the uncertainty about the filing dates to which the respective parties are entitled A party may discover after an interference has been declared that he is made the junior party theiein

55

where as he should have been made the senior party by reason of an earlier application filed by him, or by reason of his application being a continuing one, and which discloses exactly the same invention as that involved in interference. Under such circumstances he may make a motion to shift the burden of proof. This motion is within the jurisdiction of the Examiner of Interferences and not the Primary Examiner, and there is no appeal from his decision prior to final hearing. *Roulet & Nicholson v Adams.* 114 O. G. 1827; *Scott v. Southgate,* 121 O. G. 689, *Osborne v Armstrong,* 114 O. G. 2091.

Evidence to Support the Motion. No evidence is necessary to support the motion where the record in the respective cases show all the facts necessary to determine the question. *Bundy v Rumbarger.* 92 O. G. 2001.

99. Foreign Application—Burden. Where a party claims the benefit of a foreign application, the notice of interference will be prepared in accordance with the date of filing of the applications in this country, but the Examiner of Interferences may, upon a proper showing, shift the burden of proof and give the party the benefit of the filing date of his foreign application. *Steel & Steel v Myers.* 205 O. G. 1021, 1914 C. D. 74.

100. Priority—Evidence in Interferences. The testimony taken in an interference must be confined to the question of priority of invention of the issue. *Brill v. Adams v Uebelacher,* 99 O. G. 2966; 1902 C. D. 220.

Priority means priority in point of time to make the invention. *Trufant v. Brindle v Brown,* 101 O. G. 1608, 1902 C. D. 397.

Testimony must not be at variance with the preliminary statement, as to conception disclosure and reduction to practice. and testimony taken tending to establish earlier dates, if admitted, will be effective only for the purpose of establishing the dates alleged. *Cross v. Phillips.* 14 App D C 228, 87 O. G. 1399; 1899 C D 342, *Funk v Matterson v Haines,* 100 O G. 1563; 1902

56

C. D. 297, 20 App. D. C 285, 100 O G 1764, 1902 C D
553, *Lowrie v Taylor & Taylor*, 118 O. G 1681 (1905),
Fowler v Boyce, 118 O G 2534 (1905), 27 App D C.
55, 122 O G. 1726 (1906), 121 O G 1014, *Fowler v
McBerty*, 121 O G 1015 (1906), *Lowrie v Taylor &
Taylor*, 27 App D C 522, 123 O G 1665 (1906); *Herman v Fullman*, 109 O G 1888; *Hammond v Basch*,
115 O G 804, 24 App D C 469

101. Conception—Evidence of A conception of the
mind is not an invention until represented in some phy-
sical form *Clark Thread Co v Williamantic Linen Co*,
140 U S. 489, 35 L Ed 521, 525, *Voightmann, et al.,
v Perkinson, et al.,* 138 Fed 56, *Mergenthaler v Scudder*, 11 App D C. 264, 81 O G. 1417 (1897) In some
instances statements and conversations of the inventor
may be shown to establish conception of the invention.
In many cases of inventions, it is hardly possible in any
other manner to ascertain in the precise time and exact
origin of the particular invention The invention itself
is an intellectual process or operation, and, like all other
expressions of thought, can in many cases be scarcely
made known, except by speech The invention may be
consummated and perfect, and may be susceptible of
complete description in words, a month, or even a year
before it can be embodied in visible form, machine or
composition of matter Conversations and declarations
of the inventor that he made a certain invention, and describing its details and explaining its operations, are
properly to be deemed an assertion of his right, at that
time, as an inventor to the extent of the facts and details
which he then makes known, although the date of his
invention in such case would be the time when he makes
known the invention and not the time when he claims to
have first had it in mind, if that be a previous time
Philadelphia & Trenton Railroad Co v Stimpson, 14
Peters 448, 10 U S Law Ed 535, 542 If the inventor
orally describes his invention with sufficient clearness,

57

even though he does not state all the details, that an artisan can work out the details, he has disclosed an invention. *Westinghouse Electric & Mfg. Co v Stanley Instrument Co*, 133 Fed. 167.

Where an oral statement by the inventor is relied upon to prove invention it must be shown not only that the statement was sufficiently clear and complete to enable one skilled in the art to make the machine, or practice the process or art, but also that it was made to one who understood it and remembered it with sufficient accuracy to enable him to communicate it to the world. *Stephens v Salisbury*, 1 *McArthur's Patent Cases*, 385.

102. Kinds of Evidence to Prove Conception. The evidence may consist of oral or written description of the invention, or drawing or model or partly of one of these forms of evidence and partly of another But we have already seen that the description or drawing, or model, must be known to some one other than the inventor and the date of invention is the date upon which it is made known to such other person or persons, hence this brings us to the consideration of the question of disclosure, and, later the corroboration of the inventor

Disclosure Disclosure in the sense of the patent law must be made ordinarily to persons competent to understand and appreciate the alleged invention. Merely showing a device or drawing to witnesses who had no understanding of the invention, can not be considered a disclosure It is therefore plain that in proving disclosure it should be shown clearly that the person to whom the disclosure was made, understood the invention, remembered it with sufficient accuracy to communicate it to others, or could recognize the identical drawings or device exhibited to him and explain their meaning, or operation, or construction. Furthermore in order to make such evidence available to establish a date of invention, the witness or witnesses to whom the disclosure was made must be able to in some manner fix the time of

58

such disclosure with reasonable certainty, and, where they are called upon to testify some years after the event, great care should be exercised to establish, as near as possible, a definite time of disclosure which will not be dependent upon the uncertainties of memory as to when such event took place. *Eastman v Houston*, 95 O. G 2064, 1902 C D 386, 18 App D C. 135-140, *Henggi v. Dallmeyer*, 253 O. G. 514. A disclosure to one skilled in the art to which the invention belongs, is sufficient. Persons "skilled in the art" includes careful workmen who are skilled in the particular line of business in which they are engaged. *Pupin v. Hutin & Leblanc v. Stone*, 100 O G 931, 1902 C D 269 Where the witnesses make it appear that the inventor had in mind the result to be accomplished, but not the means by which it was to be done, conception and disclosure is not established *Cobb v Goebel*, 23 App D C 75, 108 O. G. 1591, *Brooks v Hillard*, 106 O G 1237 (1903): *Fenner v Blake*, 30 App D C 507, 134 O G 2244 (1908). The disclosure must be full and clear as to all essential elements of the invention and such as was sufficient in itself to enable the party to whom the disclosure was made to give the invention practical form and effect without the exercise of invention on his part. *Sendelbach v. Gillette*, 22 App D. C. 168, 109 O G 276. Disclosing matters which are old in the art, is not disclosing invention. *French v Holcomb*, 115 O G. 506 (1905). Where the inventor presents drawings witnessed and dated, it should appear that the witnesses whose names are signed thereto not only signed them on the date appearing on the drawings, but that they understood the invention and that the drawings at the time they are offered in evidence are in the same condition that they were when they were witnessed *Kukeguard & Jebsen v Ries*, 125 O G 1700 (1906). Where the wife of an inventor is offered as a witness to prove disclosure, it has been held that her testimony should be corroborated. The soundness of this

59

ruling may well be doubted *Harter v. Barrett,* 114 O.
G 975. Where an original application is relied upon for
disclosure it must appear that the invention in issue is
disclosed in that application as originally filed *Mc-
Knight v Pohle.* 30 App D C 92, 130 O. G. 2069 (1907),
McMulkin v Bollee, 126 O. G 1356 (1906) (See Reduction to Practice and Dates) It is not necessary that an
apparatus used to carry out a process be disclosed in
order to constitute a disclosure of the process *Osborne
v. Armstrong.* 19 Gour. 3-8 (Jan , 1907). Work done on
an invention in a foreign country is not available as evidence to prove conception or reduction to practice in the
United States R S Sec 4923 *DeKando v. Armstrong,*
37 App D C 314, 169 O. G 1185 A disclosure to one
of two joint inventors is a disclosure to both. *General
Electric Co v Steinberger,* 208 Fed 699-714. Circumstances surrounding an alleged disclosure of invention
may be such as to discredit the evidence as where Jenner
saw a notice of Dickinson s invention in 1900, and did
not file his own application for patent until he was induced to do so by Hildreth in 1902, it was held that no
value can be attached to testimony on his behalf that he
made the invention in 1899 *Jenner v. Dickinson, Thibodeau v Dickinson.* 117 O. G. 600 (1905) And where
for several years after the alleged conception. as appeared from the evidence. manufacturers were demanding a device of the kind in issue and the party made no
disclosure to such manufacturers nor any attempt to reduce to practice. but endeavored to sell patents upon
prior devices and failed on the express ground that they
did not possess the advantages found in the present invention, it was held that his claims to early conception
and disclosure are not entitled to consideration *Hope,
Jr.. v Voigt.* 115 O G 1585 (1905), 25 App D C. 22

103 **Corroboration of Inventor.** Corroborating evidence means evidence which tends to support and render
more probable some other evidence—generally that al-

ready produced—to the same point and like in character. Encyclopedia of Evidence, Vol 3, page 674

The mere uncorroborated statements of an inventor are not sufficient to show conception, disclosure or reduction to practice. The same rule holds true as to joint inventors because joint inventors constitute but a single party and their minds and interests become one, hence they can not corroborate each other *Freeman v Garrels & Kimball,* 102 O G 1777 (1903); *Mergenthaler v Scudder,* 11 App D C 264, 81 O G. 1477, *Garrels, et al, v Freeman,* 103 O G 1683, 21 App D. C 207, *Paul v Hess,* 113 O G 847, *Podelsak & Podelsak v McInnerney,* 26 App D C 399, 118 O G. 835 (1905), 120 O. G 2127. A witness may be able to corroborate the inventor as to certain details of his invention, even though his testimony does not corroborate him as to every detail sought to be established *Dunbar v Schellengers,* 125 O G. 348 (1906). Statements in an inventor's note book, alleged to disclose the invention in issue, are insufficient to prove conception, where it does not appear that the entry was ever shown to anyone *French v Holcomb,* 26 App D. C 307, 120 O G 1824 (1905) Vague and indefinite corroborating evidence of witnesses is insufficient to overcome a prior filing date of an opposing party *McKnight v Pohle & Croasdale,* 105 O. G. 977, *Steinmetz v Thomas,* 31 App. D C 574, 137 O. G 479 (1908), *Smith v Foley, et al,* 136 O G. 847 (1907), *Burson v Vogel,* 125 O G. 2361 (1906) The evidence should be clear and specific and not dependent upon inferences *Robinson v. Thresher,* 18 Gour. 21-21 (March, 1906); *Lotz v Kenny,* 19 Gour. 51-10 (July 13, 1907) The making of drawings on a specific date is not established by witnesses who have not had possession of the drawings since they were shown to them and who are not able to testify that they are in the same condition at the time their testimony is given as they were at the time they were shown to them. *Miller v Blackburn,* 172 O

61

G. 549 (1911); *Kirkegaard & Jebsen v. Ries,* 125 O G. 1700 (1906); *Freeman v Garrels & Kimball,* 102 O. G. 1777

104. Who May Be Corroborating Witnesses. An assignee may testify as a corroborating witness, though his testimony would not be given the same weight as it would if he were disinterested. *Turnbull v. Curtis,* 120 O G. 2442 (1905) The wife of the inventor. *Harter v Barrett,* 114 O. G. 975. One joint inventor can not corroborate another joint inventor. *Freeman v. Garrels & Kimball,* 102 O G. 1777 (1903).

105. Importance of Date of Conception in Interference Cases. In an interference case, the date of conception and disclosure becomes important on the question of priority, to the party who was last to file his application or last to reduce to practice, so when he is the first to conceive but the last to reduce to practice, he is entitled to an award of priority where he has followed up his conception and disclosure by due diligence, more particularly diligence in reducing his invention to actual practice than in filing his application for a patent or manufacturing his device for public use *Oliver v Felbel,* 20 App D C 255, 100 O G 2384; 1902 C D 565; *Cooke v Jones & Taylor,* 116 O G 1181 (1904)

106. Diligence. Many interference cases turn on the question as to which of the parties exercised diligence in following up his invention and putting it into practical, useful form. We have seen that invention is a mental process, in the first instance, and that so long as it remains in the mind of the inventor, undisclosed to anyone else, it serves the world no purpose and does not advance the arts or sciences The inventor may refuse to disclose his discoveries The object of the public in granting a patent is to obtain the benefit of the discovery and therefore inventors are encouraged to put their discoveries into practical useful form. Not only in patents, but in many other affairs of life, the law rewards the

62

diligent. An inventor may conceive an invention and make drawings of it, but he will not be permitted to stop at that point and through utter carelessness give it no more consideration for a long period of time, if while he is sitting idly by, another, more industrious, makes the same discovery that he has made and proceeds with due dispatch to put the discovery into form in which the public can obtain the benefit thereof There can be no good reason for depriving this later, diligent, industrious inventor of a reward in the form of a patent, merely to accommodate the doless, idle inventor who has no excuse for holding back his invention

There are, however, many circumstances which may contribute to prevent an inventor from putting his invention into useful form, and for this reason we hear the apparently delinquent as to what excuse he may have to offer for not being more diligent in reducing his invention to actual practice or what excuse he may have for not filing his application for a patent at an earlier date. The excuses which have been offered cover a wide range, and some have been found to be reasonable and legitimate while others have been found to be insufficient as against another inventor who has been diligent and has no need to offer excuses Diligence is therefore the essence of the proper relation between conception and reduction to practice, and must consist of the degree of effort that can fairly be characterized as substantially one continuous act *Twentieth Century Machinery Co v Loew Mfg Co*, 243 Fed 373 There is no fixed rule of diligence applicable to all cases alike Whether the delay shown shall be regarded as excusable or inexcusable, must necessarily depend upon the special circumstances surrounding the actions of the party in the particular case wherein the application of the rule may be sought *Christensen v. Ellis,* 94 O. G 2561; 1901 C. D. 326, 17 App. D. C 498

Whoever first perfects a machine is entitled to the

63

patent therefor and is the real inventor, although others may have previously had the idea and made some experiments toward putting it in practice, subject, however, to this qualification, that if the party who conceives the invention was at the time of a second invention by another party using reasonable diligence in perfecting the same, he is entitled to be recognized as the first inventor, although the second to conceive may have been the first to reduce to practice, either actually or constructively. In other words, the inventor who starts work on an invention is required to keep working at it or show a good reason for not working at it or applying for a patent. *Funk v Matteson v Haines*, 20 App. D C. 285, 100 O G. 1764, 1902 C D 553; *Agawam Co v Jordan*, 7 Wall. 583.

107. To What Diligence Relates Diligence relates to the efforts of a party to perfect his invention mechanically and not to efforts to exploit the invention commercially, so where a party is in straightened financial condition, he should devote his attention to securing means necessary to construct his machine, or, if unable to do that, to securing assistance to apply for a patent. *Seeberger v Dodge*, 113 O. G. 1415; *Turnbull v. Curtis*, 120 O G 2442 (1905).

108. Of Whom a Showing of Diligence Is Required. Diligence is required of the first to conceive but last to reduce to practice. Under our patent system, he who first arrives at a complete conception of an invention is entitled to a patent therefor unless the interest of the public is compromised by his lack of diligence in demonstrating that his invention is capable of useful operation As between two inventors of the same thing, the one who first reduces the discovery to practical operation is deemed prima facie the true inventor without regard to the date of his conception, but the earlier inventor may overcome such presumption by satisfactory evidence that he used due diligence to perfect and utilize the in-

64

vention, and actual reduction to practice is preferable to that which is constructive merely. *Laas, et al., v. Scott, et al*, 161 Fed. 122. *Eastern Paper Bag Co v Continental Paper Bag Co*, 142 Fed 479, 516; *Continental Rubber Works v Single Tube, etc., Co*, 178 Fed 452, *Gabowsky v Gallaher*, 191 O. G. 835.

109. **When Not Applicable.** A showing of diligence is not required of the inventor who was the first to reduce his invention to practice *Grabowsky v Gallaher*, 39 App D C 548, 191 O G 835, *Paul v Johnson*, 23 App. D C 187, 109 O G 807, *Thompson v Storrie*, 245 O G 845, 46 App D C 324, *Henderson v Gilpin*, 186 O G 289.

110. **At What Time Diligence Is Required.** One who is the first to conceive but the last to reduce to practice, must show due diligence from a time just previous to the entry of his opponent into the field. *Scott v Laas & Sponenburg.* 118 O G. 1367 (1905); *Braun v. Wahl*, 45 App D. C 291, 228 O G. 1458; *Givens v Warren*, 216 O G 1013, 44 App. D. C. 10, *Christie v Seybold*, 55 Fed 69

111. **Comparative Diligence.** Comparative diligence of the parties is not material. *Paul v Johnson*, 109 O G. 807, 23 App D. C 187.

112. **Work On Auxiliary Inventions** That the inventor was engaged in work on an auxiliary invention is generally no excuse except where it is necessary to have the auxiliary invention perfected in order to use the invention in issue *Stapleton v. Kinney*, 18 App D C. 394, 96 O G 1432; 1901 C. D 414; *Lotterhand v Hanson*, 23 App D. C. 372, 110 O. G. 861, *Luby v. Taylor*, 118 O G 835 (1905), *Turnbull v Curtis*, 120 O G 2442 (1905).

113. **Work on Other Forms of the Device.** That the inventor was at work on other forms of the device is ordinarily no valid excuse for doing nothing on the form of device in issue *Clement v Richards, etc*, 113 O G.

7 65

1143; *Briggs v. Lillie, etc*, 116 O. G. 871 (1904); *Jones v Wolff*, 17 Gour. 53-8 (July, 1905).

114. Work on Other Inventions. That the inventor was engaged in perfecting other inventions is no valid excuse for laying aside the invention in issue. *Robinson v Copeland*, 111 O G 579; *Liberman v Williams*, 23 App D. C 223, 109 O G. 1610, *Taylor v Westinghouse*, 119 O G 1257 (1905); *Kilbourn v Hiner*, 124 O G 1841 (1906), *Tower v. Yost*, 19 Gour 66-3 (July, 1907).

115. Business Convenience. While the inventor is not required to devote his entire time to the reduction of his invention to practice under circumstances which would ordinarily deprive him of the means whereby he obtains a livelihood, still he will not be permitted to offer as a valid excuse that because of a certain contract he had entered into he was prevented from perfecting his invention, or applying for a patent, or that his personal business commanded his time in another direction, or that he delayed action for the purpose of interesting some person of large capital for exploitation of the invention. *Watson v Thomas*, 106 O G. 1776 (1903); *Miehle v Read*, 18 App D C 128, 96 O. G 426, 1901 C D. 396; *Clement v Richards, etc*, 113 O G. 1143, *Robinson v Copeland*, 24 App D C 68, 112 O G. 501, *Taylor v. Westinghouse*, 119 O G 1257 (1905); *Seeberger v Dodge*, 114 O. G 2382, 24 App D C. 476-485, *Wyman v Donnelly*, 21 App D. C. 81, 87, *Wilson & Willard Mfg. Co. v. Bole, et al.*, 227 Fed 607, 610

116. Poverty. Where poverty is offered as an excuse for inactivity the claim will be carefully scrutinized, including the credit of the applicant, his expenditures in other directions, his earnings, his efforts to obtain assistance from others, and if too poor to construct his machine it must also appear that he was too poor to apply for a patent at an earlier date Usually this excuse has not been established *Turnbull v Curtis*, 123

66

O G 2312 (1906); *Feinberg v Cowan*, 29 App D C 80, 125 O. G. 667 (1906), 128 O G 889, *Woods v Poor*, 126 O G 391 (1906) ; *Donnelly v Wyman*, 103 O G. 657 (1903) Where poverty is the alleged excuse for not filing an application, it must be shown that the circumstances were of a compelling nature and not merely a matter of business convenience, and the filing of other applications in the meantime would rebut any such claim. *Paul v Hess*, 113 O G 847, 115 O G 251, *Turnbull v Curtis*, 120 O G 2442 (1905), *McNeal v Macey*, 106 O G 2287 (1903), *Gibbons v Peller*, 124 O G 624 (1906)

117 Commercial Diligence Is of No Consequence. Where the inventor spends his time and efforts to get investors interested in exploiting his invention commercially, or in trying to interest a corporation in adopting his invention, and does nothing to perfect his invention mechanically and test its efficiency, he is not diligent in the direction which the law requires. *Seeberger v. Dodge*, 113 O. G. 1415, 24 App D. C. 476, 114 O. G 2382, *Gallagher v. Hein*, 25 App D. C 77, 115 O. G 1330 (1905), *Turnbull v. Curtis*, 120 O. G. 2442 (1905), *Laas & Sponenburg v Scott*, 122 O. G. 352 (1905)

118. Shifting Responsibility to Guardian or Assignee Since responsibility must rest upon someone, if a minor attributes his lack of diligence to his guardian, then the guardian must explain the reasons for delay If through the intervention of the guardian the minor was prevented from perfecting his invention, then the minor must show diligence after he became of age. *Fuller v Jones*, 115 O G 1066; *Fuller v Hewlett*, 17 Gour 3-6 Nor can responsibility for lack of diligence be shifted to an assignee *O'Connel v Schmidt*, 118 O G 588 (1905)

119. Making of Drawings and Blue Prints. The making of drawings and blue prints is no evidence of diligence unless it is followed promptly by construction and testing of the device, or by application for a patent. *Watson v Thomas*, 108 O G. 1590, 23 App D C 65

Large Cost. The great cost of building and testing an invention is no valid excuse, if within the means of the inventor. *Sceberger v Dodge*, 113 O. G. 1415.

Infringement Suit. Where a party relies upon the existence of an infringement suit as the cause of his delay, he must show what there was in that infringement suit to prevent his reducing to practice the invention in issue. *Hammond v Basch*, 115 O. G. 804, 24 App D C 469 Belief that a prior patent covered the issue is no excuse *Secberger v. Dodge*, 114 O G. 2382, 24 App. D C 476

Sickness. Where one gives the excuse of sickness for his inactivity, he must show that he was diligent up to the time of his illness and subsequent thereto. *Paul v. Johnson*, 106 O. G. 2013 (1903)

120. Time for Experimenting. Long delay in producing an invention will not be tolerated, especially where it is shown that the inventor had, or could readily have obtained facilities for speedy construction of his invention. *Courson v. O'Connor*, 38 App D C 484, 181 O G 544; *Slick v Hansen*, 39 App D. C. 131, 181 O. G. 1076; *Bradley v Miggett*, 179 O G. 1108 (1911).

121 Reasonable Diligence—What Is. Reasonable diligence, like "reasonable doubt" is not capable of any exact definition What is a reasonable time in one case, may under other circumstances be unreasonable The court will grant great latitude when the inventor is delayed by reason of circumstances over which he has no control; but where the delay is caused by the negligence of the inventor, or for a manifest ulterior purpose, no leniency whatever should be extended. *Nelson v Faucette*, 143 O G. 1348, 33 App D. C. 217

Reasonable Diligence Shown. For particular cases where the parties have been held to have exercised reasonable diligence under the circumstances shown, see *Rowe v Brinkman*, 172 O. G. 1090, *Cragg v Strickland*, 250 O. G. 255, *Sauer v Groebli*, 239 O G 653, *Oakes*

68

v *Young*, 152 O G 1225, *Davis v Horton*, 136 O. G 1768, *Woods v Poor*, 130 O G 1313; *Dunbar v Schetlenberger*, 125 O G. 348 (1906), *Davis v Garrett*, 123 O G 1991 (1906) *Christensen v Ellis*, 94 O G 2561 1901 C D 326, *Roe v. Hanson*, 99 O G 2550, 1902 C. D 546, *Jones & Taylor v Cooke*, 117 O G 1493 (1905).

122. Diligence in Filing Application for Patent. After reduction to practice of the invention, a mere delay of the inventor in applying for a patent, in the absence of concealment (see Title Concealment), abandonment (see Title Abandonment), or suppression, will not prevent an inventor from obtaining a patent based on priority of invention *Rose v Clifford, etc*, 135 O G 1361 (1908); *Hubbard v. Berg,* 195 O G. 818. So he is allowed a reasonable time to perfect his invention before applying for a patent *Mead v Davis & Varney*, 31 App. D. C 590, 136 O G 2001 (1908) . Even a delay of six years was permitted, where, notwithstanding the long delay, he was the first to file his application *Kellogg, etc, Co. v International Telephone Mfg. Co, et al.*, 158 Fed. 104-108, 171 Fed. 651, 656. A delay of four years in filing an application, in the absence of evidence showing actual abandonment of the invention, was held not to estop the applicant on the ground of concealment stated in (*Mason v Hepburn*, 13 App. D. C 86, 84 O G. 147) *Rolfe v Kaisling v Leeper*, 143 O G 562, *Walker v. Lederer*, 179 O G. 851.

123. Intervening Rights. Inventors striving, in good faith, and with due diligence to perfect their inventions, instead of engaging in a race of diligence to reach the Patent Office with crude and probably inoperative devices, should be commended for their delay rather than be charged with laches, but there is sometimes a tendency to hold back applications for patents in order to circumvent rival claimants and to prolong the life of the monopolies granted, which tendency should be rebuked whenever it is possible to do so. *Fefel v Stock-*

er. 17 App D C 317. 94 O G. 433, 1901 C D 269, *McNeal v Macey*, 106 O G 2257 (1903) Where during a delay of six years a rival had entered the field, widely advertised the device and sold several thousand of them, it was held that the first to reduce to practice but who had secreted his invention, never made public use of it or otherwise gave it to the public had lost his rights *Davis, etc. v National Steam Specialty Co*, 164 Fed 191 One who conceives a broad invention but fails to claim it broadly leaves the field open to specific inventions other than his own He can not control all specific inventions by procuring a broad patent on the broad invention the claim to which he did not advance prior to the making of a specific invention by a later inventor *Wood v Beckman*, 89 O G 2459, 15 App D C 484

124. **Unexplained Delay in Filing Application.** Long delay, unexplained, creates a presumption that what was done amounted merely to an abandoned experiment (See Abandoned Experiment) *Smith v Brooks*, 21 App D C 75, 112 O G 953. *Sendelbach v Gillette*, 22 App D. C. 168, 109 O. G. 276, *Warner v. Smith*, 13 App D C 111, 94 O G 311. *McDonald v Edison*, 105 O. G. 973 (1903), *Winter v Slick, etc*. 107 O. G. 1659 (1903) *Oliver v Felbel*, 100 O G 2384, 1902 C. D 565, 20 App D. C 255

125 **Diligence of Attorney in Filing Application.** Where the attorney was given the invention in February to prepare an application, the Patent Office drawings were made in July and the specifications were prepared in October, it was held that the party was not diligent, and that a showing that his attorney was sick for six weeks during that time, was not a sufficient excuse *Briggs v Lillie, etc*. 116 O G 871 (1904) A delay of three months by an attorney in filing an application was held not to constitute a lack of diligence. *Poe v. Scharf*, 130 O. G. 1309 (1907).

126. **Diligence in Prosecuting Application.** After a

70

party has filed his application his rights become fixed and he can not be charged with a lack of diligence because of delays in the prosecution of his application *Mehle v Read*, 18 App D C 128, 96 O G 426, 1901 C. D. 396, *McDuffec v Hestonville, etc, Co*, 181 Fed. 503-512, *Young v Struble*, 153 O. G 1223, *Shreeve v Grissinger*, 202 O. G 951 (1914).

127. Documentary Evidence—Letters. Where letters are offered in evidence accompanied by proof that they were received in the ordinary course of business, that the recipient was familiar with the signature of the party who purports to have written them; that they are in his handwriting or signed by him, they are admissible *Royce v. Kempshall*, 125 O G 1347 (1906). Where letters were introduced as collateral evidence relating to the conduct of a party, and it was shown that they were received in the due course of business and acted upon by the writer and the person to whom they were sent, no other proof of their genuineness was necessary. *Jones & Taylor v Cooke*, 25 App D C. 524, 117 O G 1493 (1905) A letter properly deposited in the United States mail will be presumed to have reached its destination and to have been received by the addressee in due course, but such presumption may be rebutted by evidence. Abbott's Proof of Facts, page 664. This presumption is overcome by testimony of the addressee that he never received it. *Aull v. Interstate Sav & Loan Ass'n*, 15 Wash 627, 47 Pac. 13 Letters from an agent are admissible if the agency is established. *Beaver v Taylor*, 1 Wall 637, 17 Law Ed 601 Where a party testified that letters offered in evidence were received by him through the mail in answer to letters written by himself, they will be presumed in the absence of any showing to the contrary, to be the letters of the party whose name is signed to them *Briggs v Lillie, etc.*, 116 O G 871 (1904), Abbott's Proof of Facts, page 660 If one party offers part of a connected correspondence, the

71

other party may offer the remainder thereof. Abbott's Proof of Facts, page 557.

Copies of Letters. Where the original letters are in possession of an adverse party and it is desired to introduce them in evidence, notice should be served on the adverse party or his attorney to produce them at a certain time and place, or on failure to do so, letter press or other copies thereof will be offered, but in such case proof should be offered that the copies are correct copies of the original *Boyce v Kempshall,* 125 O G 1347 The writer's execution of the letter must be shown before it is admissible in evidence, unless it is shown to have been mailed at the writer's place of residence and to be in answer to a letter previously written to him Abbott's Proof of Facts, page 659.

128. Refreshing Memory of Witness. Books, memoranda, letters or documents of most any kind may be used by the witness to refresh his memory as to the date of the happening of an event, but such means of refreshing the memory are not in themselves evidence proper to be introduced in evidence by the party who offers the witness, for the contents of such instruments, etc, may not in any manner bear upon the issue and may be wholly foreign to the issues, but on cross-examination opposing counsel may require the production of the memoranda used by the witness, in order that he may cross-examine upon the same. Abbott's Proof of Facts, pages 403 and 487 *Laas & Sponenburg v Scott,* 122 O. G 352, *Lowrie v. Taylor & Taylor,* 123 O G. 1665 (1906), 27 App D C 522

129. Photographs—Secondary Evidence. In most cases photographs are secondary evidence. The thing photographed is the primary evidence unless the photograph itself is the thing in dispute, but it would seem that photographs of things which it is manifestly impossible to produce before the tribunal should be received if they are accompanied by proper proof that

72

they are correct representations of such things or are offered as a part of the oral testimony of a witness. Abbott's Proof of Facts, pages 792, 793

130. **Blue Prints** are copies of some original, but they may be introduced as a part of the testimony of a witness and as such are made a part of his oral testimony *Fessenden v Pierce*, 21 Gour. 21-11 (Mar , 1909)

131. **Drawings.** One relying upon drawings to fix the time of conception or disclosure, must not only produce the drawings but he must also establish the fact as to when the drawings were made or disclosed to others, and the inventor's own statements, uncorroborated, are not sufficient to show when the drawings were made or when the drawings were exhibited to another. *Freeman v Gartels & Kimball*, 102 O. G. 1777 (1903).

132. **Exhibits.** Exhibits not properly marked, though filed in the Patent Office, need not be considered However the party was permitted to offer ex parte affidavits as furnishing a foundation for proof that they are the identical exhibits offered in evidence and the party was permitted to take proofs to establish such fact *Hendler v. Graf*, 96 O G 2063; 1901 C D 130

Exhibits, except by consent of the parties to the cause, can not be taken from the Patent Office They will, however, be sent in charge of an employee of the office. *Seiler v Goldberg*, 116 O G 595

Identification of Exhibits. Where the witnesses identify an exhibit by its general appearance and have no knowledge of the invention embodied in it and it appears that the invention in controversy is a feature of construction almost hidden from view and having no effect upon the general appearance, such testimony does not prove the existence of the invention in controversy at the date stated. *Harris v. Stern & Lotz*, 105 O. G. 259 (1903)

The claim has often been made that exhibits were changed after being introduced in evidence, or after fil-

73

ing To avoid such controversies, the exhibit should be carefully described at the time of its introduction

133. **Reduction to Practice—Actual.** To constitute actual reduction to practice it is necessary (except in certain cases where actual test is manifestly unnecessary) to do more than make the device or machine It must be shown that the machine was capable of performing the work for which it was designed, at least to a small degree of efficiency *Macdonald v Edison*, 105 O G. 973 (1903). **Sale Commercially.** So where the evidence showed that the machine had been built, practically tested and sold commercially as an operative machine, the facts were held to establish beyond a reasonable doubt a reduction to practice. *Otis Elevator Co , et al , v. Interborough, etc , Co*, 222 Fed. 501 The machine must embody the elements of the issue, be put to practical use and operated successfully to perform the particular work for which it was intended The fact that the inventor afterwards constructed one or more other machines with a view to greater mechanical perfection, or where the inventor constructs a cheaper or lighter machine, or changes certain details to perfect it for the trade, such subsequent constructions do not alter the fact that the former construction was a reduction to practice *Thomas v. Trissel*, 107 O G 265 (1903) ; *Trissel v. Thomas*, 109 O G. 809, 23 App. D. C. 219; *Hein v Buhoup*, 81 O. G. 2088, *Blackford v Wilder*, 104 O. G 578 (1903), 21 App D. C. 1.

Mere progress to an end is not sufficient, however near that progress may have been to the end in view The law requires certainty and the inventor must show that his machine was actually capable of performing the work for which it was intended *Funk v Matteson v Haines*, 20 App. D. C 285, 100 O. G 1764, 1902 C. D 553, *Macdonald v Edison*, 21 App D C 527, 105 O G 1263 (1903).

The Mechanism Claimed Must Operate Successfully.

Though it is not necessary that the machine be perfect or that all parts of the machine in which it is used shall be mechanically perfect, still, as to that part of the machine which is in issue, there must be successful operation A failure can not be excused by making the claim that a skilled mechanic could have made it operate successfully. *Swerhart v Mauldin*, 99 O. G. 665, 1902 C. D. 137 (See Tests)

134. Imperfections. To constitute a reduction to practice it is not necessary that a machine be perfect, but it must appear that a structure embodying all the essential elements of the invention did accomplish the result for which it was intended, in a reasonably practical way. A machine may be even crude and not made with materials which would ordinarily and naturally be used by a manufacturer and still be a reduction to practice, if in such form it is practically operative and performs the function for which it is intended *Cummings v McKenzie*, 110 O G. 1167, *American Co v Tool Co*, 4 Fisher 299, *Halwood v. Lalor v. Bockhoff*, 21 App D. C 61, 103 O G. 887 (1903), *Spaulding v. Norden*, 24 App D. C. 286, 112 O. G 2091, 114 O G 1828, *Smith v. Brooks*, 24 App D C. 75, 112 O G. 953, *Hope, Jr., v Voight*, 25 App D. C 22, 115 O G 1585 (1905); *Lowrie v. Taylor & Taylor*, 27 App. D. C 522, 123 O. G. 1665 (1906); *Burson v Vogel*, 29 App. D. C 388, 131 O. G 942 (1907).

135. Crude Structure. Where a structure was so crude as to make it necessary to make further experiments before undertaking to build machines in accordance with the exhibit and it appears that it is essentially an experimental device, it is not a reduction to practice *Ocumpaugh v Norton*, 25 App D C 90, 115 O. G 1850; *Lindemeyer v Hoffman, et al.*, 18 App D C 1, 95 O G. 838 (1901)

136 Reduction to Practice in a Foreign Country. The construction of a successful device in a foreign country is not a reduction to practice in this country, even when the inventor conceives the invention here and goes abroad to install the apparatus *Lorimer v Erickson,* 227 O G. 1445, 44 App. D C 503, *Bell v Brooks,* 1881 C D. 8, *Tucker v Davis,* 2 O G 224; *DeKando v Armstrong,* 169 O G 1185, 37 App. D C 314, *Bradley v Miggett,* 179 O G 1108 (1911)

137. Reduction to Practice by An Assignee. Where an invention has been assigned, the assignee may reduce it to practice and such reduction inures to the benefit of such assignee, whether the inventor contributes to the reduction or not, and even though the machine constructed may embody features patentably different from the original *Thomas v Stewart* 202 O G 1259 (1913), 42 App D C 222

138. Agent Reducing to Practice. A reduction to practice by an agent inures to the benefit of the principal, but it is not enough to entitle an applicant to a patent that someone else, not his agent, has shown the practicability of the invention by reducing it to practice *Hunter v Stikeman,* 13 App D C 214, 226, *Robinson v McCormick,* 128 O G. 3289, 29 App. D. C 98, 111, *Shuman v Beall,* 123 O G 1664, *Howell v Hess,* 30 App D. C 194, 132 O G. 1074 (1907), *Hathaway v. Field,* 261 O G 413 (1919). Where an invention is reduced to practice by one not authorized to do so, such reduction to practice does not inure to the benefit of the inventor *Howell v Hess,* 122 O. G 2393 (1906)

139. Model. While a model, in the strict meaning of that term, is not a reduction to practice, nevertheless, where a device was called a model but was actually used for the purpose intended and completely demonstrated its practicability, even though but half size of a commercial machine, it was held to be a reduction to practice. *Gallagher v Hein,* 25 App D. C. 77, 115 O. G. 1330 (1905), *Hammond v. Basch,* 115 O G 804, 24 App. D. C 460, *Hope, Jr, v. Voight,* 25 App. D C 22; 115 O.

76

G. 1585 *Robinson v Thresher*, 123 O G 2975, 28 App
D C 22

140. **Machine Incomplete at the Time of Taking Testimony.** Though a machine may not be complete at the
time of taking testimony, if it is clearly established that
the missing parts were present at the time it was operated, and where it also appears that the test showed successful operation, it would be a reduction to practice
Basch v. Hammond, 113 O G. 551; *Brooks v. Seelinger,*
116 O G 1735 (1905), *Wyman v Donnelly,* 104 O. G.
310 (1903), 21 App. D. C. 81. And where the device
only required the addition of a mechanical detail which
any mechanic skilled in the art would have supplied and
such detail itself is old in the art, it was held a reduction
to practice *Howard v Bowes,* 137 O. G. 733 (1908), 31
App D C 619

TESTS.

141. **Tests Are Required as a General Rule.** As a general rule a machine must be tested to demonstrate its
fitness to accomplish the result for which it was designed.
Macdonald v. Edison, 105 O. G. 1263 (1903), 21 App.
D. C 527; *Paul v Hess,* 115 O G 251; *Gallagher v.
Hein,* 115 O G. 1330, *O'Connell v. Schmidt,* 122 O G.
2065 (1906); *Wickers & Furlong v McKee,* 129 O. G
869 (1907); *Pool v Dunn,* 151 O G 450 The condition
of the prior art must be considered in determining necessity of test. *Sachs v Haskins,* 21 Gour 17-1 (Mar,
1909)

When Tests Are Not Necessary. When a device is so
simple that it is apparent upon inspection that it will
perform the intended function no test is necessary to
establish a reduction to practice *Mason v Hepburn,* 13
App D C 86, 84 O. G 147; 1898 C. D. 510, *Lindemeyer v Hoffman, et al,* 18 App D. C 1, 95 O G 838;
1901 C. D 353, *Loomis v Hauser,* 19 App D C 401, 99
O G 1172, 1902 C. D 530; *Landa v Kavle,* 158 O G.
228 (1910), *Gaisman v Gillette,* 165 O G 244; *Cham-*

bers & King v. Frost, 170 O. G. 244, 246, 37 App. D C. 332.

Particular Devices, Tests of Which Were Held Necessary:

Type-bars for typewriters *Paul v Hess*, 115 O G. 251.

Graduated printing plate *Wickers & Furlong v McKee*, 129 O. G 860.

Mechanism to be put in a telephone circuit *O'Connell v Schmidt*, 122 O G. 2065.

Bottle cap so crude as not to be capable of actual use. *Lindemeyer v. Hoffman*, 95 O. G. 838.

A cloth cased horse-collar stuffed with cotton. *Couch v Barnett*, 110 O. G. 1431

Ticket holder for theater tickets. *Loomis v. Hauser*, 99 O G 1172

Electrical circuit protector *Rolfe v Hoffman*, 121 O. G 1350.

Roller bearing. *Winter v Slick, etc*, 107 O G. 1659.

Typewriting machine. *Paul v Hess*, 113 O G. 847.

Garment hook. *Lowrie v Taylor & Taylor*, 118 O G. 1681

Cover-strip for the ends of the blades of a turbine wheel *Emmett v Fullagar*, 124 O G 2178

Inverted gas-mantle *Daggett, Jr., v. Kauffman*, 145 O. G. 1024.

Fuse for electric lighting circuit *Sachs v Haskins*, 21 Gour. 17-2 (March, 1909)

Casing for transmission gearing. *Huff v. Gulick*, 177 O. G 525

Sound boxes for phonograph *Rinehart v Gibson*, 185 O G. 527

Printing press *Miehle v Scott & Scott*, 190 O. G. 1030.

Rail-anchor *Laas, et al, v Scott, et al*, 161 Fed 122, 126.

78

Linked bracelet *Hadley v Ellis*, 265 O. G. 458 (1919), 258 Fed 984

142. Kind of Test Required. The kind of test that is required is a test which will show that the machine as constructed did perform the work which it was intended to perform, and though it is safer practice to show a test under actual service conditions such showing may not be necessary if its practicability can be established by a test elsewhere *Roe v Hanson*, 99 O. G 2550, 1902 C D 546, *Rolfe v Hoffman*, 121 O G 1350 (1905) *Ebersole v Durkin*, 132 O G 842 (1907).

A shop test may in some cases be sufficient *Wyman v Donnelly*, 21 App. D C 81, 104 O G 310 But it was held that a shop test of a rail anchor was not sufficient. *Laas, et al v Scott, et al*, 161 Fed 122, 127. Nor was a test of a garment stay not under actual service conditions. *Barcley v. Schuler*, 41 App. D. C. 250, 199 O G 309 Nor was a test of a tire-holding device by merely bouncing upon the floor a wheel having the device and a tire attached *Jobski, etc v Johnson*, 247 O. G 479. Nor a test of an electric lighting system for railway cars not tested on railway cars *Bliss v. Thompson*, 20 Gour. 19-8 (March, 1908). But for contrary view see decision of Court of Appeals, D C *Creveling v Jepson*, 226 O G 339, 44 App D C 445 Commercial practicability not necessary if it be shown that the device accomplished the end desired *Laas, et al v Scott, et al*, 161 Fed 122, *Roe v Hanson*, 19 App D C 559, 99 O G 2550, 1902 C D 546, *Emerson v Sanderson*, 174 O. G 831 (1911).

An experimental test may or may not establish a reduction to practice, depending upon the nature of the invention and the results shown by the test. *Mills v Torrance*, 17 Gour. 67-6 (Oct., 1905); *Dashiell v. Tasker*, 21 App D C 64, 103 O. G 2147 (1903), 102 O G 1551

Mechanical changes may be necessary and still constitute a reduction to practice It is only necessary that

79

the device reasonably meet the requirements of the specification. *Pool v Dunn*, 151 O G. 450, 34 App D. C 132

143   Parts Broken. The mere fact that some part was broken during the test does not necessarily show an unsuccessful operation, if it was ordinary breakage which might be expected of similar machines under similar conditions. *Double v Mills*, 112 O G 1747. But where, as a result of breaking the materials had to be changed, as well as the shape of the device, the test was held insufficient. *Gilman & Brown v Hinson*, 118 O G. 1933 (1905). And where in the test the device was crushed to fragments, it was held not a sufficient test *Gallagher v Heine*, 114 O. G 974 Where the device was embodied in an automobile and after a run of eighty miles, certain parts were broken, even though the injury did not appear to be to the novel parts, it was held an insufficient test. *Huff v. Gulick*, 38 App. D C 334, 179 O G 579 But where a machine had been used for six months and the only broken part was a rivet supporting one of the parts, the test was held sufficient. *Foote v. Wenk*, 118 O. G 1366 (1905)

144.   Must Include All the Elements of the Issue. The test must generally include all the elements of the issue *Henderson v Gilpin*, 186 O. G 289 (1911), 39 App D. C 428, 187 O G. 231, *Miehle v Scott & Scott*, 40 App. D C 17, 190 O G 1030, *Hett v. Swinnerton*, 181 O. G. 542 (1911) But where some of the elements were old and the nature of the invention was such that a test was hardly necessary, it was held that the test established a successful reduction to practice even though lacking some elements of the issue *Stewart v Thomas*. 202 O G 1262, 42 App D C 222

145.   When Test Must Be Made. To overcome a prior filing date, the test must have been made prior to the filing date of the opposing party *Miehle v. Scott & Scott*, 190 O. G 1030, 40 App. D C. 17.

80

146. Chemical Compound Test. It is sufficient to show that the compound had some apparent usefulness *Potter v. Tone,* 163 O G 729 (1911), *Silverman v Hendrickson,* 99 O G 445, 1902 C D 123

147 Process Test. A process may be shown to have been successfully reduced to practice even though the product was defective, due to defective material and not to the fact that the process was not successfully carried out. *Appert v. Brownsville Plate Glass Co,* 144 Fed 115, 118

148. Two Forms of Machine—One Test Where after making a successful test of one form of machine, the inventor made an improved form and showed the second form in his application, making broad claims, including the first form, it was held a reduction to practice *Wyman v Donnelly,* 21 App. D C 81, 104 O G 310 (1903) Affirming Commissioner, 103 O G 657

149 Evidence of Success of Test. In proving successful operation, care should be exercised to avoid introducing merely the conclusions or opinions of the witnesses (unless they are persons skilled in the art) without stating the facts upon which such opinions or conclusions are based, and it is not sufficient for the witnesses to state that a machine was tested and found satisfactory While such evidence may be entitled to some weight, it is plain that in most cases such evidence would be merely the opinion or conclusions of the witnesses arrived at from what they observed during the test. The tribunal trying the case is the ultimate judge of whether the tests were satisfactory, and therefore such tribunal is entitled to know what was done at such tests and particularly what results were obtained. *Robinson v Thresher,* 123 O. G. 2627, 28 App D C. 22, 123 O. G. 2976 (1906); *Daggett v Kaufmann,* 33 App D C. 450, 145 O G 1024 Where the invention was a friction spring and the evidence showed that it was put in a vice and subjected to pressure, but there were no facts appearing of record which showed what the pressure was, nor any facts stated which would enable the court to determine whether the statement of the inventor that the test was satisfactory, was justified, it was held insufficient to show a reduction to practice *Gallagher, Jr v Hein,* 25 App D C. 77, 115 O G 1330 (1905), *Emmet v Fullager,* 124 O G. 2178 (1906).

150. Opinions of Witnesses Skilled in the Art. The Court of Appeals, D C, in the case of *Seeberger v Russell,* 121 O. G. 2328, 26 App D C 344, held that the opinions of witnesses skilled in the art and who were shown to have understood the invention or construction, that the device operated successfully, was sufficient to show reduction to practice though the facts upon which such conclusions were based were not stated *Horton v Zimmer,* 32 App D C. 217, 137 O G 2223 (1908), *Hopkins v Peters & Demont,* 199 O G 1243, 41 App. D C 302; *Ebersole v Durkin,* 132 O G 842 (1907).

151. Description of Invention Tested. It must of course clearly appear that the invention in issue is what was tested, and the witnesses who testify to its successful operation must be shown to have understood the invention *Schmidt v Clark,* 138 O G. 768, 32 App. D. C. 290

152. Tests Made at Time of Trial. Where a machine is operated at the time of trial for the purpose of showing that it will operate successfully, and witnesses are produced who testify that the machine is in the same condition as when it was first operated, and that the last operation is the same as the first, such facts would establish a reduction to practice. *Gordon v Wentworth,* 130 O. G. 2065 (1907); *Putnam v. Wetmore & Niemann,* 181 O G 269, 39 App. D. C 138 But where a party has failed to prove successful operation, he can not at the final hearing, operate an exhibit to show that it is in operative condition and would have so operated when first constructed *Taylor v. Gilman,* 158 O. G. 883

82

(1910), *Fefel v Stocker*, 94 O. G. 433, 1901 C D. 269, 17 App D C 317.

153. Organized Machine Successful—Presumption as to Subsidiary Parts. If an organized machine was successfully operated, it will be presumed that its subsidiary parts also operated successfully. *United Shoe Machinery Co. v Greenman*, 153 Fed 283, 286.

Adoption for Commercial Use Where an invention had been tested by the government and adopted as a model for the production of others like it, it was held to show a reduction to practice. *Schneider v. Driggs*, 162 O G. 1000, 36 App D C 116 Commissioner's decision, 162 O. G. 269.

154. Circumstances Discrediting Test. Where a witness after having used a tool, recommended the adoption of another similar tool, it was held that such conduct was stronger evidence that the test was unsatisfactory than his testimony that it was satisfactory. *Double v Mills*, 112 O. G 1747 The construction of another device to obviate defects in a prior device, tends to show that the first device was unsatisfactory *Marconi v Shoemaker*, 131 O G. 1939 (1907) So work on a similar device or devices tends to show that the first was unsatisfactory *Jobski, etc v Johnson*, 247 O G 479, 47 App D. C 230 Where a machine was constructed and tested for a short time but subsequently dismantled and parts of the same were lost and the machine was never again used or other similar machines made for several years, a presumption arises that the machine was unsatisfactory. *Gallagher v Hien*, 25 App. D. C. 77, 83, 1905 C. D. 624; *Seeberger v. Russell*, 117 O G 2086 But on the facts in the latter case the Court of Appeals, D C, arrived at a different conclusion. 26 App D C 344 But the mere fact that a machine was used but little and was then dismantled, is not conclusive that it was not successfully operated, for failure to use the machine may be satisfactorily explained *Stanbon v. Howe*,

83

etc , 153 O G. 823, 34 App. D C. 413· *United Shoe Machinery Co v. Greeneman*, 153 Fed 283, 286, *Funk, et al v Whitely*, 117 O G 280 (1905).

Long Delay in Putting a Machine in Actual Use—Effect. Long delay in putting a machine in actual use for the purposes intended, has always been regarded as a potent circumstance in determining whether the test was successful or only an abandoned experiment—*Sydeman & Meade v Thoma*, 141 O G 866, 32 App. D. C 362; *Thomas v. Weston*, 99 O G 864, 1902 C D 521, *Greenwood v Dover*, 1904 C D. 66 108 O. G. 2143; *Quist v. Ostrom*, 106 O. G. 1501.

Weight of Evidence. Ex parte tests will not be given as much weight as tests made in the presence of both parties *Bethlehem Steel Co v Niles, etc*, 160 Fed. 880 Affirmed, 173 Fed. 1019.

154a. Patentability of the Issue—Rule 130. One who desires to question the patentability of the issue to his opponent should first make a motion to dissolve **under** Rule 122. upon the ground that the claims are not patentable to his opponent, or in other words, that his opponent has no right to make the claims, and he may then argue the question on final hearing Rule 130 is intended to provide for the contingency that one party may have the right to make the claims and another party may not have the right to make them It can not be urged under this rule that none of the parties, including the moving party, have a right to make the claims, or that the counts are not patentable generally over the prior art But where a motion to dissolve assails the right of one of the parties for any reason to make the claims, the question of priority is directly involved, since one who can not make the claims would not in any event be entitled to an award of priority *Elsom v Bonner & Golde*, 246 O G 299 46 App D C 230 Rule 130 only gives a party the right to argue at final hearing the unpatentability of the claims to an opponent, and then only when it is material

to the right of such party to a patent, and other questions
arising on motion to dissolve, may not be presented on
final hearing, nor can a party argue the patentability of
the issue over the prior art *Molyneux v Onderdonk*,
191 O G. 292 (1918), *Havemeyer v Coryell*, 186 O G
558 (1912), *Weis v Mack*, 185 O G 830 (1912), *Smith
& Larsen v Hill*, 177 O G. 523 (1912) The right of a
party to argue at final hearing the right of his opponent
to make the claims, is conditioned upon his having first
moved to dissolve upon that ground, or having presented
a sufficient reason for his failure to do so. *Weis v Mack*,
185 O. G 830 (1912), *Broadwell v Long*, 164 O G. 252,
36 App D C 418 However, the office may consider the
question upon its own motion, even though no motion to
dissolve has been made *Smith v. Foley, etc*, 136 O G
847 (1907). A cause will not be set down for final hearing under Rule 130 except upon motion, which motion
should be made before, but may be made after, entry of
judgment upon the record *Noble v. Levine*, 180 O G.
602 (1912). Where a party moves to amend the issue
under Rule 109, and his opponent opposes the motion
upon the ground that the moving party has no right to
make the claims, such opponent may urge at final hearing
under Rule 130, the nonpatentability of the claims presented by such amendment *Leonard v Pardee*, 164 O
G. 249 (1911). Since the operativeness of an opponent's
device goes to his right to make the claims, this question
may be presented on final hearing under Rule 130, where
the question has previously been presented on motion to
dissolve. *Barber v Wood*, 127 O G 1991 (1907)

155. Operation of Similar Devices. Proof may be made
that another device of substantially the same construction operated successfully *Laas, et al. v. Scott, et al*,
161 Fed 126.

156. Abandoned Experiment. The proofs tending to
establish a reduction to practice must be considered as
a whole with all the surrounding circumstances of the

case and the action of the inventor with respect to his invention, whether he made or attempted to make use of it, or pursue his object to any final conclusion, whether he made any attempt to apply for a patent, whether he gave up his original structure and proceeded to work on some other or similar device for similar use, after testing the original, or threw the original on the scrap heap, permitting parts thereof to be lost, or delayed giving it any further consideration until he learned of a rival in the field It would therefore be quite impossible to state any general rule as to what is and what is not merely an abandoned experiment, since each case must rest upon the particular facts and circumstances shown *Ocumpaugh v. Norton*, 25 App. D C. 90, 115 O G 1850 (1905) Where an inventor does not use his machine, but permits it to slumber and does not apply for a patent, he can not resort to such invention as an anticipation of a subsequent patent by another *Welshbach Light Co v Cohn*, 181 Fed 122, 125. And where an invention is laid aside for six years until it is discovered that another has entered the field with a similar device, such inaction would strongly tend to show that the invention was impractical, or if operative, had been abandoned *Curtain Supply Co. v National Lock Washer Co*, 178 Fed 95

Discarding the Invention After Test. Where one throws aside his invention after test and does nothing more until he learns of others making a similar device, such action would indicate that the alleged invention was merely an experiment. *Lawrence v Voight*, 147 O. G 235 (1909); *Lemp v Mudge*, 114 O G. 763, 24 App. D C. 282; *Gilman & Brown v. Hinson*, 201 O G 1219 (1913), *Whipple v Sharp*, 112 O. G. 1749.

Another Device Put Upon the Market After Test. The circumstance that another device was put upon the market by the inventor, or those who were given charge thereof, after test of the invention in question, would indicate that the test was unsatisfactory and the invention merely an experiment *Paul v Hess*, 24 App D. C. 462, 115 O G. 251 (1905), *Quist v Ostrom*, 108 O G 2147; *Hilliard v Brooks*, 111 O G 302, 23 App D C 526, *Bliss v McElroy*, 122 O. G. 2687 (1906), *Gordon v Wentworth*, 31 App D C 150, 135 O. G 1125 (1908); *Gillman & Brown v. Hinson*, 122 O. G. 731, 26 App D C 409. Where the invention is laid aside for a long period after alleged reduction to practice, while the inventor works on other inventions, a presumption arises that his first invention was merely an abandoned experiment. *Adams v Murphy*, 96 O. G. 845, 1901 C. D. 401.

Inaction in the Face of Demand for the Invention. Total abandonment of effort in the face of a strong demand for the invention is proof positive that the device amounted only to an abandoned experiment. *Lemp v Mudge*, 24 App D. C 282, 114 O G 763, *Reichenbach v Kelley*, 94 O G 1185, 1901 C. D 282.

Delay as Evidence of Abandoned Experiment. A long delay after alleged reduction to practice, during which time the inventor develops other inventions, is convincing evidence that the alleged reduction to practice was merely an abandoned experiment. *Moore v. Hewitt*, 31 App. D. C 577, 136 O G. 1535 (1908) A delay of four years in applying for a patent is strong evidence that the device was not successful *Fefel v Stocker*, 94 O. G. 433; 1901 C. D 269, *Quist v Ostrom*, 108 O. G. 2147, 23 App D C 69.

Refusal to Adopt After Test. Where those who were relied upon to market the device abandoned the enterprise after test and refuse further assistance thereafter and nothing further was done by the inventor for several years, the invention was held to be an abandoned experiment *Pohle v McKnight*, 119 O G. 2519 (1905).

Abandoned for Financial Reasons. Where a party can make satisfactory proof showing that his inactivity was

87

due to lack of finances and it is further shown that his device was practically operated, such inactivity will not be regarded as an abandonment of the invention, nor as proof that his reduction to practice was merely an abandoned experiment. *Columbia Motor Car Co , et al. v C A Duerr & Co , et al ,* 184 Fed 893, 900.

Work Done by Hand After Alleged Reduction to Practice. Where the invention is intended to dispense with hand work and for three years after the alleged reduction to practice the inventor continued to do the work by hand, such circumstance was held to show that the invention was merely an abandoned experiment and not a reduction to practice. *Jenner v Dickinson, etc.,* 116 O. G 1181 (1904)

Making a Second Machine Where the inventor makes a second machine differing from the first merely in improvement in details, such fact does not show that the first machine was not successful *Brooks v. Smith,* 110 O. G 2013.

157. Concealment. The man who secretes an invention contributes nothing to the public The law owes nothing to the inventor who hides away his invention, and it is the settled doctrine of the Court of Appeals of the District of Columbia, and of the Patent Office, that when an inventor perfects and reduces to practice an invention, and fails for an unreasonable period to take steps to give it to the public, and until some one else has independently invented and patented it, the earlier inventor forfeits his right to a patent as against the later and more diligent inventor *Brown v. Campbell,* 201 O. G 905, 41 App D C 499, *Mower v Crisp,* 83 O G. 155, *Mason v Hepburn,* 84 O. G 147, 13 App D. C. 86; *Davis v Forsythe & Forsythe,* 87 O G 516; *Mower v Duell, Com'r,* 88 O G. 191; *Thomas v. Weston,* 94 O. G 985, 19 App. D. C. 373, *Wright v Lorenz,* 101 O G 661, *Macdonald v Edison,* 105 O G 973; *Kendall v. Winsor,* 21 How 322, 327, 328, *Matthes v Burt,* 114 O

88

G. 764, 24 App D. C 265   *Curtain Supply Co v National Lock Washer Co*, 174 Fed 45, 47, Robinson on Patents, Sec. 389

The doctrine of concealment is however, a strict one which will not be enforced except in cases which come clearly within it   So where there is nothing to indicate that a party was induced to file because of knowledge of activity on the part of another, and there are no circumstances to impugn his good faith, or he can satisfactorily explain his inaction and such explanation appears reasonable and in accord with conduct which might be reasonably expected of a person who was honestly seeking to give the public the benefit of his invention he can not be charged with concealment   *Brown v Blood*, 105 O. G. 976 (1903) ; *Gaisman v Gillette*, 36 App D. C. 440; *Hubbard v Berg*, 40 App D C 577; *Stewart v Thomas*, 42 App D. C. 222, *Piermann v. Chisholm*, 44 App D C 460, *Lederer v Walker*, 182 O. G 511; *Hathaway v Field*, 261 O G 413, 1919 C D. 460, *Aufiero v. Monnot*, 242 O. G. 750, 46 App D C. 297

The fact that an inventor conceals and suppresses his invention after reduction to practice and does nothing more with it in the way of giving the public the benefit of it, or applying for a patent, until he obtains some definite knowledge that another party has made the same invention and put it into use, or has applied for a patent, is usually sufficient to cause the first inventor to lose any rights he may have originally had in such invention. *Matthes v Burt*, 24 App D C 265, 114 O G. 764, *Gordon v. Wentworth*, 31 App D C 150, 135 O G 1125 (1908) ; *Dreckschmidt v Schaefer & Holmes*, 246 O G. 301, *Whitney v Brewer*, 177 O. G. 1296. So where a party after reducing his invention to practice, put it aside for more than a year until he discovered that his rival had put his invention upon the market, it was held that he must be charged with concealment.   *Howard v. Bowes*, 31 App D C 619, 137 O. G. 733 (1908).   The

89

question as to who was first to file his application is not material as to one who is properly chargeable with concealment *Whitney v Brewer*, 177 O. G 1296.

Disclosing to Others as Affecting Concealment. Where the inventor does not keep his invention secret but discloses it to others, there is no abandonment of the invention by concealment. *Chisholm v Pierman*, 225 O. G 1105 (1915) Nor where the inventor showed his invention to his opponent *Meyer v. Sarfert*, 102 O G 1555 (1903)

158. Originality. One of the questions which may arise in an interference and which is pertinent to the issue of priority, is that of originality It is plain that one who has derived his knowledge of the invention from his opponent is not an inventor Evidence that a third party, who is not a party to the record, invented the device in issue, is not material, hence evidence as to originality will be confined to the parties to the interference. *Foster v. Antisdel*, 88 O G 1527, 14 App D C. 552; *Pope v McKenzie*, 38 App D C 111, 176 O G 1072, *Thomas v Weintraub*, 175 O G 1097 (1911); *Herman v Fullman*, 107 O G 1094, *Bauer v Crone*. 118 O. G. 1071, *Doble v Henry*, 118 O G 2249 (1905)

159. Burden of Proof The burden of proving lack of originality is upon the one who asserts it, and the fact must be established by clear evidence in any case, but where the party against whom the charge is made has a patent which was granted prior to applicant's filing date, then the applicant must prove beyond a reasonable doubt, want of originality in such patentee *Kreag v Green*, 124 O G 1208 (1906); *Funk v Matteson v. Haines*, 100 O. G. 1764 (1902), 20 App D C 235, 100 O G 1563; 1902 C D. 297: *Swinglehurst v. Ballard*, 265 O G 459 (1919), 258 Fed 973

160. How Established. Lack of originality is a difficult fact to prove since direct evidence is not ordinarily obtainable and resort must be had to circumstantial

90

evidence As has often been said in criminal cases, circumstantial evidence is as reliable as any other evidence, provided the circumstances pointing to the existence of the fact in question are so complete in detail that no other reasonable conclusion can be drawn from them than that such fact exists *Reinhart v Gibson*, 185 O. G 1383, 39 App D C 358

161 **Opportunity of Derivation.** It is proper to show that a party had an opportunity of deriving his knowledge of the invention from his opponent, and the fact that he had such opportunity would be a strong circumstance tending to establish lack of originality, but the mere existence of such opportunity would not of itself be sufficient to establish lack of originality. *Wood v Poor*, 126 O G 391 (1906) , *Cutler v Keeney*, 17 Gour. 66-2 (Aug , 1905) Where two parties appear with the same invention, identical in many novel details, there would be a strong suspicion that one derived his knowledge from the other, if it also be shown that he had an opportunity to so derive such knowledge *Beal v Shuman,* 120 O G. 655 (1905)

162 **Failure to Rebut Evidence of Lack of Originality —Effect.** The failure of a party to rebut the sworn statement of his adversary that he fully disclosed the invention to him, is conclusive evidence that the latter was not the first inventor, and the oath filed with the application of the party so charged, is not sufficient to overcome the effect of such testimony *Winslow v Austin,* 14 App. D. C. 137 , *Hewlett v. Steinberger,* 40 App D. C 287, 190 O G 270; *Royce v Kempshall,* 125 O. G. 1347 (1906)

163. **Sufficiency of Disclosure to Prove the Charge.** Where one alleged that he communicated the invention to his opponent, he must show exactly what the nature of the communication was and that is was full and clear as to all essential elements of the invention, so as to enable the party to whom such disclosure was made to give it

91

practical form and effect without the exercise of invention on his part *Anderson v Wells*, 122 O G. 3014 (1906) , *Podelsak v McInnerney*, 26 App. D C 399, 120 O G 2127 (1906).

Reduction to Practice by One Inures to the Benefit of the Other. Where one who has derived his knowledge of an invention from another reduces it to practice, such reduction to practice inures to the benefit of the one who made the disclosure *Shuman v. Beall*, 123 O. G 1664.

164. Employer and Employee. Where one employs another to construct or improve a machine, the presumption is that the resulting machine or improvement is the invention of the employer, in the absence of satisfactory proof to the contrary *Thibodeau v Hildreth* 117 O. G. 601, 25 App. D C 320. The burden of proof that the invention is that of the employee rather than that of the employer, is upon the employee in such cases, but the employer must show that he disclosed to the employee more than the result desired and that he did not leave it to the employee to invent the means of accomplishing the result. He must show that his instructions not only embodied the result to be attained but also the means of accomplishing the result. *Corry, et al. v McDermott*, 117 O G 279, 25 App. D C 305 , *Robinson v McCormick*, 128 O G 3289 (1907) . *McKeen v. Jerdone*, 34 App. D C. 163, 153 O G 272; *Ludoff v Dempster*, 166 O G. 511, 36 App D C 520 , *Eshelman v. Shantz.* 189 O G. 1282, 39 App. D C 434.

When the Rule Does Not Apply. The rule does not apply unless the employee is engaged in perfecting the device under the direction of the employer *Soley v Hebbard*, 5 App D C. 99 , *Jameson & Yeserba v Ellsworth*, 192 O G 218, 40 App D C. 164 , *Schroeder v Wageley & Stocke*, 118 O. G 268 (1905). Nor where one is employed merely as a draughtsman *Miller v. Blackburn*, 172 O. G. 549 (1911) Nor where the making of the improvement is not within the line of the duties of the employee. *Peckham v Price*, 118 O. G 1934 (1905).

Ancillary Features to the Main Invention Belong to the Employer. *Orcutt v McDonald & McDonald*, 118 O G 591 (1905), 27 App D. C. 228, 123 O G. 1287 (1906), *Moody v Colby*, 198 O G 899, 41 App D C 248, *Libby v Farmer & Turner* 18 Gour 37-14 (May, 1906), *Kreag v Green*, 127 O. G 1581 (1906); *Agewan v Jordan*, 7 Wall 583, 602, *Gedge v Cromwell*, 19 App D C 198, *Milton v Kingsley*, 7 App D C 531; *Larkin v Richardson*, 127 O G. 2394 (1906)

To What Improvements an Employee Is Entitled. The employer is entitled to any improvements made by the employee in the discharge of his duties in constructing or improving a machine which are due to the exercise of his mechanical skill, but if the employee goes farther than mechanical skill enables him to do, and makes an actual invention, he is entitled to the benefit thereof. *McKeen v Jordone*, 153 O. G. 272, 34 App D C. 163; *Ladoff v Dempster*, 166 O G. 511, 36 App D C. 520, *Sparkman v Higgins*, 1 Blatch 206; *Yoder v Mills*, 34 O G 1048, *Huebel v Bernard*, 90 O G 751, 15 App D C 510, *Neth & Tamplin v Ohmer, etc*, 135 O G 662 (1908), 30 App. D. C 478

Fellow Employees—Principal and Assistant. The same rule of law that applies to employer and employee, applies with like force to principal and assistant, though they are fellow employees. *Braunstein v Holmes*, 133 O. G 1937 (1908).

165. Inoperativeness. Where a party to an interference desires to present evidence that the structure of his opponent is inoperative, and since the question of the operativeness of the device goes to the question of the right to make the claims, he should proceed in accordance with Rule 130, first to prosecute a motion to dissolve before the Primary Examiner (Law Examiner), and subsequently, if necessary, bring a motion before the Examiner of Interferences for leave to take testimony as to the operativeness of his opponent's device *Pym v Hadaway*, 125 O G 1702, *Lowry & Cowley v Spoon*, 122 O G 2687, *Brown v Stroud*, 122 O G 2688 But in *Ritter v Krahau*, 104 O G 1897, it was held that a party must anticipate ordinary attacks upon his evidence and that testimony taken as to the operativeness of a device offered in evidence by a senior party would not be stricken out

Character of Showing Required—Motion to Take Testimony as to Operativeness. As a prerequisite to the right to take testimony as to the operativeness of an opponent s device it is not necessary that the moving party make an absolutely conclusive showing of inoperativeness, but if he makes out a prima facie case of inoperativeness thereof which does not extend to his own, and it appears that it would be a matter of great difficulty to decide the question of operativeness from a mere inspection of the application and it can not be determined that a decision so arrived at would be the same as would be reached in the light of information that might be derived from witnesses expert in the art to which the invention relates, a motion for leave to take testimony should be granted *Lowry & Cowley v Spoon*, 124 O G 1846 (1906); *Brown v Stroud*, 122 O. G. 2688.

Counter Affidavits. While an opposing party may attack the sufficiency of the motion, he should not present counter affidavits *Clement v. Browne v Stroud*, 126 O. G 2589 (1907)

166. Public Use It may not be possible to give any accurate definition of the term 'public use,' but the general principles by which we may determine whether or not a certain use is a public use or otherwise, are fairly well established by the decisions

The use of an invention by the inventor himself, or of another person under his direction, by way of experiment, and in order to bring the invention to perfection, has never been regarded as a public use. When the subject of the invention is a machine, it may be tested and tried in a building either with or without closed doors, in either case, such use is not a public use within the meaning of the statute so long as the inventor is engaged, in good faith, in testing its operation. He may see cause to alter it or improve it or not. His experiments will reveal the fact whether any alterations may be necessary, if durability is one of the qualities to be attained, a long period, perhaps years, may be necessary to enable the inventor to discover whether his purpose is accomplished. And though during all that period he may not find that any changes are necessary, yet he may be justly said to be using the machine only by way of experiment, and no one would say that such use, pursued with a bona fide intent of testing the quality of the machine, would be public use, within the meaning of the statute. So long as he does not voluntarily allow others to use it, and so long as it is not on sale for general use, he keeps the invention under his own control and does not lose his right to a patent. It would not be necessary in such case that his machine be put up and used only in the inventor's own shop or premises. He may have it put up and used on the premises of another, and the use may inure to the benefit of the owner of the establishment. Still, if used under the surveillance of the inventor, and for the purpose of enabling him to test the machine and ascertain whether it will answer the purpose intended, and make such alterations and improvements as experience demonstrates to be necessary, it will still be an experimental use and not a public use, within the meaning of the statute. But if the inventor allows his machine to be used by other persons generally, either with or without compensation, or if it is with his consent, put on sale for such use, then it will be in public use and on public sale within the meaning of the law.

95

Elizabeth v American Nicholson Paving Co, 97 U S 135, 24 L Ed. 1004; *Beedle v Bennet*, 122 U S. 77, 30 L Ed. 1074.

Whether the use of an invention is public or private, does not necessarily depend upon the number of persons to whom its use is known If the inventor, having made his device, gives or sells it to another, to be used by the donee or vendee, without limitation or restriction, or injunction of secrecy, and it is so used, such use is public, within the meaning of the statute, even though the use and knowledge of the use may be confined to one person. *Eggbert v Lippman*, 104 U S 333, 336, *Root v Third Ave R Co*, 146 U S 221, 36 L Ed. 951. So where one uses the invention himself for his own profit and advantage, it is public use. *International Tooth Crown Co v. Gaylord*, 140 U S 63, 35 L Ed 347.

Where the invention is a machine designed to manufacture articles, the inventor may make use of or sell such product as he may make while so experimenting, without bringing himself within the statute as to public use. But if the invention is upon the article, the sale of the article would be public use *Bryce Bros Co. v Seneca Glass Co*, 140 Fed. 161.

167. Character of Evidence as to Experimental Use. Where use for more than two years prior to the application for a patent is established, it is incumbent upon the patentee to show by clear, unequivocal and convincing evidence that such use was experimental with a view to perfecting the mechanism and improve its operation or test its qualities *Smith & Griggs Mfg Co v. Sprague*, 123 U. S 264, 31 L Ed 146.

Public Use in Interference Cases. It seems that the action of the Patent Office relating to public use is not conclusive against the parties and a review may be had in an action in equity under Section 4918, Revised St. *Dittgen v. Racine Paper Goods Co, et al*, 181 Fed. 394

The fact that a party to an interference proceeding

has been awarded a judgment of priority does not necessarily mean that he is entitled to a patent, for it may
appear in the course of the proceedings that there is a
statutory bar to a grant of a patent to him *Sobey v
Holschlaw*, 28 App. D C. 65, 126 O G 3041; 1907 C D
465, *Burson v Vogel*, 29 App. D C 348, 131 O G 942,
United States ex rel, Dunkley v. Ewing, Com'r, 203 O.
G 603, 42 App D C 176

**168. Public Use Proceedings When and How Insti-
tuted.** Since the institution of public use proceedings is
within the discretion of the Commissioner, after consideration of the prima facie proofs presented, the petitioner should present with his petition sufficient affidavits to make out a prima facie case of public use
against the applicant, serve the other party or parties
with due notice of the filing and hearing of the petition,
offer to produce the witnesses for examination and bear
the expense And where such petition is filed before the
taking of testimony as to priority, the public use proceeding will take precedence *In re United States Wood
Preserving Co*, 153 O G 271 (1910), *Schrum v Baumgarten*, 104 O G 577

Petition Presented Pending Motion to Dissolve. If a
motion to dissolve is pending at the time of the filing of
the petition to institute public use proceedings, such motion should be determined before proceeding to determine the question of public use The reason for this is
that a ruling on the motion to dissolve may make it unnecessary to incur the expense which might be involved
in the public use proceeding *Snyder v Woodward*, 173
O G 863 (1911), *In re United States Wood Preserving
Co*, 153 O. G 271.

After Testimony Has Been Taken as to Priority. After
the parties have taken their testimony as to priority, the
interference should not be suspended for the purpose of
instituting public use proceedings, since a ruling on the
question of priority may make it unnecessary to deter-

mine the question of public use, unless the testimony shows that the party against whom the public use proceeding is to be instituted, knew of the public use and his application was therefore fraudulently filed *Luellen v. Claussen & Claus,* 190 O. G 265 (1913), *Kneisly v. Kaisling.* 174 O G 830 (1911); *Doble v Henry,* 118 O G 2249. *Weit v Boist, etc,* 122 O. G 2062; *Brenzer v. Robinson.* 166 O G 1281 (1911).

As Between Applicants. In *Surfert v Meyer,* 98 O G 793; 1902 C. D 30, Commissioner Moore said. "Where the interference is between pending applications, the institution of public use proceedings prior to the final determination of priority is uniformly refused, for the reason that if the bar of public use or sale be established against one of the parties, it might leave the road clear to the grant of a patent to the other, who might perhaps not be the prior inventor."

When Shown by the Evidence in an Interference—Action Under Rule 126 The Examiner of Interferences, or Board of Examiners in Chief, may either before or in their decision on the question of priority, direct the attention of the Commissioner to the fact that in their opinion the issue is not patentable because of two years' public use. In such case the Commissioner refers the question to the Primary Examiner for a report thereon. If the Primary Examiner reports that in his opinion the issue is not patentable because the evidence shows more than two years' public use prior to the filing of the application, the office will not be justified in continuing the interference without investigating and finally determining the question of public use. But the evidence taken in the interference can not be used as a basis for final judgment as to that question without giving the parties an opportunity to take further testimony thereon. The Commissioner will then notify the parties that the testimony already taken will be used as prima facie case in support of the allegation of public use and if any of

98

them wishes to take testimony, to notify the Commissioner within a specified time If such notice is given time will be given by the Commissioner in which the parties may take their further proofs *Niedringhaus v McConnell,* 121 O G 338 (1905) Allegations as to public use must apply to all the counts to warrant a suspension of proceedings *Moss v Blaisdell,* 113 O G 1703, *Patee v Cook,* 16 Gour. 2-1

WITNESSES

170. Subpœna for Witnesses By the provisions of Section 4906 R S , the clerk of any court of the United States for any district wherein testimony is taken for use in a contested cause in the Patent Office, shall, upon application of any party thereto, or of his agent or attorney, issue a subpœna for any witness residing or being within such district, commanding him to appear and testify before any officer in such district authorized to take depositions and affidavits, at any time and place in the subpœna stated But no witness shall be required to attend at any place more than forty miles from the place where the subpœna is served upon him His fees and expenses must be paid or tendered unless he waives them, and his failure to demand them is not a waiver. *In re Boeshore,* 125 Fed 651

The Patent Office has no power to compel the attendance of witnesses, nor to compel a party to an interference to submit himself for examination by subpœna or render a judgment against him for failure to do so. *Henderson & Cantley v Kindervater,* 192 O G 741, *Lindstrom v Lipschutz,* 120 O G. 904, *Kelly, et al v Park, et al,* 81 O G 1931, *Bay State Belting Co v Kelton-Bruce Mfg Co,* 127 O G 1580.

171. Application to Force Obedience. The proper form of application to enforce obedience to a subpœna issued under this section is a petition to the court for an

99

attachment for contempt *Brungger v Smith*, 49 Fed. 124

Subpœna duces tecum. This section does not authorize the issue of a subpœna duces tecum. *Ex parte Moses*, 53 Fed 348; *In re Outcalt*, 149 Fed 228

Failure to attend or refusal to testify Sec. 4908 R. S provides that one who has been served with a subpœna and neglects or refuses to appear, or after appearing, refuses to testify, may be punished by the judge of the court whose clerk issued the subpœna But a witness shall not be required to disclose any secret invention or discovery made or owned by himself.

172 Refusal to Testify—Suppression of Testimony. It has been held that the testimony of a witness may be suppressed on account of his refusal to furnish material evidence. *Lindstrom v Lipschutz,* 120 O. G. 904 (1905).

173. Solicitor of Patents as a Witness. A solicitor of patents who is not an attorney-at-law, is not privileged from answering questions under this section, as he can not invoke the privilege of confidential communication between attorney and client *Brungger v Smith*, 59 Fed 124.

174. Cross-Examination of Witnesses. There will be no attempt here to discuss in detail matters pertaining to the cross-examination of witnesses, but merely to state some of the general rules

Leading Questions It is well settled that the cross-examiner is entitled to ask leading questions *Hempton v. State,* 111 Wis 127, 86 N W. 596

Assuming Facts Not Proved Counsel in his cross-questions should not assume that the witness has testified to facts to which he has not testified *Howland v Oakland etc., R R Co ,* 115 Cal 487, 47 Pac. 120

Argumentative Questions. Questions should not be argumentative *People v Harlan,* 133 Cal. 16, 65 Pac. 9

Bringing Out New Matter. Where on cross-examination counsel goes outside the direct examination and inquires about new matters, not related thereto, he makes the witnesses his own as to such new matter and he is not entitled to ask leading questions in relation thereto. though this is a matter within the discretion of the court according to the circumstances *Legg v Drake,* 1 Ohio St 286 29 Ala 558

Immaterial Matters. Where on direct examination a witness has been asked about immaterial matters, the other party has a right to cross-examine with reference thereto *L & N R Co v Hill,* 115 Ala 334, 22 South 163

175. Acts and Conversations. Where an act or a statement or a part of a conversation of a witness is put in evidence, he may be cross-examined respecting everything connected with that act, or all the circumstances under which the statement was made, or the entire conversation may be brought out, even though parts of it may be immaterial In other words, when the party calling a witness opens up a subject, his opponent is entitled to inquire all about that subject. *Vogel v Harris,* 112 Ind 494, 14 N E 385, *State v Pancoast,* 35 L R A. 518; *Hartness v Goddard,* 176 Mass 326, 57 N E 677; *Gilmer v Higley,* 110 U S 47

176. Showing Hostility, Bias and Prejudice. Great latitude is permitted in cross-examining a witness with a view to showing hostility to a party, hence he may be asked as to his interest in the case, his relations to the party calling him, his feeling toward the opposing party, or any facts or circumstances which would tend to reveal his state of mind with reference to the parties. *People v. Thompson,* 92 Cal 506, 28 Pac. 589

177. Impeachment of Witness. A witness may be impeached by showing that he made statements at some other time and place which are contrary to those testified to, but it is necessary to ask the witness on cross-examination whether he made such statements at a certain time and place and to a certain person. If he denies hav-

101

ing made the statement, the person to whom he is alleged
to have made them, may be called to prove the facts as
laid in the impeaching question   Conrad v Griffey, 16
How. (U. S) 38; Ancals v People, 134 Ill. 401, Mc-
Culloch v Dobson, 133 N Y 114, Shelton v Fenton
Electric Light etc. Co , 100 Mich. 87.

Evidence Must Be Material.   You cannot impeach a
witness upon an immaterial matter, that is, matter not
material to the issue on trial   U S v Dickinson, 2 Mc-
Lean (U S) 325; People v. Tipley, 84 Cal 651, Elbert
v Witman, 122 Ind 538, Com v. Jones, 155 Mass 170

178   Surprise by Hostile Witness   It not infrequently
happens that a party calling a witness is surprised by the
witness testifying directly opposite to what he indicated
to the party calling him   In such case the party calling
him is usually permitted to cross-examine him to a limited extent, and, in some jurisdictions, to impeach him,
not for the purpose of showing that his original statement to the party calling him was true, but for the purpose of setting the party who called him right before the
court or jury.

179.   **Party as a Witness—Presumptions Arising From
Failure to Testify or Produce Evidence.**   Where a party
refuses to answer questions, it will be presumed that the
facts are against him   Perri v Thoma, 188 O G 1053,
39 App D. C 460.

180.   **Failure to Call a Material Witness.**   Where a
party fails to call a material witness and offers no explanation for not calling him, the presumption is that his
testimony would have been unfavorable.   McConnell v
Wood, 250 O G 767; Blackman v Alexander, 113 O G
1703, 26 App D C 541, 121 O G 1979, Turnbull v
Curtis, 120 O G 2442 (1905)   Schmidt v Clark, 138
O G 768, 32 App D C 290   But where the witness
might have been called by either party and such witness
was the only person, aside from the parties, who knew
certain facts, and it appeared that the witness was in the

102

employ of one of the parties, it was held that the party in whose employ he was would have called him, if his testimony would have been favorable to such party. *Gallaghe v Hastings,* 103 O G 1165, 21 App D C. 88.

Failure to Call a Hostile Witness. Where an assignee failed to call the inventor and it was shown that the inventor was hostile to such assignee, and it was within the power of the opposing party to have called such applicant, no unfavorable presumption arises against the assignee *Stoetzel v Fordyce,* 21 Gom. 2-4 (Jan, 1909); *Silverman v. Hendrickson,* 99 O. G 445, 1902 C. D. 123

181. Failure to Deny Charges of Lack of Originality. When the facts are peculiarly within the knowledge of a party and he fails to take the stand and testify thereto, the presumption is that he could not deny the truth of the evidence offered against him *Steinberger v Hewlett,* 183 O G 1308 (1912), *Winslow v Austin,* 86 O. G 2171, *Royce v Kempshall,* 125 O. G 1347 (1906); *Rollfe v Kaisling v Lecper,* 143 O. G. 562, 32 App. D. C 582 So also a failure to produce evidence clearly within the control of a party, raises a presumption that if produced, it would have been unfavorable. *Huff v Gulic,* 179 O G 579, 38 App D C 334 And where the circumstances are such that a party might easily disprove the facts sought to be established by his opponent, if untrue, and he fails to make any effort to disprove them, the presumption is that they could not be disproved *Schneider v Driggs,* 162 O G. 1000, 36 App D C 116. *Whitman v King,* 160 O. G. 260, 35 App D C 449

182 Failure to Produce Sketches or Devices Where a party claims to have produced certain sketches, drawings, or to have completed a certain device, he should produce the same or make a satisfactory explanation for not doing so In the absence of a showing of any reason for not producing such evidence, an unfavorable presumption arises. *Saunders v Miller,* 146 O G 505, 33

App D. C 456, *Turnbull v Curtis,* 120 O G 2442 (1905).

183 Failure to Rebut. Where the circumstances show that the evidence produced by a party might readily be disproved, if untrue, and his opponent makes no effort to disprove the facts, such failure raises an unfavorable presumption against such opponent So where the evidence clearly showed that a certain machine embodying every element of the issue was in existence and readily accessible to the party who might be expected to disprove its existence if he entertained any doubt of the truth of such evidence. but he offers no evidence upon that subject, the existence of the machine will be regarded as established. *Smith v. Kilgren,* 215 O. G. 324, 43 App D C. 193.

Employee and Employer—Independent Inventorship The unexplained failure of an employer to take the stand, necessitates an inference in favor of the employees' independent inventorship *Peckham v Price,* 118 O G 1934 (1905). 26 App D C. 556

184 Conduct Inconsistent With Claims to Invention. The conduct of a party, acts as well as words, is often more potent in revealing the truth than the testimony he renders after becoming involved in a controversy with another Hence it is important in weighing the testimony to consider what happened prior to as well as after the controversy arose, and where a party claimed to have made an invention at a certain time, but continued thereafter to experiment upon other inventions for securing the same ultimate results. and full records at the time do not mention the invention in issue. and patents were taken out on other inventions, but no application was filed on the invention in issue, it was held that the conduct of the inventor at the time is stronger evidence against his claim to invention than is the testimony of himself and witnesses in favor of the same *Sherwood v Dreusen,* 124 O G 1205 (1906), *Gibbons v Peller,* 124

O G 624 (1906), *Larkin v Richardson*, 122 O G. 2390 (1906)

185 Failure to Assert Claim to Invention Where a party fails to assert any claim to an invention under circumstances which would indicate that another is claiming it, and the former constructed no device embodying the issue, the presumption is that he did not invent it *Hansen v Dean*, 129 O G 483 (1907), 29 App. D C 112 Where a senior party informed a junior party that he had applied for a patent on the invention and the junior party made no protest and signified neither by word nor act that the invention was his own, it was held that then, if ever, he should have spoken. *Scott v. Scott*, 96 O. G 1650, 1901 C D 419 And where a party testified in favor of another in an interference, making no claim at the time to his own invention of the issue, but afterward filed an application therefor, it was held that it was his duty to have asserted his claim earlier *Lloyd v Antisdel*, 95 O G. 1645, 1901 C. D 371

And where a party fails to assert his claim to an invention after knowledge that others are claiming it, his silence at a time when he should have spoken, discredits his testimony *McKnight v. Pohl & Croasdale*, 22 App. D C 219, 105 O G 977 (1903), *Harter v. Barrett*, 114 O G 975, 24 App D C 300.

Delay in Copying Claims of a Patent—Estoppel. In *Chapman v Wintroath*, decided March 1, 1920 (not yet reported), the United States Supreme Court held that an applicant has two years from the date of filing of a divisional application, in which to copy the claims of an issued patent for the purpose of interference Up to 1916. it had been the practice to allow two years in which to copy the claims of a published patent, but at that time the Court of Appeals, D C, in *Rowntree v Sloan*, 45 App. D C 207, held that one who delayed for more than one year to copy the claims of a published patent, was guilty of laches and estopped from copying such claims for the purpose of interference This ruling was followed by the office until the reversal of the Court of Appeals D C by the United States Supreme Court, in *Chapman v Wintroath,* March 1, 1920.

186 Failure to Disclose Invention. And where a party fails to disclose the invention in issue under circumstances which would naturally induce him to do so, the presumption is that he did not have the invention. *Slaughter v. Halle,* 102 O. G. 469 (1903), *Hope, Jr. v. Voight,* 115 O G 1585 (1905), 25 App D C 22 ·

187. Delay in Filing Application and Failure to Assert Alleged Right. Where a party permitted a manufacturer to manufacture the device in issue for a period of nearly two years, without claiming the invention, or making protest, and did not file an application for.patent for over four years after the alleged discovery and not until after he had difficulties with such manufacturer, such silence and failure to earlier file an application, was held to discredit his claim to inventorship *Wilson & Willard Mfg Co v Bole, et al.* 227 Fed 607, 610

188. Testimony Impeached by Previous Declarations Where the testimony of an inventor is shown to be at variance with his preliminary statement and with affidavits filed during the progress of his application, or in conflict with the oath filed with the application, such facts should weigh strongly against the credibility of the witness, unless a satisfactory explanation is made of such variance *Barnes v Swartwout,* 161 O. G 1045 (1910); *Tripler v Linde,* 102 O. G. 1297 (1903)

189. Presumption Arising From Knowledge and Experience of a Party. The knowledge and experience of a party in general, and particularly his experience in and familiarity with the subject in issue, will be considered in weighing the testimony Therefore, as between two parties, each claiming a disclosure of an invention to the other, where one of such parties is shown to have a prac-

106

tical knowledge of the art and the other has not, a strong presumption arises that the one having such practical knowledge would be the more likely to have conceived the invention (See subject Originality) *Alexander v Blackman*, 26 App D C 541, 121 O G 1979 (1906), *Flather v. Weber*, 21 App D C 179, 104 O G 312 (1903), *Miller v Kelley*, 96 O G 1038; 1901 C D 405, 18 App D C 163

190. Presumption as to Originality—Following the Line of Invention of Another. Where one is shown to have gained his knowledge of the art from the invention or series of inventions of the other party, and a dispute as to the inventorship of a specific improvement arises, both parties claiming it, a question of veracity is presented, and under such circumstances, to determine to whom the greater weight should be given, the presumption will be that the party experienced in the art is the more likely inventor. *French v Holcomb*, 115 O G. 506; *Scott v. Scott*, 96 O G. 1650; 1901 C. D. 419.

And where there is an issue of originality, and all that one of the parties did grew out of and was dependent upon the disclosure of the other party, the presumption is that the party making such disclosure was the inventor of the issue *Granger v Richardson*, 110 O G 722, *Scott v Scott*, 96 O. G. 1650, 1901 C. D 419, 18 App D C 420

191. Irrelevant Testimony. Testimony is irrelevant when it has no bearing on the matter in dispute, does not affect the subject matter of the controversy, and can in no way assist the court in deciding the case The Court of Appeals D C, has called attention to the fact that the practice of encumbering the record in interference cases with irrelevant matters is general, and has strongly condemned the practice *Connor v Dean*, 24 App D C 277, 142 O G 856, *Scott v Scott*, 96 O. G. 1650, 1901 C D 419, 18 App D C 420.

Testimony to show non-patentability of the issue or the

107

scope of the issue, is irrelevant *Von Keller v Hayden, et al*, 173 O G. 285 (1911) That a stranger to the record made the invention is immaterial *Steinmetz v Hewitt*, 107 O. G 1972 (1903)

191a. Expert Testimony It is not the practice of the office to permit expert testimony to explain what an application discloses, and it should be permitted only in very exceptional cases, if at all *Cooper v Downing*, 222 O G 727 (1915) But in *Hopkins v. Newman*, 134 O. G 2028, 30 App D C 402, such testimony was considered In *Cooper v Downing*, 230 O. G. 909, 45 App. D-C. 345, it was held that the Commissioner properly refused to consider evidence of what was intended by the disclosure of one of the parties, since it is the duty of the office experts to determine what an application discloses

191b. Objections to Evidence. A party who desires to oppose the admission of any evidence produced or offered by his opponent, should make his objection and state the grounds therefor at the time the evidence is offered If he fails to object he waives his right to have the evidence excluded He should also be considered to have waived his right if he fails to state a legitimate ground of objection, unless there is a stipulation in the record that he may afterward state the grounds of objection All objections, whether to the proceedings or to specific evidence, should be timely made in order that the opposing party may be placed on his guard *Badger v Morgan*, 117 O G 598 (1905) In many instances the answer of the witness is not responsive to the question, in which case there is no opportunity to object to the evidence by objecting to the question, since the question may have been proper, but in that event the aggrieved party should move to strike out the answer, or so much of it as is irresponsive to the question

Form of Objection An objection should be positive and should state what principle of evidence the question, or an answer thereto, would violate A general objection, such as—that the evidence is inadmissible—would hardly present any question unless the evidence is such that it could not be admissible for any purpose whatever If objection is made and no valid ground of objection is stated, it will not be available to exclude the evidence because there was another and valid ground of objection which might have been made but was not It would seem that objections to the materiality or relevancy of evidence may be made at any time, for a party is bound to know whether the evidence tends to prove or disprove any issue in the cause. Furthermore the court will not decide a cause upon immaterial or irrelevant evidence, because if it is immaterial or irrelevant it does not prove anything in relation to the issue. Wigmore's Ev Sec. 18.

192. Relevant Testimony—What Is. In an interference the ultimate question to be determined is, who was the prior inventor of the issue, and the evidence should be confined to the question of priority *Brill & Adams v Ucbelacher*, 99 O. G. 2966, 1902 C. D. 220; *Trufant v Brindle, etc*, 101 O G 1608, 1902 C. D 397. As to what facts and circumstances have a tendency to prove priority there has been much controversy The Court of Appeals D C. has repeatedly declared that it would not take into consideration, in interferences, questions which do not relate to priority Out of the numerous questions which parties to interferences have attempted to bring before that court on appeal, we have a number of decisions defining what is regarded by the court as material to the determination of the question of priority, or what facts or circumstances may be introduced to establish the ultimate fact of who, as between the parties, was the first inventor of the issue

Laches. It has been held that the question of whether a party has been guilty of laches is one proper to be determined as relating to priority *Wintroath v Chapman*, 248 O G 1004, 47 App D C. 428

109

Originality It would seem to be obvious that the question of fact as to whether one party derived his knowledge of the invention from the other party, is one which relates to priority *Milton v Kingsley,* 7 App D C. 531, 75 O. G. 2193.

Reduction to Practice Whether a party reduced an invention to practice and the date of such reduction to practice, relate to priority *Stevens v Scher,* 11 App. D C 245, 81 O. G. 1932

The court has also considered as relating to priority the following questions. Whether the evidence shows a lack of reasonable diligence on the part of one of the parties *Paul v. Johnson,* 23 App D C 187, 109 O G 807, *Wickers v McKee,* 29 App D C 4, 129 O G. 869. Whether a party has concealed or suppressed his invention *Matthes v Burt,* 24 App D C 265, 111 O G. 1363 Whether a party has exercised reasonable diligence, where diligence is required of him *Yates v Huson,* 8 App D C. 93, 74 O G 1732 What effect the filing dates of the applications shall have in determining the question of priority. *Sherwood v Drewson,* 29 App D C 161, 130 O G 657 Whether one party was acting as the agent of another in what he did in relation to the invention *Milton v Kingsley,* 7 App. D C 531, 75 O. G 2193; *Huebel v Bernard,* 15 App. D C 510, 90 O. G. 751. Whether a party has the right to make the claims *Podelsack v. McInnerney,* 26 App. D C 399, 120 O G. 2127, *Wickers v McKee,* 29 App D. C. 4, 120 O. G. 869. Whether one of the parties failed to disclose the invention *Manley v Williams,* 168 O G 1034, 37 App D. C 194 Whether the application of one of the parties, as originally filed, disclosed the invention in issue. *Mc-Knight v Pohl,* 130 O G 2067 (1907), 30 App D C 92 Whether a party is a joint or sole inventor. *Lemp v Randall,* 146 O G 255, 35 App D C. 430 Whether the applications had been altered after execution. *Lindstrom v Ames,* 168 O G. 250, 37 App D C. 365 The invalidity of an oath executed before a notary who was the attorney for the applicant *Dalton v Wilson*, 224 O G 741, 44 App D C 249, and whether an application was abandoned during prosecution *Kinsman v Strohm*, 136 O G 1769, 31 App D C 581 All of the foregoing questions being material to the determination of priority, it is proper to introduce evidence thereon

193 Rebuttal Testimony. The word rebutting has a two-fold signification, both in common and legal parlance It sometimes means contradictory evidence only At other times overcoming testimony It may be employed as contravening, or opposing, as well as overcoming proof. *Fain v Cornett*, 25 Ga 184. Words & Phrases, Vol 7, page 5987

The party on whom the burden of proof rests is required to produce sufficient evidence to sustain his case The defendant meets this proof by evidence to explain or disprove the evidence already put in 10 Fed. Cases No 5452, *Achlin v. McCalmont Oil Co*, 201 Pa St. 257, 50 Atl 955

Where a party anticipates a defense and puts in evidence which he is not required to put in in chief, and thereby undertakes to meet the evidence of the defendant before it is produced, he can not thereafter introduce cumulative evidence upon the same subject, as rebuttal *York v Pease*, 2 Gray (Mass) 282 Nor can a party under the guise of rebuttal, put in cumulative evidence which merely goes to sustain and support that which he has introduced to sustain his original case, nor evidence on an essential point which he failed to prove in his original case. *Swinglehurst v Ballard*, 265 O G 459, 258 Fed 973; *Kohler v Wells-Fargo & Co*, 26 Cal 606, 613 The admission or rejection of evidence offered in rebuttal, is however, a matter largely in the discretion of the court, the circumstances under which it is offered and the good faith of the party being taken into account. Enc of Ev Vol 10, page 651

111

Where a junior party filed interrogatories in rebuttal by which it was sought to prove that the senior party was not the original inventor, it was held that the testimony should be suppressed because it constitutes a part of the junior party's original case. *Goldschmidt & Weber v. Von Schutz*, 192 O G 743 (1913) Testimony taken in rebuttal will not be suppressed on motion or objection of the defendant upon the ground that it was not proper rebuttal after the defendant has, by leave of court, taken surrebuttal testimony *American Bank Protection Co v. City Nat Bank*, 181 Fed 375

Where a senior party proved dates later than those set up in his preliminary statement, it was held not proper for the junior party to make out a different prima facie case in his rebuttal testimony *Woodbridge v Winship*, 21 Gour 19-7 (Feb., 1909)

Where one party fails to take testimony it is improper for his opponent to put in additional testimony as rebuttal *Kinsman v Strohm*, 125 O G 1699 (1906).

Rebuttal testimony relating to the patentability of the issue will be stricken out on motion *Parker v Lewis*, 120 O G 323 (1905).

193a. Surrebuttal Evidence. In setting dates for the taking of testimony, no provision is made for taking surrebuttal testimony, and if the evidence previously produced warrants the taking of surrebuttal testimony, the party desiring to take the same should file a motion for permission to do so Whether this motion shall be granted or refused is a matter within the discretion of the Examiner of Interferences The privilege of taking such testimony will be extended to a party whenever he has been surprised by evidence or a line of defense in rebuttal which he has had no reason to anticipate or an opportunity to prepare against *Donning v. Stackpole and Laganke*, 106 O. G. 264, 1903 C D 298 Such motions have been denied wherein it was not shown that the rebuttal testimony constituted a surprise *Howard v.*

112

Spare, 21 Gour 19-8 (Mar , 1909) , *Ruthven v Christ-ensen*, 138 O G 257 (1908)

In Wigmore on Evidence, See 1874, it is said "For the opponent's case in surrebuttal there remain properly only two sorts of evidence, namely, evidence explaining away the effect of new facts brought forward by the proponent in rebuttal, and evidence impeaching the witnesses testifying in rebuttal All other evidence could and should have been put in in reply Evidence legitimately receivable in surrebuttal would be evidence impeaching rebuttal witnesses"

SUPPRESSION OF TESTIMONY.

194. Motion to Suppress. Where a party desires to suppress certain testimony, he may make a motion to suppress, designating the parts that he desires to have suppressed, giving the grounds for such suppression The motion should be made before final hearing and before printing of the record, but a ruling thereon may, and will be reserved for final hearing in cases where a reading of the record would be required for the Examiner of Interferences to determine whether or not the testimony should be suppressed. The motion should be noted for hearing with proof of service upon the opposing party. *Talbot v Monell*, 99 O G 2965; 1902 C D. 216; *Hall v Alvord*, 101 O. G 1833; 1902 C D 418; *Dyson v Land, etc* , 130 O. G. 1690 (1907) ; *Andrews v. Nilson*, 111 O G. 1038; *Keith v Erickson, etc* , 157 O. G 754 (1910).

Whether a ruling on the motion should be reserved for final hearing is a matter within the discretion of the Examiner of Interferences *Royce v Kempshall*, 119 O. G 338 (1905)

Refusal to suppress is not reversible error. *Kempshall v Royce*, 129 O G 3162.

194a Retaking Testimony A party may be permitted to retake his testimony where an irregularity in taking the same arose through inadvertence and not through any desire to delay the proceedings or take any unfair advantage over the opposing party. Where a party finds that he has not taken his testimony in accordance with the rules it is incumbent on him, in support of a motion to retake the testimony, to show why he failed to comply with the rules in the first instance and that the granting of the motion will result in no hardship to his opponent. *Jones v Starr*, 111 O G. 2221, *Shaw & Welty Shirt Co v Quaker City Shirt Co*, 157 O G 1000 (1910). *Goodfellow v Jolly*, 111 O ·G. 1940 (See Sec 220)

The granting or refusing of a motion to retake testimony is a matter within the discretion of the Examiner of Interferences or the Commissioner on appeal, and the Court of Appeals. D. C , will not interfere with the exercise of that discretion *Jones v Starr*, 1905 C D 694, 25 App. D. C. 529.

Since the primary reason for refusing a motion to retake testimony is the expense, inconvenience or disadvantage it might impose upon the opposing party, it would seem that the Examiner of Interferences or the Commissioner might properly impose conditions upon which the moving party would be permitted to retake the testimony. The moving party should act promptly upon discovery of the necessity to retake his testimony, to the end that his opponent be not delayed, inconvenienced or put to a disadvantage other than such as would necessarily result when the moving party is acting in good faith and with as much promptitude as the circumstances will permit.

195. Grounds for Suppression. The following facts and circumstances may be valid grounds for suppressing testimony. That the interrogatories are not proper rebuttal *Goldschmidt & Weber v Von Schutz*, 192 O. G. 743 (1913), that the testimony relates solely to the patentability of the counts and the state of the prior art.

114

Felbel v. Oliver, 13 Goш 4-11 (Jan, 1901), *Dıron & Marsh v. Graces, etc*, 127 O G 1993 (1907); that the testimony was not taken ın accordance with the rules *Blackman v Alexander*, 98 O. G 1281, 1902 C. D 41, that the notary s certificate is defectıve in that ıt does not certify that the depositions were read by or to the wıtnesses before signing and that the notaı y dıd not seal the depositions and forward them to the office *Blackman v Alexander*, 98 O G 1281 1902 C D 41; or faılure to certify the date on which the package was sealed, oı the name of the person who transcribed the stenographer's notes, or that they were written out ın presence of the notary, oı that the notaı y failed to foı waı d the exhibits to the office, ın the absence of a stipu-latıon that they may be retained by counsel *Rolfe v Taylor*, 111 O. G 1938, that the deposıtions were taken wıthout propeı notıce. *Potter v Ochs*, 95 O G 1049; 1901 C D 39, that a party served notıce to take testi-mony and taıled to appear and subsequently served an-other notıce and took the testimony *Denton v Burn-ham*, 18 Gonr 83-11 (Nov, 1906), that the cross-exam-ınatıon sought to be strıcken out is not propeг cross-examınatıon, *Marconı v Shocmaher, etc*, 121 O G 2664 (1906), that the testimony ıs not proper rebuttal, *Kınsman v Strohm*, 125 O. G. 1699 (1906), 135 O G 1121 (1908), that a paı ty was not given an opportunit\ to cross-examine the wıtnesses; *Munster v. Aınswoı th*, 128 O G 2085 (1906), 128 O G 2088, *Hattıce v Lang-woı thy*, 140 O. G 507 (1909), that the testımony ıelates solely to publıc use, *Stroud v Mıller*, 101 O. G 2075, 1902 (D. 423, that corrections and addıtıons were made long afteı the testımony was taken and wıthout notıce to the movıng party. *Independent Bahıng Pow-deı Co v Fıdclıty Mfg. Co*. 94 O G. 222, 1901 C D 7

196 Grounds Insufficient. The fact that the notary dıd not wrıte the names of the wıtnesses at the top oɪ each page, ıs not sufficıent grounds for suppressıon of a

115

deposition; *Rolfe v. Taylor*, 111 O. G. 1938; nor that
the notary delayed filing the testimony, where such delay
is properly explained; *Moss v Blaisdell*, 113 O G 2505;
nor that certain words in the printed record are itali-
cized, *Faller v. Lorimer*, 16 Gour. 37-11; nor that the
testimony was adduced by leading questions, though testimony adduced by leading questions will be critically
scanned, *Smith v Brooks*, 112 O. G. 953, nor that the
notary acted out of his jurisdiction, no objection being
made at the time the testimony was taken · *Badger v.
Morgan, etc*, 117 O. G. 598 (1905); nor the fact that
the notary was in the employ of the attorney for the opposing party, where no objection was made on that
ground at the time the testimony was taken, *Royce v.
Kempshall*, 117 O G 2090, nor that the notary failed to
certify whether one of the parties was present in person
or by attorney, *Royce v Kempshall*, 117 O G. 2090;
nor that a party refused to produce or introduce in evidence certain books about which he testified for the purpose of refreshing his recollection, where it appears that
he offered the same to opposing counsel for inspection
at the time he testified. *Bay State Belting Co v Kelton
Bruce Mfg Co*, 127 O. C. 1580 (1907); nor that a certain witness was not named in the notice *Keith, etc v.
Lundquist, etc*, 156 O. G. 798 (1910).

197. **Suppressed Testimony—How Retained in the Record.** When testimony is stricken out on motion in an
interference proceeding, that part which is cancelled
should be shown by red lines and proper marginal notes,
as when matter is cancelled in a specification of an application for a patent When the record is printed, that
portion which is stricken out should not be printed in
the body of the testimony, but notice should be inserted
in the printed record that certain questions and answers
or other evidence was stricken out, giving the date of the
decision or order striking it out. The party whose testimony has been stricken out may print the parts stricken

116

out as an appendix to his record   *Marconi v Shoemaker, etc*, 121 O. G 2664 (1906)

In an infringement suit, a party may move to strike out or he may insist upon his objections at the hearing In either event the matter stricken out remains in the record for the purposes of appeal   *Blease v. Garlington,* 92 U S 1; *Nelson v U. S.,* 201 U S 92, 114, *Wolff Truch Frame Co v American Steel Foundries,* 195 Fed 940, 946   However, it was held in *Felbel v Oliver,* 100 O G 1975; 1902 C D 309, that where a party prints in his record depositions which have been suppressed, such depositions will be expunged upon motion

198. Testimony Taken in Another Interference—As Evidence. Rule 157 provides that testimony taken in an interference proceeding may be used in any other or subsequent interference proceeding, so far as relevant and material, subject to the right of the contesting party to recall the witnesses whose testimony has been taken and to take other testimony in rebuttal of the same

For What Purpose Material or Relevant. Testimony taken in another interference may be introduced for the purpose of discrediting or impeaching the testimony of the witness in a later interference   This is upon the well established principle of evidence that the testimony of a witness may be discredited or impeached by showing declarations made at other times and places by the same witness relating to the same subject which are not consistent with his later testimony or are contradictory thereof   *Talbott v Monell,* 99 O G 2965, 1902 C D. 217; *Hewitt v. Weintraub,* 134 O G. 1561 (1908). Such testimony may also be introduced where the issues in the interferences are substantially the same and the parties are the same and the provisions of Rule 157 are otherwise complied with and a proper showing made It is for the office to determine whether the circumstances are such as to permit the use of such testimony   This rule is similar to the rules of evidence in the trial of

117

causes in court In *Clow v Baker, et al.*, 36 Fed. 692, the court said "To prevent a failure of justice that might result, it is permissible for the court, when cause is shown therefor, to permit the depositions taken in one case to be read on the trial of another, if it appears that the parties to the later case were the parties or privies with the parties to the former suit, that the issues upon which the testimony was taken are substantially the same, and that every opportunity for thorough examination and cross-examination was afforded both parties when the testimony was taken *Kenny & Thordarson v O'Connell, et al*, 117 O G 1163 (1905), *Beall v Lyon*, 127 O G 3215 (1907). *Strauble v Young*, 119 O. G. 338 (1905).

199. **The Hearing.** The extent to which the Examiner of Interferences will grant a hearing or re-hearing of a case, is a matter ordinarily within his discretion. *Dunlap v. Creveling, etc*, 160 O G 774 (1910)

200. **Postponement of Final Hearing.** It is within the discretion of the Examiner of Interferences and the Commissioner to extend the time for final hearing *Dunkley v Beckhuis,* 158 O G. 886 (1910). But a postponement will not be granted to permit a party to intervene *In re Columbian Carbide Co* 20 Gour 17-1 (March 27, 1908).

201. **Admissions Made by Counsel at Hearing.** Admissions made by counsel at or before final hearing are binding upon his client *Horton v Zimmer*, 32 App D C 217, 137 O G 2233 (1908); *Mortimer v Thomas, etc*, 192 O G. 215 (1913)

No Hearing After Expiration of Limit of Appeal. Rule 126 does not provide for a hearing before the Commissioner, and no hearing will be granted after the expiration of the limit of appeal to an applicant whose claims are found unpatentable by the Board of Examiners in Chief in consideration of the claim in connection with the question of priority *Holtz v Hewitt*, 127 O G 1992

.(1907) The length of time which will be granted for a hearing is within the discretion of the Examiner of Interferences *Moore v Curtis*, 120 O G 324 (1905), *Cazin v Von Welshbach*, 119 O G 650 (1905)

202. **Petition to Restore Jurisdiction.** A petition to restore jurisdiction to the Examiner of Interferences will not be set down for hearing but briefs may be filed *Adams v. Randall*, 125 O G 1700 (1906).

203. **Judgment Without a Hearing—Disclaimer.** Where there is a disclaimer filed the Examiner of Interferences will render judgment of priority without setting a date for hearing *Townsend v Corey*, 119 O. G 2237 (1905)

204 **Questions Raised But Not Argued.** Where a party moves to dissolve upon all grounds mentioned in Rule 122, but only argues part of them, judgment will be rendered against him on the grounds not argued *Harnish v Guenifet, et al*, 117 O G 1492 (1905)

205. **Statements of Examiner of Interferences Made at Hearing—When Not Reviewable on Appeal.** Where the Examiner of Interferences makes a statement as to admissions and waivers of counsel at a hearing, error therein, if any, will not be reviewed on appeal unless there was a motion for a re-hearing presented to the Examiner of Interferences and ruled upon *Hansel v Wardwell*, 116 O. G. 2008 (1905)

206. **Hearing on Motion to Dissolve—New Grounds and Notice.** Patents referred to by one of the parties which are not of record and have not been served upon the opposing party at least five days before the hearing will not be considered on motion to dissolve unless service is waived by the opposing party *Young v Eich*, 113 O G. 547, *Lake v Cahill*, 110 O G 2235, *Wells v Packer*, 1900 C D 35, 90 O. G. 1947, *Whitlock & Huson v Scott*, 99 O G 1385, 1902 C D 166

What Will Be Considered on Motion to Dissolve. Nothing can be considered which is not contained in the

119

record of the case unless timely notice (five days before the hearing) of such matter is served upon the opposing party. *Summers v Hart,* 98 O G 2585, 1902 C. D 104.

207. **Notice of New Matter—Postponement of Hearing to Give.** Upon a proper showing of facts that the new matter could not have been earlier discovered, a postponement of the hearing will be granted to enable a party to give the proper notice *Summers v Hart,* 98 O G 2585, 1902 C. D 104

JURISDICTION.

208. **Jurisdiction of Examiner of Interferences.** The Examiner of Interferences has jurisdiction to determine questions of priority and all matters which relate to the question of priority, but not to dissolve an interference. *Brodwell v Long,* 21 Gour 2-5 (Dec, 1908) Where jurisdiction by the Primary Examiner is desired, it can only be obtained by the order of the Commissioner and the Primary Examiner should make his request of the Commissioner. *Hildreth,* 97 O G. 1374, 1901 C. D 186 He has not jurisdiction to grant amendments to applications *Moore v Hewitt,* 115 O G 509 Nor to require the filing of a new oath. *Dukesmith v Carrington v Turner,* 125 O G 348 (1906)

209. **Jurisdiction of Examiners in Chief.** The Examiners in Chief have appellate jurisdiction in all matters properly brought before them on appeal, but have no jurisdiction to extend the time within which such appeal may be taken *Blackman v Alexander,* 105 O G. 2059 (1903)

210. **Jurisdiction of Commissioner Pending Appeal to Court of Appeals** The Commissioner of Patents has jurisdiction pending an appeal to the Court of Appeals to hear and determine a motion to reopen a case for the purpose of taking additional testimony *Clement v Richards, etc,* 111 O G 1627

211. **Jurisdiction of Courts Over Witnesses in Inter-**

ferences When a witness goes upon the stand in an interference case he submits to the jurisdiction of the U. S District Court in the district in which he testifies and remains under that jurisdiction until his cross-examination is concluded *Lobel v Cossey*, 157 Fed 664, 666

212. Restoring Jurisdiction—Petition For. When it is desired to restore jurisdiction of the Examiner of Interferences to consider certain motions, copies of the motions which the petitioner desires the Examiner of Interferences to consider and decide should accompany the petition, and service of the papers should be made on the opposite party The petition should be addressed to the Commissioner, but the Commissioner will not pass upon the merits of the motion but merely upon the form of it *Adams v Randall*, 125 O G 1700 (1906)

Restoring Jurisdiction After Limit of Appeal Even after the limit of appeal has expired upon a judgment against the moving party, a motion to restore the jurisdiction of the Examiner of Interferences to hear a motion to reopen the case, may be granted upon proper showing *Lipscomb v Pfeiffer*, 122 O. G. 351 (1906) After time for appeal has expired the Commissioner has sole power to restore jurisdiction *Hough v Gordon*, 108 O G 797.

Restoring Jurisdiction Pending Appeal Though an appeal is pending before the Examiners in Chief on the question of priority, the jurisdiction of the Examiner of Interferences may be restored to consider a motion to reopen the case to offer newly discovered evidence *Newell v Clifford v Rose*, 122 O. G 730 (1905) ; *Dunbar v Schellenger*, 118 O G 2536 (1905)

Restoring Jurisdiction to Hear Motions to Dissolve Under the former rules motions to transmit motions to dissolve were heard by the Examiner of Interferences, but under the present practice such motions to transmit are heard first by the Commissioner and if in his

121

opinion such motion should be transmitted it is so ordered and the motion then goes to the Law Examiner instead of the Primary Examiner Under the present rules the motions are heard by different officials than formerly heard such motions, but the time for making such motions and the character of showing required are not changed and the old decisions may therefore be important guides as to the practice

Where a party fails to make a motion to dissolve under Rule 122 within the time provided, but waits until testimony has been taken and judgment has been rendered on priority, the jurisdiction of the Examiner of Interferences will not be restored to consider a motion to transmit a motion to dissolve *Fessenden v Potter*, 101 O G. 2823, 1902 C D 466. While under the present rules the Examiner of Interferences does not have jurisdiction of motions to transmit motions to dissolve, still a similar question might arise under the present rules where the motion to transmit is heard by the Commissioner.

213. Rehearings. The various tribunals of the Patent Office stand upon the same footing respecting their judgments and decisions as do the courts In *Donning v Fisher*, 125 O G 2765 (1906), it was said "A court has control over its own judgments and decrees during the term at which they were rendered and may at any time before the expiration of the term, in the exercise of its discretion, open, amend, correct, revise, vacate, or supplement any judgment or decree rendered during such term. The tribunals of the Patent Office have this power over their judgments within the limits of appeal They also have the power in analogy to the practice of the courts, of requesting a rehearing of any point upon which they desire further light The granting of a rehearing or refusal to grant the same are matters within the discretion of the tribunal having jurisdiction of the case at the time "

122

In *Robinson v Townsend v Copeland*, 106 O. G. 997, a motion was filed before the Commissioner to suspend proceedings in the interference and remand the same to the Examiner of Interferences to hear and determine a motion to reopen the interference for the purpose of introducing newly discovered evidence. At the time the motion was brought, decisions had been rendered by the Examiner of Interferences and by the Examiners in Chief on the question of priority and at the time this motion was brought one of the parties had appealed to the Commissioner. It was therefore held that there was no necessity of suspending proceedings, since there was no limit of appeal running against any of the parties, but the hearing on the appeal was continued until the final determination of the motion. It was further held that the motion to open the case for further testimony should be heard in the first instance by the Examiner of Interferences and therefore the motion to transmit the motion to reopen, to the Examiner of Interferences, was granted.

214. When Motion May Be Brought. A motion for rehearing may be brought at any time before the expiration of the time fixed for appeal and the motion may be heard and decided after the limit of appeal has expired. The filing of the motion does not stay the running of the limit of appeal and if a party desires to appeal he must do so within the limit of appeal notwithstanding his motion for a rehearing. *Naulty v Cutler*, 126 O. G. 389 (1907).

215. Appeal. There is no appeal from a decision denying a motion for a rehearing, though the right to a rehearing may be considered on appeal on the entire record. *Macey v Laning v Casler*, 101 O. G. 1608, *Carmichael v Fox*, 104 O. G. 1656. *Cole v Zarbock v Green*, 116 O. G. 1451, *Hewitt v Thomas, etc*, 122 O. G. 1045 Approved in *Naulty v Cutler*, 126 O. G. 389

216. Newly Discovered Evidence as Ground for Re-

hearing. Where the ground upon which a rehearing is sought is newly discovered evidence. the motion must show that the evidence sought to be introduced was not known at the time the original testimony was taken and could not have been discovered at that time by the exercise of reasonable diligence. *Mosher v. Tully & Clark,* 99 O G. 2968, 1902 C D 224. *Dudley v. Blickinsderfer, etc.* 99 O G 228. 1902 C. D. 119. *Latshaw v. Duff v Kaplan,* 130 O G 980 (1907)

The motion must also show what the newly discovered evidence consists of. that is if it is the testimony of witnesses, what the witnesses will testify to. if exhibits, what the exhibits are that will be introduced in evidence. that the evidence is material, and that the moving party was diligent in bringing the motion *Robinson v. Townsend v Copeland.* 100 O G 683 1902 C D. 263 *Allis v Stowell.* 85 Fed 481 *Parker v Spoon,* 14 Gour 19-8 (April, 1902), *Crescent Oil Co v W C Robinson & Son Co,* 142 O. G. 1113 (1909)

It must also be shown that the newly discovered evidence is of such character that the establishment of the facts alleged would likely result in a change or modification of the decision *French v Halcomb.* 110 O. G 1727, *Ball v Flora,* 117 O G 2088 (1905). *Struble v Young, etc,* 139 O G. 729 (1909)

It must also appear that due diligence was exercised in presenting the motion *Beckert v. Currier.* 104 O G. 2439 (1903). *Newell v Clifford v Rose.* 125 O G 665 (1906) *Claussen v Dunbar, etc,* 129 O G 2499 (1907), *Townsend v Thullen.* 21 Gour 37-12 (May. 1909) A delay of two weeks held not unreasonable. *Robinson v. Townsend v Copeland.* 107 O G 1376.

217. By Whom the Motion Shall Be Heard The motion must be heard in the first instance by the Examiner of Interferences and where the cause has passed out of his jurisdiction, there must be a motion to restore his jurisdiction *Bowen v Bradley,* 58 O. G 386; *Robinson*

124

v Townsend v Copeland, 106 O G 997 (1903), *Clement v Richards, etc .* 111 O G. 1626. *Dunbar v. Schellenger,* 19 Gour. 37-17 (April, 1907), *Rolfe v Leeper,* 159 O. G. 991 (1910) Can not be granted by the Court of Appeals D C *DeFerranti v Lindmark,* 32 App D C 6, 137 O G 733 (1908) A motion to transmit a motion to take further testimony, made pending an appeal to the Court of Appeals, will be granted upon a proper showing *Clements v Richards v Meissner,* 111 O G. 1626

Official Request for Rehearing. Where the request is made by the tribunal before whom the case was previously heard, it will be granted jurisdiction. *Bettendorf,* 17 Gour 41-22 (May, 1905)

218. Insufficient Grounds for Rehearing. There is no sufficient ground for a rehearing where there is an absence of a showing why the evidence was not produced when the testimony was originally taken *Mosler v Tully & Clark,* 99 O. G. 2968, 1902 C. D 224 Or where the evidence sought to be introduced is immaterial, or relates wholly to expert testimony *Robinson v Townsend v Copeland,* 107 O G 1376 (1903) Or where the showing is merely that a party failed to produce his best evidence, or the object is merely to strengthen the testimony already in the record *Sutton v McDonald, etc .* 98 O G 1418, 1902 C D 47, *Harris v Stern & Lotz.* 101 O G 1132, 1902 C D 386 Or where the purpose is to explain certain exhibits which are in evidence *Blackman v Alexander,* 104 O. G. 2441 (1903) Or where it appears that the evidence is unimportant or could have been discovered by the exercise of reasonable diligence *Shaffer v Dolan,* 100 O G 3012; 1902 C D 344 Or where a party failed to produce the evidence because he did not regard it as material *Roberts v Bachelle,* 101 O. G. 1831, 1902 C D 415. Or that a party did not recall certain facts at the time his testimony was taken. *French v Halcomb,* 110 O. G.

125

1727   Or where it appears that a party knew of the evidence but did not introduce it because of the expense which he would have had to incur in securing it   *Greuter v Mathieu,* 111 O. G 582   Or where the proposed evidence relates solely to a statutory bar. *Ritter v Krakau & Conner,* 108 O G 1050   Or where the evidence relates to the right of a party to make the claims and not to priority   *Osborn v Austin,* 115 O. G. 1065   Or where it is based on the fact that a party misjudged her ability to prove her case and for that reason took no testimony *Hull v McGill,* 117 O. G. 597.   Nor is the fact that one of the witnesses of a party was sick, another was hostile and another was out of town at the time the original testimony was taken, sufficient ground for rehearing, though such facts may have been sufficient to support a motion or extension of time for taking testimony *Newell v Clifford v. Rose,* 125 O. G 665 (1906)   Or where the purpose is merely to introduce an earlier application *Cutler v. Hall,* 135 O G 449 (1908).   Or where it appears that the testimony was improperly taken as rebuttal and thereafter stricken out. *McNeil v Stephenson,* 192 O. G. 517 (1913).   Or where the testimony was known and available when the original testimony was taken   *Webber v. Wood,* 181 O G 553 (1912)

219. Stay of Proceedings. A motion for rehearing does not of itself operate as a stay of proceedings. *Charmichael v Fox,* 104 O. G. 1656 (1903)   Nor stay the running of time for appeal   *Naulty v Cutler,* 126 O. G. 389 (1907)   If future proceedings require that a party take some action before his motion for rehearing can be heard, and the proceedings are such as may be suspended, a motion to suspend proceedings should be made   *Robinson v Townsend v Copeland,* 106 O G 997.

220   Suppression of Testimony—Rehearing   Where testimony is suppressed because of irregularities in taking thereof due entirely to inadvertence and not intention to delay proceedings, the party should be given an opportunity to retake the testimony. *Blackman v. Alexander*, 100 O G 2383; 1902 C D 323 But where testimony is improperly taken as rebuttal and due notice is given that a motion will be presented to suppress the same, the case will not be reopened to take such testimony *McNeil v Stephenson*, 192 O. G 517 (1913)

221. Motion to Dissolve—Rehearnig A party may obtain a reconsideration of a motion to dissolve by showing good cause which justifies a rehearing *Newcomb v Lemp*, 110 O G 307 But where a party fails to cite all the references which he might have cited on his motion to dissolve, such failure does not entitle him to a rehearing *White v Powell*, 160 O G 776 (1910) Where a motion to dissolve on the ground that a party has no right to make the claims was not presented at the proper time, but after all the testimony had been taken, the case will not be reopened to consider such motion or a motion for permission to take testimony as to the operativeness of an opponent's device *Broadwell v Long*, 164 O G. 252.

222. Second Interference Improperly Declared—Rehearing of First Interference. Where a second interference was improperly declared, the first interference will not be reheard for the purpose of including the issue in the second interference *Wende v Horine*, 130 O G 1311 (1907).

223. Stay of Proceedings—How Obtained. Motions brought under Rules 109 and 122, when set for hearing, stay proceedings pending the determination of the motions. Rule 123. In all other cases a motion to stay proceedings must be brought under Rule 123, which motion should set forth with particularity the circumstances of the case which make it necessary that the proceedings be stayed *Hoegh v Gordon*, 108 O. G 797 Proceedings may be suspended by stipulation *McKean v Morse*, 94 O G 1557, 1901 C D. 33.

224. Insufficient Grounds An interference proceed-

127

ing will not be suspended to permit a party to take out a patent upon a closely allied invention, merely because through the interference the opposing party might learn of such other application *Field,* 130 O G 1687 (1906)

The taking of testimony on the question of priority will not be suspended until the question of the right to make the claims has been determined *Hewitt v Weintraub, etc,* 128 O G. 1689 (1907)

Ex Parte Rights. Proceedings will not be stayed to consider ex parte rights, since such rights should be considered after decision on priority. *Dunbar v Schellenger,* 121 O G 687 (1905), *Mark v Greenewalt,* 118 O G 1068 (1905).

The fact that one of the parties to an interference has a patent and has an infringement suit pending against the other party, is no ground for suspending the proceedings in the interference *McBride v Kemp,* 109 O G. 1069 Nor is the fact that it is alleged that joint applicants are not joint inventors. since that is a question which may be determined on final hearing *Robinson v Muller & Bonnet,* 110 O G 1429

225 **Interference Terminated as to Some Parties—Effect of Stay.** A stay of proceedings after the termination of an interference as to some of the parties only operates as to the remainder of such parties *Swaren v Sandage, etc,* 17 Gour. 34-1 (April, 1905)

226 **Resumption—Suspended to Hear Motion** Where proceedings are suspended to hear a motion, they are resumed on the date the motion is finally determined, and no notice of resumption. other than notice of the decision, is necessary. *Greuter v Mathieu,* 112 O G. 253; *Blackman v Alexander,* 103 O G. 2059 (1903) But in *Hewitt v Steinmetz,* 122 O. G 1396 (1906), it was held that times fixed for taking testimony do not commence to run after suspension of proceedings for consideration of motions for dissolution, until the cases are returned to

128

the Examiner of Interferences and formal notice of resumption of proceedings is noted

227 **Appeal—Effect of Stay.** If a stay of proceedings is obtained after a decision is made and the time for appeal is fixed, such stay stops the running of time for appeal, but the time for appeal begins to run again as soon as the stay is ended and whatever time shall have expired between the time the limit of appeal was fixed and the granting of the stay, is lost to the party who obtains the stay, and he has only the remainder of the time originally fixed for appeal *Blackman v Alexander*, 105 O. G 2059 (1903).

Order of Suspension Modified After Appeal. An order suspending proceedings may be modified after appeal, provided the questions presented on appeal are not affected thereby *Herreshoff v Kmetsch*, 111 O G 1624

After Appeal Stay Unnecessary. After a party has appealed no stay of proceedings is necessary, but if the circumstances make it necessary to have more time for taking some action, the proper practice would be to ask that the hearing on appeal be continued *Robinson v Townsend v. Copeland*, 106 O G 997 (1903).

Appeal to the Court of Appeals—Time For Not Stayed The office can not stay the running of time for appeal to the Court of Appeals, D C , because that is a matter controlled by the rules of the court *Clement v Richards v. Weissner*, 16 Gour 52-10

RES ADJUDICATA.

228. **Successive Interferences—Res Adjudicata.** Where after final decision in an interference, claims are presented by the losing party which are such that they would dominate the subject matter upon which the other party prevailed, the decision in the interference would be res adjudicata *In re Curtiss*, 238 O. G 650, 46 App. D C. 183

As to claims involved in a second interference between

the same parties which could have been made in the first interference on the question of priority, the first decision is res adjudicata *Hopkins v. Newman*, 131 O. G 1161 (1907)

229. What Questions Are Determined by Interference. A final decision in an interference proceeding, as between the parties thereto, is conclusive as to all questions which were or could have been presented and determined by that proceeding *Blackford v Wilder*, 28 App D. C. 535, 127 O G. 1255 (1907), *Sarfert v Meyer*, 109 O G. 1885; *Cross v Rusby*, 42 App D C 227, 204 O. G. 1347, *Horine v Wende*, 29 App D C 415; 1907 C D 615

230. Second Interference—When Allowed. Second interferences will be allowed only under exceptional circumstances and will not ordinarily be declared upon claims to the same device differing from the first issue merely in scope *Corey & Baker v. Trout v McDermott*, 110 O G 306

Second Interference—Rule 109. The purpose of Rule 109 is to avoid second interferences, and where a party fails to take advantage of that rule he loses the right to contest the question of priority as to the claims made by his opponent *Sutton, Steele & Steele*, 121 O. G. 1012 (1906)

231. Judgments in Interferences. There are two kinds of judgments in interferences, interlocutory and final judgments

A final judgment is one which determines the rights of the parties in the matter in controversy, or a definite branch of it and reserves no further question for future determination, but a judgment may be final though it does not determine the rights of the parties if it ends the suit

An interlocutory judgment is one which does not dispose of the suit but reserves some further question for future determination

130

An interference is for the purpose of determining who, as between the parties to it, was the first in point of time to invent the subject matter in issue

In declaring the interference the Examiner settles to his own satisfaction all preliminary questions which must be determined in order that the question of priority may be investigated and determined by final judgment To do this he determines that the issue is patentable, that it is properly declared so that there may be a proper determination of the question of priority, that each of the parties has the right to make the claims and who are the senior and junior parties If any party desires to question the correctness of his conclusions he should do so by appropriate motions provided by the rules of practice, as for instance, if he wishes to question the decision as to whether he is a junior or the senior party, he should move to shift the burden of proof. A decision on this motion would be an interlocutory judgment from which there is no appeal, but which may be presented again on appeal from the final decision on priority. If a party believes the issue is not patentable he moves to dissolve the interference for that reason and if upon this motion the Law Examiner holds the issue is not patentable, this is a final judgment and puts an end to the interference unless one or more of the parties appeal and obtain a reversal of the judgment This though a final judgment, is not a final judgment on priority, there being no question of priority involved The foregoing are given as illustrations of interlocutory and final judgments

231a. What Questions Should Be Presented by Motions All questions, except those involving priority, should be presented by appropriate motions as provided in the rules Some questions which should first be presented by motion may also be urged at final hearing as involving the question of priority, illustrations of which will be

131

found in Sec 154a   Questions ancillary to the question of priority are set forth in Sec 192

232. Res Adjudicata. When a second suit is upon the same cause of action, and between the same parties as the first, the judgment in the former is conclusive in the latter as to every question which was or might have been presented and determined in the first action, but when the second suit is upon a different cause of action, though between the same parties, the judgment in the former action operates as an estoppel only as to the point or question actually litigated and determined, and not as to other matters which might have been litigated and determined   *Nesbit v Riverside Independent District,* 144 U. S 610, 618; *New Orleans v Citizen's Bank,* 167 U S 371, 386, *S P R R v U S,* 168 U S 1, 48   It was held that the doctrine as above stated is applicable to decisions of the Patent Office   It was therefore held in *Blackford v Wilder,* 127 O. G 1255 (1907), 28 App. D C 535; *Wende v Horine,* 129 O G. 2858, 29 App D C 415, and *In re Marconi,* 179 O G 577, 38 App. D C 286, that the losing party in an interference can not, after the interference, present claims which will dominate the issue involved in the interference   In other words, the party who prevails in the interference is by reason of the judgment of priority given the right to the subject matter involved and it can not afterward be given to another without taking it from him, and the question of his right to it having been fairly tried, he should not and can not be forced to retry the question, except upon appeal   See also *Carroll v Halwood,* 135 O G 896, 31 App D C 165

The fact that a party has a right under the statute to bring an action in equity to obtain a patent notwithstanding such judgment of priority, does not lessen the force of the foregoing decisions, since this is a right granted by statute to retry the issues and must be

132

availed of in accordance with the provisions of the statute

In harmony also with the foregoing decisions is the later case of *Rusby v Cross*, 204 O G 321, 42 App D. C. 341. Rusby prevailed in the interference. He then presented claims dominating certain claims of a patent inadvertently issued to Cross, the claims of which were not involved in the interference. Because Cross could have presented these claims but failed to do so, it was held that the judgment of priority awarded Rusby was res adjudicata as to those claims. Each party was demanding a right to the claims which formed the subject matter of the interference and it was incumbent on each party to present whatever facts he could to sustain his right therto. A winning party in an interference should not be disturbed in the full enjoyment of that which he has won, nor should he be penalized by further litigation for which there is no excuse other than that his opponent neglected to present all the facts which he could have presented

233. Broad Claims Presented After Termination of Interference—Res Adjudicata. Where after termination of an interference involving only narrow claims, the winning party takes out a patent on the narrow claims, not claiming the invention broadly, and the losing party establishes by competent evidence that he made another species of the invention patentably different from that involved in the interference prior to the date of invention established by his opponent, he is entitled to a claim broad enough to cover both forms of the invention notwithstanding the adverse decision in the interference Such is the holding by the Board of Examiners in Chief *In re Klahn*, 241 O G. 623, 1917 C D 7 (See Estoppel, Sec 242)

In *Temple v Goodrum*, 176 O G 526, the losing party in the interference, after judgment on priority, presented claims which read upon his own case and the two

133

other cases with which he had been involved but which could not have been added to that interference because of a decision in another interference adverse to one of the parties These claims were held res adjudicata because the applicant could have presented and contested them with the other party who could have made them, concurrently with the other interfering subject matter

In *Frickey v. Ogden*, 199 O G 307, it was held that where during the pendency of an interference between Ogden and Cornwall, but too late to be added thereto, an application was filed by Frickey which was assigned to the same party as that of Cornwall and it appeared that the assignee controlled both inventions and could have filed the application of Frickey in time for it to have been included in the interference between Ogden and Cornwall, but neglected to do so, he was estopped to contest further with Ogden the subject matter thereof.

234. **Motion to Dissolve—When Judgment is Res Adjudicata.** When a motion to dissolve on the ground that a party has no right to make the claims is sustained and no appeal is taken, such judgment is final as to the right of the losing party to a patent, or in other words, it is res adjudicata in the further prosecution of his application. *U S ex rel. Newcomb Motor Co v Moore*, 133 O. G. 1680, 30 App D C. 464

Motion to Dissolve—Unpatentability Since every applicant is entitled to appeal to the Court of Appeals on the patentability of his claims and since motions to dissolve can be carried no farther than the Commissioner, the dissolution on this ground is not conclusive against the parties *Gold v Gold*, 150 O G 570 34 App D C. 229

Right of Prevailing Party to Patent—Not Res Adjudicata. The right of the prevailing party in an interference to a patent is not conclusively determined by a judgment of priority because it may be that a statutory bar exists such as public use After the interference is terminated public use proceedings may be instituted and the issue in such case is not one of priority, nor is it confined to the structures or parties to the interference. *In re Pittsburgh Brake Shoe Co*, 176 O. G. 750 (1912), *Guempfet, etc v Wictorsohn*, 134 O. G. 255, 131 O. G. 779, 30 App. D. C. 432.

235. **Prior Motion—Res Adjudicata** Where a party makes a motion he must set up all that he can offer in support thereof as he is precluded from bringing another motion upon the same ground *Townsend v Ehret, etc.*, 137 O. G. 1485 (1908), *Townsend v. Thullen v. Young*, 137 O. G. 1710 (1908)

236. **Judgment of Priority—Effect.** Under the rules and practice of the Patent Office the decision of the Examiner of Interferences on a declared interference determines only the question of priority of invention in time as between the parties, and the party against whom the decision is rendered may still contend that the successful party is not entitled to the claims made, and he is not concluded upon the question of his right to a patent until the expiration of the time allowed him by statute for an appeal from the final order rejecting his application *Westinghouse v Hien, et al*, 159 Fed. 936

A judgment in an interference is to the effect that the losing party is not the first inventor of the subject matter in issue and he is therefore not entitled to a patent as to that issue. But such judgment is not conclusive against the losing party under all circumstances, for, it may appear that subsequent to the rendition of the judgment the prevailing party abandoned his application, never in any way gave his invention to the public and never took out his patent And where the judgment was rendered upon the record because the losing party failed to produce any testimony to support his preliminary statement, the prevailing party was not required to take testimony and the judgment was therefore based upon the applications, there being no evidence of actual

135

reduction to practice by either party. In such case, if the prevailing party, after judgment, permits his application to become abandoned and has in no way given his invention to the public, he has not completed the act of invention by in any manner giving the public the benefit of his invention. Since an abandoned application is not a bar to the granting of a patent to another, the losing party in such interference, if he has kept his application alive, is entitled to a patent on the issue notwithstanding such judgment of priority. It was held in *Ex parte Phelps*, 176 O. G. 525, that a judgment of priority was a bar to the claims of the losing party, even though the prevailing party had permitted his application to become abandoned after judgment and there was no testimony taken in the interference to show an actual reduction to practice by the prevailing party. But in *Jolliffe v. Waldo v. Vermer & Schorich*, 234 O. G. 671 (1916), Commissioner Ewing did not agree with the reasoning in *Ex parte Phelps*, 176 O. G. 525, and held that the losing party under such circumstances was entitled to a patent notwithstanding the judgment of priority against him. See also *Fanslow v. Whitney*, 266 O. G. 742 (1910).

237. **Judgment on the Record—When Not Permissible.** Where a junior party to an interference alleges in his preliminary statement a date of conception of the invention in issue prior to the senior party's filing date, but the other dates alleged are subsequent thereto, an order to show cause why judgment should not be rendered on the record should not be granted, as, conception might be proved as alleged. *Peters v. Hopkins & Dement*, 150 O. G. 1044, 34 App. D. C. 141.

238. **Motion for Judgment on the Record—Question Raised.** A motion for judgment on the record in an interference does not present the case for final hearing on the merits, but raises only the question of the sufficiency of the allegations of the preliminary statements of the opposing parties, admitting their truth for the purposes

136

of the motion only *Lindmark v De Ferranti*, 153 O. G 1082, 34 App D. C. 445 But where the junior party in his preliminary statement fails to allege a date of conception earlier than the filing date of his opponent, judgment of priority will be awarded to the senior party on the record *Neth & Tamplin v Ohmer*, 123 O G 998

In response to a motion to show cause why judgment should not be rendered upon the record, a party may move to dissolve the interference *Field v Colman*, 131 O G 1686 (1907), *Felbel v For*, 130 O G 2375 (1907), *Jarvis v de Focatiis*, 20 Gour. 66-4 (Mar, 1908).

239. For Failure to File Preliminary Statement. Where a party fails to file any preliminary statement and his filing date is later than that of one of his opponents, an order will be made to show cause why judgment should not be entered against him If he fails to respond to this order judgment will be rendered that he is not the first inventor, but where there are several parties such judgment is not a holding that he was the last of all the parties to make the invention *Dutcher v Matthew, etc*, 118 O G 2538 (1905)

240. For Failure to Print Testimony Judgment of priority will be awarded against a junior party who fails to print his testimony. *Brown v Gillett*, 191 O G 832 (1913)

241. For Failure to Take Testimony. When the time for taking testimony has expired and no testimony has been taken or filed by either party, it is the duty of the Examiner of Interferences to award priority to the senior party under Rule 116 *Brough v Snyder*, 94 O. G. 221, 1901 C D 3.

ESTOPPEL.

242. By Judgment in Interference (See title Judgment)

By Concealment (See title Concealment)

137

To Deny Validity of Patent After Contesting an Interference. Where a party has made application for a patent on the invention and contested an interference in regard to it, the contention against his successful rival that the invention is not patentable does not come with good grace. *R Thomas & Sons Co v The Electric Porcelain & Mfg Co, et al*, 111 Fed 923, 97 O G. 1838, 1901 C. D 510 Nevertheless a defeated party in an interference is not estopped to deny the validity of the patent granted on his opponent's application *Automatic Racking Machine Co v White Racker Co*, 145 Fed. 643, 645

To Make Claim After Rights or Third Parties Have Intervened. A party is not estopped from subsequently making a claim to an invention unless there is a failure of the specification to disclose it The absence of a definite and special claim for an invention when the application was originally filed does not act as an estoppel to the subsequent making of the claim In *Bechman v Wood*, 89 O G 2462, and *Miehle v Read*, 18 App. D C 128, 96 O G 426, it was held that where there are intervening rights an applicant may not broaden his claims to destroy those rights *Furman v Dean*, 114 O G 1552.

By Failure to Appeal. Where action is taken by the office upon motion to dissolve an interference from which an appeal may be taken in the interference and the opportunity for such appeal is neglected, an ex parte appeal thereafter upon the same matter will not be entertained except where the right of appeal is statutory. *Newcomb v Thompson*, 122 O G. 3012 (1906).

242a By Failure to Make Claims Under Rule 109. The purpose of Rule 109 is to avoid a second interference, and where a party fails to take advantage of that rule he loses his right to contest the question of priority as to the claims made by his opponent *Sutton v Steele & Steele*, 121 O G 1012 (1906)

By Admissions of Solicitor in Prosecution of Applica-

138

tion. A party is estopped to deny admissions made by his solicitor in the prosecution of his application *Weissenthanner v Dodge Metallic Cap Co*, 156 Fed 365, 368

243. Judicial Notice Since the Commissioner of Patents may take judicial notice of facts adjudicated by the Supreme Court of the United States in a cause passed upon by that court, he may for a stronger reason act upon knowledge derived from a search of the records of litigation and decisions made in his own department even though such records have not been formally introduced in evidence *In Re Marconi*, 179 O. G. 577, 38 App. D. C 286, 1912 C. D 483; *In re Drawbaugh*, 1896 C. D. 527, 77 O. G. 313. 9 App D C. 219, *McDermott*, 15 Gour 88-26 (Oct 1903).

The Commissioner takes judicial notice of the decisions of the Court of Appeals, D. C. Tourmer, 108 O. G. 798.

Facts of which the tribunal before whom the cause is tried, is bound to take judicial notice, need not be proven *Ball v Flora*, 121 O G. 2668 (1905).

Judicial notice will be taken of the contents of standard books of reference *Werk v Parker*, 264 O. G 159, 249 U S 130

While the court takes notice of its own records, it can not travel for this purpose out of the records relating to the particular case Thus in one case the court can not take notice of the proceedings in another case, unless such proceedings are put in evidence Wharton on Evidence, Vol 1, Sec 326

The court can not in one case take judicial notice of the records in a different case, even though pending in the same court Nor will it take judicial notice in a given case of the pendency of proceedings in other causes in the same court, much less of those of other courts Jones on Evidence, Sec. 129.

Special Knowledge of the Judge A judge has no right to act upon his own personal or special knowledge of

139

facts, as distinguished from that general knowledge which might be important to other persons of intelligence, since if the judge knows anything which would aid one of the parties he should be called from his place as judge and become a witness Jones on Evidence, Sec 133

MOTIONS.

244. (See Forms, Dissolution, Preliminary Statement, Hearing, Burden of Proof, Stay of Proceedings.)

Interlocutory Motions—What Are Permitted. ' Interlocutory motions are not permitted upon matters which can not be determined from a consideration of the application and office records and which require the taking of proofs *Cory, etc v Blakey,* 115 O G. 1328

Piecemeal prosecution is against the policy of the office, and hence a party may not make a motion which embodies but a part of his grounds for relief and after that has been determined, file other motions for other reasons which could have been and should have been included in the first motion *Williams v Webster v Sprague,* 148 O G. 280 (1909), *Egly v. Schultz,* 117 O. G 276 (1905).

To Dissolve Interference. (See Dissolution)

To Transmit Motions. Where a party desires to present a question which can not be passed upon by the particular tribunal before whom the case is at the time pending because of lack of jurisdiction to hear the motion, it is necessary to make a motion to transmit the motion to such tribunal. A motion to transmit should be accompanied by the motion which is to be transmitted Under the present rules such motions are filed before and passed upon by the Commissioner If in the opinion of the Commissioner the motion be not in proper form, or if it be not brought within the time specified and no satisfactory reason be given for the delay, it will not be transmitted Rule 122 If the motion is transmitted,

140

it is sent to the Law Examiner for his opinion thereon Under the former practice and under which most of the decisions elsewhere considered under the head of "dissolution" were rendered, a motion to transmit a motion to dissolve was filed before the Examiner of Interferences and if granted, the original motion then went to the Primary Examiner for determination. Since the change in the rules relate to the jurisdiction of the official who is authorized to pass upon the same, it is believed that the decisions under the old rules will apply under the new rules in so far as the form and merits of such motions are concerned

To Shift the Burden of Proof. Motions to shift the burden of proof should be filed before and decided by the Examiner of Interferences Rule 122 (See Burden of Proof)

To Amend Preliminary Statement. (See Preliminary Statement—Amendment of)

To Postpone Time for Filing Preliminary Statement. Rule 104. (See Preliminary Statement)

To Postpone Hearing. (Rules 120-153 See Hearing)

To Extend Time for Taking Testimony. The granting or refusing of a motion to extend time for taking of testimony is wholly within the discretion of the Examiner of Interferences and no appeal lies from his decision upon such motion, though in extreme cases where an abuse of discretion is shown, resulting in great hardship to a party, the ruling may be reviewed on appeal *Goodfellow v Jolly*, 115 O. G 1064, 1905 C D 105, *Christensen v McKenzie*. 117 O G 277, 1905 C D 238; *Dalton v Hopkins*, 121 O G 2666 (1906)

Delay in bringing the motion may result in its refusal *Donning v Anderson*, 111 O. G 582 And where a party made no effort to take testimony as to priority within the time set, but devoted his time to the investigation of public use of the invention, it was held

141

that an extension of time was properly refused. *Perrault v Pierce*, 108 O. G 2146

The motion should clearly set forth the grounds upon which the extension is asked and state why the testimony could not be taken during the time originally allowed. *Reynolds v Bean*, 101 O G 2821; 1902 C D 461. The motion should be brought before the time originally set has expired *Turner v Benzinger*, 102 O G 1552 (1903); *Byron v. Henry.* 104 O. G. 1895 (1903). A party may not voluntarily put himself in a position where his testimony can not be taken and then ask to be relieved of his own fault or negligence, as such action will be regarded as a waiver of his right to take testimony *Davis v Cody*, 101 O G 1369; 1902 C. D. 220

Since the granting or refusing a motion to extend time for taking testimony is a matter within the discretion of the Examiner of Interferences, each motion presented must rest upon its own inherent merits It would seem that the rules of the courts in granting continuances should be made applicable to motions of this character, though it seems that the office has not thus far applied such rules as where an extension is asked because of the inability of a party to procure the testimony of a certain witness, three elements should concur: (1) Materiality and admissibility of the evidence (2) due diligence, (3) an affirmative showing that the absent witness can and will be produced at a future time

To Suppress Testimony. (See Testimony—Suppression of)

To Take Testimony in a Foreign Country. Rule 158

To Amend Issue. Rule 109 (See Issue—Amendment)

To Add Further Counts. (See Issue)

For Rehearing. (See Hearing)

244a. To Amend a Motion. Where a party makes a motion which if found to be not in proper form, he may cure the defect by a motion to amend the motion, provided it appears that he is acting in good faith and that the same was brought within the time for appeal from the decision upon the former motion *Gold v Gold,* 131 O G. 1422 (1907), *Rochstroh v Warnock,* 132 O. G. 234, *McQuarrie v Manson.* 142 O G 288 (1909).

For Judgment of the Record. Rule 119. (See Judgment)

To Take Testimony as to Operativeness. (See Inoperativeness) *Lowry & Cowley v Spoon,* 122 O. G. 2687; *Barber v Wood,* 132 O G 1588

APPEALS

245 **To the Examiners in Chief** Sec 4909 R S "Every party to an interference may appeal from the decision of the Primary Examiner, or of the Examiner in charge of interferences in such case, to the Board of Examiners in Chief " Rules 143, 144, 145 and 146

Sec 4910 R S "If such party is dissatisfied with the decision of the Examiners in Chief, he may appeal to the Commissioner in person "

Extent of Right to Appeal. The right to appeal to the Examiners in Chief in interference cases created by statute was to review the question of priority and such ancillary questions as the Examiner had passed upon in deciding the question of priority for which the interference is instituted *Allen Comr. v. U S ex rel Lowry, et al ,* 116 O. G 2253 (1905)

Ancillary questions which go to the question of priority and which have been passed upon by the various tribunals of the Patent Office and Court of Appeals, D. C., are set forth in this work under title of Relevant Testimony, See 192

Judgment on the Record Appeal lies to Examiners-in-Chief *McHarg v. Schmidt & Mayland,* 106 O G. 1780 (1903); *Brown v Lindmark,* 109 O G 1071

246 **To the Court of Appeals. D. C.** In interference cases the Court of Appeals has jurisdiction to review the decision of the Commissioner in but one class of decisions, viz, final awards of priority. Decisions on motions are interlocutory judgments on which no appeal lies to the Court of Appeals. No award of priority may be made on motion to dissolve and before proofs are taken, not even in a case where the motion is based upon the ground that a party has no right to make the claims. If the motion is denied, the soundness of the ruling is a question ancillary to the final judgment of priority, as in *Podelsak v. McInnerney*, 26 App. D. C. 399 - If the motion is sustained, it ends the interference and no cause of action survives or exists upon which an order of priority can be based. Since the statute imposes on the Commissioner the power to declare in interference without right of appeal, he may also dissolve it without right of appeal. In *Cosper v Gold*, 34 App. D. C. 194, the Commissioner dissolved the interference on the ground that Cosper had no right to make the claims. On the first appeal the Court of Appeals declined jurisdiction because there had been no judgment of priority rendered. Thereupon the Commissioner entered a judgment of priority upon the ground that Cosper had no right to make the claims, and the question of priority hinged upon the question as to whether Cosper had a right to make the claims. Where there has been no hearing upon the question of priority no award of priority can be made on motion to dissolve. *Carlin v Goldberg*, 45 App. D. C. 540, 236 O. G. 1222, 1917 C. D. 128

Questions Which May Be Presented on Appeal on Priority as Ancillary Thereto. (See Sec 192.)

247. Questions Not Considered. As we have already seen, no question will be considered on appeal except that of priority and such questions as are ancillary thereto. The court has declined to consider that a showing made is not sufficient to establish that the delay in prosecution of the application was unavoidable. *In re Carvalho*, 250 O. G. 514, 47 App. D. C. 584. Patentability

144

of the issue *Hathoway & Lea v Colman*, 245 O. G.
1025, 46 App D C. 40, *Lautenschlager v. Glass*, 249 O.
G. 1223, 47 App D C. 443, *Elsom v Bonner & Golde*,
246 O G. 299 (1917), *Slingluff v Sweet, et al*, 230 O.
G 659; 1916 C D 224, 45 App D C 302; *Sobey v
Holschlaw*, 1907 C D 465, 126 O G. 3041, 28 App D.
C 65; *Mell v Midgley*, 1908 C D 512, 136 O G 1534,
31 App D C 534   Whether a statutory bar existed to
the granting of a patent to the successful party   *Burson
v Vogel*, 1907 C D 669, 131 O G 942, 29 App D C.
388   *Lacroir v Tybery*, 150 O G 267, 33 App D C 586;
Norling v Hayes, 1911 C D 347, 166 O G 1282, 37 App
D C. 169   Whether either party will have a right to a
patent   *Guenifett v Wictorsohn*, 1908 C D 367, 134 O.
G 779, 30 App D C 432   The refusal of the Commissioner to exercise his supervisory authority or of the Examiners in Chief to act under Rule 126   *Elsom v Bonner
& Golde*, 246 O G 299 (1917)   The court has frequently
refused to consider the identity of the inventions claimed
or the right of a party to make the claims, except in extreme cases where it has been held that the right to make
the claims is a question ancillary to the question of
priority. *Podelsak v McInnerney*, 120 O. G 1689, 26
App D C. 405; *U S ex rel Newcomb Motor Co v
Moore*, 133 O G 1680 (1908), 30 App. D. C. 464, *Secberger v Dodge*, 24 App D C 481; *Bechman v Southgate*, 127 O G 1254 (1906), 28 App D C 405, *Swihart
v Mauldin*, 99 O G 2332, 19 App D C 570, *Schup-
phaus v. Stevens*, 95 O G 1452, 17 App D C. 548   *Herman v Fullman*, 109 O G. 1888, 23 App D C 259,
Cosper v Gold, 151 O G 194, 34 App D C 194   The
question of operativeness   *Lotterhand v Hanson*, 110
O G 861, 23 App D C 372, *Duryea v Rice*, 126 O G
1357 (1906), 28 App. D. C. 423   An order dissolving an
interference. *The Union Distilling Co v Schneider*, 129
O G 2503 (1907), 29 App D C 1, *Brooks v Hillard*,
111 O G 302, 23 App D. C. 526   Granting or refusing

12   145

a rehearing *Greenwood v. Dover*, 109 O G 2172, 23 App. D C. 251, *Richards v Meissner*, 114 O G. 1831. Or any interlocutory motion except in extreme cases where it is plain that there has been an abuse of discretion exercised by the lower tribunals. *Ritter v Krakau & Conner*, 114 O G 1553, 24 App D C. 271, *Parker v Craft & Reynolds*, 265 O. G. 309, 258 Fed 988, *Dunbar v Schellenger*, 128 O G 2837 (1907), 29 App D C 129, *Kinsman v Strohm*, 136 O. G 1769 (1908), 31 App. D C 581, *Universal Motor Truck Co v Universal Motor Car Co*, 197 O G. 535, 41 App. D C. 261 Refusal to extend the time within which a preliminary statement may be filed, except where it clearly appears that there was an abuse of discretion. *Churchill v. Goodwin*, 141 O G 568, 32 App D C 428

The right to take expert testimony. *Weintraub v. Hewitt*, 154 O G. 254, 34 App. D C 487 Whether there was sufficient reason for delay in presenting a motion to dissolve. *Broadwell v. Long*, 164 O. G. 252, 36 App D C 418

247a. Questions Presented for the First Time on Appeal Only questions presented below will be considered on appeal *McFarland v Watson*, 146 O. G. 257, 33 App D C 445, *Lacroix v Tyberg*, 150 O. G. 267, 33 App D. C 586, *Field v. Coleman*, 193 O G 221, 40 App. D. C. 598, *Luckett v Straub*, 250 O. G 999 (1918)

248. Assignment of Errors—Scope of. On an appeal to the Examiners in Chief from a decision of the Examiner of Interferences, an assignment of error which assails the decision of the Examiner of Interferences in awarding priority on the whole case to the opposing party is sufficient to preserve the appellant's right to argue the question of res adjudicata by reason of a judgment in a prior interference *Carroll v Halwood*, 135 O G 896 (1908), 31 App D C. 165.

Amendment of Assignment of Errors. No provision is made in either the Court Rules or the Rules of the Patent Office for amendment of assignment of errors, but amendment may be permitted upon a proper showing, where no injury could be done the opposing party *Horine v Wende,* 129 O G 2858 (1907), 29 App D C 415.

249. Reversal on Question of Fact. Where the concurrent decisions of the Patent Office are the same on a question of fact, it is necessary for the appellant to make out a clear case of error to obtain a reversal. If it be left in doubt whether the ruling below is correct, the decision will be affirmed *Ries v Jebsen,* 132 O G. 845 (1907), 30 App. D C 199, *Howard v Hey,* 95 O G. 1647, 18 App. D. C. 142, *Swihart v. Mauldin,* 99 O G 2332, 19 App. D C. 570, *Flora v Powrie,* 109 O G 2443, 23 App D C 195 The court is not bound to affirm a case because the decisions below have been uniform. *O'Connell v. Schmidt,* 122 O G 2065 (1906), 27 App. D. C. 77, *Woodbridge v. Winship,* 145 O G 1250, 33 App. D C 490, *Gold v Gold,* 150 O G. 570, 34 App D C. 229, *Derr v. Gleason,* 264 O G. 864, 258 Fed 969.

250 Reversal on Questions of Law. While the decisions of the Patent Office on questions of fact will ordinarily be followed, such is not the rule where matters of law are involved *Orcutt v McDonald, Jr,* 123 O G 1287 (1906), 27 App D C 228, *Bourn v Hill,* 123 O. G 1284 (1906), 27 App D C 291

251. The Record on Appeal. The court will not consider affidavits filed either in the court or in the Patent Office, relating to changes that may have occurred, in drawings, models, or exhibits and the like, after the same have been introduced in evidence, and has pointed out that to guard against such possibility parties should describe exhibits at the time they are introduced in evidence. If any corrections are to be made in the record they should be made in the Patent Office before the record is certified to the Court of Appeals *Blackford v Wilder,* 104 O G 580 (1903), 21 App. D C 1; *Green-*

wood v Dover, 109 O G 2172, 23 App. D C 251. Where the decision of the Patent Office is based on testimony not in the record on appeal it must be assumed that the decision below was correct *Goldberg v Halle*, 151 O G 452 34 App D C 183 The record made by a party not appealing will not be considered on appeal *Richards v Meissner*. 114 O G 1831

Where error in suppressing testimony is alleged, the suppressed testimony must be made a part of the record *Jones v Starr*. 117 O. G. 1495. 26 App. D. C. 64

252. Extending Time for Filing Record The Commissioner may not extend time for giving notice of appeal, but he may extend the time for filing the transcript of the record In *Clements v Richards*, 111 O. G. 1626, it was held that the Commissioner has no authority to extend the limit of appeal to the Court of Appeals, as that is fixed by the rules of the court.

253 Appeals to the Commissioner. Appeals to the Commissioner in Interferences are permissible under Rules 124, 139 and 143 Regulations respecting the presentation of such appeals are provided in Rules 144, 145 and 146 In general a party may appeal from a judgment against him on priority of invention Certain questions have arisen in interferences and which have been designated in various decisions as questions ancillary to that of priority The questions which have been considered by the Court of Appeals D C, as ancillary to priority are referred to elsewhere under Relevant Testimony. See 192 Such questions having been taken into consideration by the court as properly relating to priority of invention, they may be presented to the various tribunals of the Patent Office and appeal taken to the Commissioner from adverse rulings thereon by the Examiners in Chief. But the jurisdiction of the Commissioner being more extensive than that of the Court of Appeals, D C, he may take into consideration on appeal matters which will not be considered by the court

148

For the sake of orderly procedure the Commissioner, with the approval of the Secretary of the Interior, has promulgated the Rules of Practice in which provision is made for appeals on certain questions and the right of appeal denied as to others The rules are designed to be in strict accordance with the Revised Statutes relating to the grant of patents Questions which are appealable under the rules should be presented by appeal in conformity with such rules, but where a party desires to present to the Commissioner a question on which the rules do not provide for appeal, he must do so by petition. (See Petitions.)

254 Patentability of the Issue. On appeals on priority, the patentability of the issue will be considered only under extraordinary circumstances which will warrant the exercise of the supervisory authority of the Commissioner to correct a manifest error *Lacroix v Tyberg,* 148 O G 831 (1908), *Dixon & Marsh v Graves,* 130 O. G. 2374 (1907), *Sorrell v Donnelly,* 129 O. G 2301 (1907), *Potter v McIntosh,* 122 O G 1721 (1906); *Sobey v. Holschlaw,* 119 O G 1922 (1905)

Where the Examiners in Chief recommend under Rule 126, that the issue is not patentable, the Commissioner will not pass upon the patentability of the issue at this stage of the proceedings, but may suspend the interference and remand the question to the Primary Examiner, from whose decision an appeal may be taken as in other cases Rule 126 *Sorrell v Donnelly,* 129 O G 2301 (1907) Where the Examiner of Interferences or the Examiners in Chief refuse to make any recommendation under Rule 126, such refusal will not be reviewed on appeal. *Wert v Borst,* 122 O G 2062 (1906).

255. Petitions in Interferences. It is well settled that a matter will not be considered on petition if the rules provide adequate remedies by appeal An aggrieved party must follow the regular course of procedure provided by the rules and should only invoke the supervi-

149

sory authority of the Commissioner under circumstances where he has no other remedy and in a clear case. *Brown v Gammeter,* 132 O G 679 (1908); *Cazin,* 20 Gour. 86-15 (Dec , 1908); *Numan v Ashley,* 175 O G 1098 (1912).

256   Right of Appeal Denied—In What Cases. No appeal lies where the rules specifically provide that a question is not appealable   And it has been held that where a motion to amend the issue is denied because the opposing party can not make the claim, no appeal lies to the Commissioner   *Stronach v Shaw,* 192 O G 989 (1913), *Mortimer v Thomas,* 192 O G 215 (1913); or from a decision which would not constitute a ground for rejecting the claims in the application of the moving party after the termination of the interference. *Mortimer v Thomas,* 192 O G. 215 (1913). Or where a motion to dissolve an interference is based on the ground of irregularity in declaring the same because of the alleged inoperativeness of the opposing party's structure. *Seacombe v Burks,* 182 O G. 973 (1912)   Or the granting of a motion to add counts under Rule 109   *Leonard v. Pardee,* 164 O. G. 249 (1911)   *Degen v Pfadt,* 133 O G 514 (1908)   Or from a decision of the Primary Examiner as to the sufficiency of a notice as to matters not of record which are to be presented at the hearing on motion to dissolve, except in cases of abuse of discretion   *Thieme v Bowen,* 21 Gour 70-13 (Aug , 1909). Or upon the admissibility of affidavits filed with a motion to dissolve, if no appeal lies from the decision on the motion to dissolve   *Brown v Inwood,* 131 O G. 1423 (1907)   Or from a decision of the Examiner of Interferences extending time for taking testimony, nor will the question be considered on petition, except in a clear case of abuse of discretion   *Withers v Weinwurm,* 129 O G 2501 (1907)   Or the granting of a motion to take testimony abroad. *Keith v Lundquist,* 128 O G 2835 (1907). Or from a decision denying a motion to

150

take testimony as to the operativeness of an opponent's device, pending a motion to dissolve the interference. *Barber v. Wood*, 127 O G 1991 (1907). Or from a decision of the Examiner of Interferences on a motion to shift the burden of proof, though the question will be considered on final hearing on priority. *Dukesmith v. Corrington*, 125 O. G. 348; *Hewitt v. Thomas, et al*, 122 O G. 1045 (1906); *McGill v Adams*, 119 O G. 1924 (1905), *Lowry v Spoon*, 14 Gour 52-7 (July, 1902) Or from a decision of the Examiner of Interferences refusing to require a party to file a supplemental oath *Dukesmith v Corrington*, 125 O G 348 (1906) Or the refusal of the Examiner of Interferences to grant a rehearing, though the right to a rehearing may be considered on appeal on the entire record *Hewitt v Thomas, et al*, 122 O G. 1045 (1906), *Dunbar v Schellenger*, 121 O G. 2663 (1906). Or from the granting or denying of a motion to extend time for filing a preliminary statement except where there is an abuse of discretion. *Ohmer v Neth*, 118 O G 1686 (1905) Or from a decision of the Examiners in Chief reversing a decision of the Primary Examiner rejecting a count of the issue and refusing to dissolve the interference as to that count *Coleman v Bullard v Struble*, 114 O G 973. Or from a favorable decision of the Examiner rendered on a motion to dissolve as to the sufficiency of an affidavit filed under Rule 75 *McChesley v Kruger*, 101 O G. 219. 1902 C D 349, *Byron v. Maxwell*, 105 O G 499 (1903) Or from a refusal of the Examiner to rehear a motion to dissolve *Macy v Laning*, 101 O G. 1608. 1902 C D 399 Or from a decision of the Examiner denying a motion to amend under Rule 109, since appeal in such case is to the Board. *Hillard v Eckert*, 101 O. G. 1831; 1902 C D. 413.

257 Right to Make the Claims and Patentability of the Issue. No appeal lies to the Commissioner, inter partes, from a favorable decision of the Law Examiner on the patentability of the issue or the right to make the claims. The Commissioner will interfere in such cases only to correct an error which is clear and evident *Niedermeyer v Walton* 98 O G 1707, 1902 C. D 56; *Miskolczy v Glibsattel.* 13 Gour 19-6 (Apr, 1901). *Kempshall v Serberling.* 104 O G 1395 (1903); *Faller v Lorimer.* 14 Gour 50-2 and 3 (July 1902), *Whipple v Sharp.* 14 Gour 66-2 (Sept 1902) *Lammers v Weinuurm.* 15 Gour 66-2 (Sept 1903) Notwithstanding numerous decision to the same effect, parties have persisted in many cases covering a period of years in such attempted appeals to the Commissioner If upon motion to dissolve on the ground that a party has no right to make the claims, it is held that he has a right to make the claims. the party who is defeated on the motion need not appeal from such interlocutory judgment, but he may present the same question for review before the Examiner of Interferences, before the Examiners in Chief before the Commissioner, and the Court of Appeals, D C as a question ancillary to that of priority. If the motion is sustained and the interference dissolved, there is then no question of priority to be determined because it has already been held that one of the parties has no right to make the claims and this holding is equivalent to saying that he never invented the issue and is therefore not entitled to a patent Under the present Rule 124 he may appeal inter partes to the Examiners in Chief and from the Board he may appeal to the Commissioner. If the Commissioner holds that he has no right to make the claims he can appeal no further inter partes, but he has a right to further prosecute his application and if his claims are rejected and patent refused. he has a statutory right to appeal through the various tribunals of the Patent Office to the Court of Appeals D C If he finally sustains his right to make the claims. the question of priority will again become an issue

Where a motion to dissolve on the ground that the

152

issue is not patentable is denied, no appeal lies because, first, Rule 124 provides that no appeal lies from such decision, and, second, because whether the issue is patentable is a matter between the applicants and the office and is not a matter of controversy between the parties. If the interference is dissolved upon this ground, the party who makes the motion confesses thereby that he is not entitled to a patent, but the other party may appeal inter partes to the Examiners in Chief, and from them to the Commissioner. It may seem that there is no valid reason for inter partes appeals in such cases, as provided in Rule 124, but it may be deemed advisable that the moving party be heard for the assistance of the office, as was held in *Griffith v Dodgson*, 116 O. G 1731 (1905), *Lipe v. Miller*, 109 O G 1608; *Robbins v Titus*, 111 O G 584, *Patterson v Neher*, 192 O. G 215 (1913) Whatever may be the reason for the provision, it is sufficient that the rule now in force so provides. It should be remembered that interlocutory motions, such as motions to dissolve, are creatures of the Rules of Practice of the Patent Office, and the rights of parties thereunder are not statutory rights, and where on such motions, which can be carried no farther than the Commissioner, the issue is held not patentable, the party has still the right to insist in the further ex parte prosecution of his application that the claims are patentable, and if his application is rejected for the reason that the claims are not patentable he has a statutory right of appeal to the various tribunals of the Patent Office and finally to the Court of Appeals, D C, and thus he has had two series of appeals within the office on the patentability of the issue and finally a decision of the Court of Appeals thereon As a practical matter it might be assumed that in the ex parte appeals, the decisions in the interference would be followed, but by this means he would finally secure a decision of the Court of Appeals on this question

153

FORMS

IN THE UNITED STATES PATENT OFFICE.

Robert A Jones,
Counterbalanced Crank Shaft,
Filed March 6, 1918,
Serial No 120,256
Commissioner of Patents,
SIR:

Affidavit of Priority.

STATE OF MICHIGAN, }
COUNTY OF WAYNE, } *ss:*

Now comes Robert A. Jones, the above-named applicant, and states that prior to January 5, 1917, the date of the filing of the application which matured into U. S. Patent No. . ... , issued February 5, 1918, to George A Allen, the said applicant disclosed to others the invention described and claimed in his pending application, and had made working drawings thereof; that thereafter and long prior to the said filing date of January 5, 1917, the said applicant had a motor constructed including a counterbalanced crank shaft which was made in accordance with the drawings of the application herein involved, that in said counterbalanced crank shaft there were counterweights fixed securely thereto, each in substantial opposition to the off-center parts of the crank shaft which the counterweights were to counterbalance, said counterweights and crank shaft being formed with shoulders which engaged and opposed that movement of the counterweights relative to the crank shaft which centrifugal force tends to produce, that in said crank shaft a counterweight was fixedly secured between the crank arms of said crank shaft by two arms which strad-

154

dled the inner end of the crank arm and were formed with inwardly projecting lugs, the said crank arm having outwardly projecting lugs which respectively engaged the lugs on the two arms of the counterweight and opposed that movement of the counterweight relative to the crank shaft which centrifugal force tends to produce, that said shaft in addition to these inter engaging shoulders of the counterweight and shaft also was welded to the counterweight at the crank arm

Deponent further states that said motor was put into actual use after a test and has been sold and is now in use commercially, that said test and actual use of the motor took place prior to the filing date of the Allen Patent, No   . ., constituting a reference against the applicant's claims

          ..   .   .
Subscribed and sworn to before me, a Notary Public, this ...   day of   .   .
. . . .
Notary Public.

My Commission Expires

IN THE UNITED STATES PATENT OFFICE.

JOHN FITCH   ⎫
  vs ⎬ Interference No   . . . . .
ROBERT FULTON.⎭

Motion to Amend the Issue.

Now comes Robert Fulton, by his attorney, and moves to amend his application, serial No. .. .., involved in the above entitled interference, by adding thereto the following proposed claims·

(Here insert the claims it is desired to have entered)

The foregoing claims are believed to be patentable, properly to describe the means disclosed by all parties and are deemed necessary to be counts of the interference in order that the question of priority respecting all pat-

155

entable means common to the parties may be adjudicated

An amendment entitled in said application and containing the said proposed claims is filed herewith.

(If the proposed claims are copied from the application of another party, so state and identify them by their ordinals in that application.)

(If the proposed amendment is for the purpose of procuring another interference, as with a divisional application of one of the opposing parties, adjust the phraseology accordingly)

. . . .

Attorney for Robert Fulton.

IN THE UNITED STATES PATENT OFFICE

JOHN FITCH,
    vs   } Interference No. . .   . .
ROBERT FULTON

Motion to Substitute an Application.

Now comes John Fitch, by his attorney, and moves that his application, Serial No   . . be substituted for application, Serial No. . .   ., now included in the above entitled interference It is believed that the counts of the issue properly describe the means disclosed in the said application it is desired to substitute

(If the moving party is an assignee and the application desired to be substituted is one of an inventor other than he whose application is already included, corresponding changes in the phraseology should be made.)

. . . . . .

Attorney for John Fitch

IN THE UNITED STATES PATENT OFFICE.

JOHN DOE
    vs   } Interference No   . . . . .
PETER SMITH

Before the Examiner of Interferences

156

Motion to Extend Time for Filing Preliminary Statement.

Now comes John Doe, one of the parties to the above entitled interference, by his attorney, and moves that his time for filing his preliminary statement herein be extended for a period of twenty days from Jan 10, 1919. The reasons for asking said extension are set forth in the attached affidavit of John Doe and are as follows: (Here state the reasons) (See Rule 104.)

Attorney for John Doe

Note One postponement of time for filing preliminary statements can ordinarily be secured by simple ex parte request

Further postponements must usually be had by motion or stipulation.

A copy of the motion and notice of hearing should be served on opposing counsel, and proof of service filed.

(Title of case)

BEFORE THE EXAMINER OF INTERFERENCES.

Motion to Amend Preliminary Statement.

And now comes the party, John Doe, by his attorney, and moves that he be permitted to amend his preliminary statement, now on file, in accordance with the preliminary statement submitted herewith, and in support of this motion files the attached affidavit of .... .. , setting forth the reasons for asking said permission to amend, which are as follows   (Set out the reasons.)

It is further moved that all other proceeding in this interference be stayed pending the determination of this motion

Attorney for John Doe

Note As to the character of showing required in the affidavit to accompany this motion, see Sec. 47

A copy of the motion (including the affidavit) and notice of hearing, should be served on the other parties.

Proof of service and notice of hearing should accompany the motion.

IN THE UNITED STATES PATENT OFFICE.

JOHN FITCH
  vs   } Interference No ....
ROBERT FULTON

Motion to Dissolve Under Rule 122.

Now comes John Fitch, by his attorney, and moves to dissolve the above-entitled interference for the reasons·

1. That there has been such informality in declaring the interference as will preclude the proper determination of the question of priority of invention.

2. That the means defined in the several (or specified) counts of the issue is not patentable.

3 That the party Fulton has no right to make the claims corresponding to the several (or specified) counts of the issue.

In support of the foregoing motion and with respect to reason 1, it will be shown (Here state what the informality is that will be relied on, which must be a fact or facts independent of those relied on to support reasons 2 and 3)

With respect to reason 2 it will be contended that all of the counts (or certain specified counts) define means that are (here state the facts that are deemed to establish want of patentability; citing by name, date and number any patent deemed to be an anticipation or, if the several counts or any of them are deemed to cover aggregations, or mere substitutions or equivalents in old combinations, specifying the aggregated or substituted parts, and citing prior patent or publications to show that the parts or equivalent elements were known in the prior art The facts relied on must be set forth with sufficient

158

particularity to enable the opposing party to prepare a defense and they must be different from facts relied on to support grounds 1 and 3   See Sec. 66).

With respect to reason 3, it will be contended that (Here set forth the facts relied on, as that the specification and drawing of the opposing party does not disclose a specified element of one or all of the counts, or that the disclosure is incomplete, or the means are inoperative and why, or that the patent is barred by a specified foreign patent to the same party, filed more than twelve months prior to the filing of the U. S. application   The facts to support ground 3 must be different from those given in support of grounds 1 and 2).

Attorney for John Fitch.

Proof of service must be filed with all motions under Rules 109 and 122

(Title of Case.)

Motion to Extend Time for Taking Testimony.

And now comes John Doe, by his attorney, and moves that the time for taking his testimony in chief be extended thirty days, and that the remaining dates and final hearing be correspondingly extended

The reasons for requesting said extension are set forth in the accompanying affidavit of .. .., and are as follows: (Here state the reasons)

It is further moved that all other proceedings be stayed pending the determination of this motion   (This paragraph may be omitted if there are no other proceedings to be stayed)

Attorney for John Doe

Note   Hearings can also be postponed and sometimes advanced by similar motion.

159

Limit of appeal can be extended by similar motion if made before limit expires

A copy of the motion (including affidavit) and notice of hearing should be served on all other parties

Proof of service and notice of hearing should accompany the motion when filed

(Title of Case)

BEFORE THE EXAMINER OF INTERFERENCES.

Motion to Use Testimony Taken in Another Interference

And now comes John Doe, by his attorney, and moves that he be permitted to use as a part of the evidence in the above-entitled interference the testimony taken in interference No. .. . , *Brown v Evans* (or if not all the testimony is to be used, specify the witnesses whose testimony is desired), subject to the right of the other parties herein to recall said witnesses, or to take other testimony in rebuttal thereof

The reason for using said testimony is set forth in the accompanying affidavit of .... , and is as follows· (Here state the reasons)

It is further moved that all other proceedings be stayed pending the determination of this motion

. .. . ,

Attorney for John Doe.

Note It should be stated in the affidavit how the testimony sought to be used is relevant and material

A copy of the motion and notice of hearing should be served on all other parties.

Proof of service and notice of hearing should be filed with the motion

(Title of Case)

BEFORE THE EXAMINER OF INTERFERENCES.

Motion to Take Special Testimony

And now comes John Doe, by his attorney, and moves that he be permitted to take testimony to prove that the device disclosed in the application of Peter Smith, is inoperative, and is not such a disclosure as is required by the statute

The reason for asking permission to take said testimony is set forth in the accompanying affidavit of .
, and is as follows (Here set out the reason)

It is further moved that all other proceedings herein be stayed pending the determination of this motion

. . . .

Attorney for John Doe.

Note. Inoperativeness goes to the right to make the claims and a motion to dissolve on that ground should first be made As to character of showing required, see Sec 165

A copy of the motion and notice of hearing should be served on all other parties

Proof of service and notice of hearing should be filed with the motion

(Title of Case)

BEFORE THE EXAMINER OF INTERFERENCES.

Motion to Shift the Burden of Proof.

And now comes John Doe by his attorney, and moves that the burden of proof in this interference be shifted to the senior party, Smith

The reason the burden of proof should be so shifted is as follows

(Here set forth the reasons relied upon)

. . . .

Attorney for John Doe.

A copy of the motion and notice of hearing should be served on the opposing parties

Proof of service and notice of hearing should accompany the motion when filed

IN THE UNITED STATES PATENT OFFICE.

DOE
  vs   } Interference No ....
SMITH

BEFORE THE EXAMINER OF INTERFERENCES.

Motion to Take Testimony Abroad.

Now comes the party Doe by his attorney, and moves that in accordance with Rule 158 a commission be issued to the United States Consul at Manchester, England, to take the depositions of John Brown, of Number 27 Woodley Street Manchester England, and of   .. .. .. ,
in behalf of John Doe, under interrogatories and cross-interrogatories to be filed by the attorneys for the parties Doe and Smith, respectively.

The particular facts to which it is expected the said Brown and   ..   ..   will testify are   (Here set out the facts)   The affidavit of John Doe is filed herewith in support of this motion

It is further moved that all other proceedings in this case be stayed pending the determination of this motion

Attorney for Doe

Motion papers and notice of hearing should be served on other parties

Proof of service and notice of hearing should accompany motion papers

Note   To have this motion granted proof must be submitted that the amount of $100 00 has been deposited with the State Department through which department the papers are forwarded

102

(Title of Case.)

BEFORE THE EXAMINER OF INTERFERENCES

Motion for Judgment on the Record.

Comes now Robert A Jones, the senior party to the above-entitled interference, and shows to the Examiner of Interferences that he is entitled to judgment on the record herein for the following reasons

1 That by the provisions of your order of November 10, 1918, the junior party, Peter Smith, was given until February 15, 1919, within which to take his testimony in chief herein, that said time has never been extended by stipulation or otherwise and that said junior party has failed and refused to take testimony herein prior to Feb 15, 1919, or at all

Wherefore the said senior party moves for judgment on the record for the reasons hereinbefore stated

Attorney for Robert A Jones

STATE OF MICHIGAN, }
COUNTY OF WAYNE, } ss.

James Bradford, being duly sworn, deposes and says that he is attorney for Robert A. Jones, the senior party to the above-entitled interference, and that the facts set forth in the foregoing motion are true, as he is informed and believes

Subscribed and sworn to before me, a Notary Public, this . . . day of .

Notary Public

My Commission Expires . . . .

Note   A copy of the motion and notice of hearing should be served on the other party

Proof of service and notice of hearing should be filed with the motion

163

For decisions on motions of this character, see Secs. 237 to 241

BEFORE THE EXAMINER OF INTERFERENCES.

Notice of Hearing.

To Messrs Bradford & Bradford, Attorneys for Peter Smith, St. Paul, Bldg., Louisville, Ky .

Please take notice that on Monday, November 3, 1919, at 10 o'clock a m, or as soon thereafter as counsel can be heard, I shall present to the Honorable Examiner of Interferences the accompanying motion to   .   .

.. . .

Attorney for John Doe.

(Title of Case)

BEFORE THE EXAMINER OF INTERFERENCES.

Proof of Service.

STATE OF MICHIGAN, } *ss* .
COUNTY OF WAYNE, }

James Bradford, being duly sworn deposes and says, that he is the attorney for John Doe in the above interference. that on the 21st day of November, 1919, he sent to Messrs Thomas & Miller, 35 Williams Street, New York City, attorneys for Peter Smith, a true copy of the annexed notice of taking testimony by depositing the said copy in the registry mail department of the general post office in the city of Detroit, State of Michigan, in a sealed envelope, postage prepaid, and addressed to the said Thomas & Miller, at the address aforesaid, registry receipt for which is hereto attached

. . . .

Subscribed and sworn to before me, a Notary Public, this   day of ...   ...
My Commission Expires on the ...   . day of   .. .   .

164

(Title of Case)

BEFORE THE EXAMINER OF INTERFERENCES.

Stipulation.

It is hereby stipulated and agreed by the attorneys for the respective parties to the above entitled interference, the Examiner of Interferences consenting thereto, that the several dates heretofore set for the taking of testimony, and final hearing, may be extended for thirty days

. . . . ..

Attorney for John Doe

New York, N Y, Jan 10, 1910

. . ..

Attorney for Peter Smith

Boston, Mass Jan 12, 1910.

Note. Time for filing preliminary statements, final hearing, interlocutory hearings and limit of appeal can be postponed by similar stipulation

(Title of Case)

BEFORE THE EXAMINER OF INTERFERENCES.

Motion to Dispense With Printing

And now comes John Doe, one of the parties to the above-entitled interference, by his attorney and moves that the printing of his testimony in this interference be dispensed with in accordance with Rule 162, for the following reasons (Here set out the reasons) and he files herewith his verified statement setting forth the reasons for dispensing with such printing of the record

(The affidavit in support of the motion should set forth the financial condition of the moving party with such particularity as to show that he is unable to defray the expense of printing the record)

It is further moved that all other proceedings in this interference be stayed pending the determination of this motion

. . . .
Attorney for John Doe

Note A copy of the motion and notice of hearing should be served on all other parties

Proof of service and notice of hearing should be filed with the motion

Printing of the record may be dispensed with by stipulation, if approved by the Commissioner

(Title of Case)

BEFORE THE EXAMINER OF INTERFERENCES.

Motion to Consolidate.

And now comes John Doe, one of the parties to the above entitled interference, by his attorney, and moves that this interference be consolidated with interference No . , . . *vs* . . . ., and No . . , . . *vs* . , and that said interferences be tried and determined as one interference, and that the times for taking testimony and the date of final hearing be set accordingly

The reasons for consolidating said interferences are as follows ·

(Here state clearly why the interferences should be consolidated)

It is further moved that all other proceedings in said interferences be stayed pending the determination of this motion

. . . .
Attorney for John Doe

Note A copy of the motion and notice of hearing should be served on all other parties

166

Proof of service and notice of hearing should be filed with the motion

The office aims to consolidate interferences when possible on its own motion.

Only interferences having the same parties, in the same order, and with closely related subject matter can be consolidated.

(Title of Case)

BEFORE THE EXAMINER OF INTERFERENCES.

Motion to Suppress Testimony.

And now comes John Doe, by his attorney, and moves that certain parts of the testimony taken by Peter Smith or in his behalf on the 10th day of January, 1910, at . . ., be suppressed and not considered in determining this interference. The testimony sought to be suppressed is as follows

(Here set out or identify particularly the testimony to be suppressed)

The following reasons are assigned for suppressing said testimony, to wit .

(Here set out the reasons for suppressing the testimony)

It is further moved that all other proceedings in this interference be stayed pending the determination of this motion

. . . .

Attorney for John Doe

Note A copy of the motion and notice of hearing should be served on all other parties

Proof of service and notice of hearing should be filed with the motion

167

(Title of Case)

BEFORE THE EXAMINER OF INTERFERENCES.

Petition for Rehearing.

And now comes John Doe, one of the parties to the above entitled interference, and prays that the Examiner of Interferences reconsider his decision of the   .   .   .   .   day of .   .   in so far as said decision related to (Set out the part of the decision to which exception is taken)

The grounds upon which a rehearing is asked are as follows   (Set out the various points to be considered, and if any point is based on matters not in the record, an affidavit in support of such facts should accompany the motion)

(If the rehearing is on an interlocutory decision, add :)

It is further moved that all other proceedings herein be stayed pending the determination of this motion.

.   .   .   .
Attorney for John Doe.

This is an ex parte matter   No notice other parties is necessary. If granted the office will set a date for hearing and notify the parties

RULES OF PRACTICE

IN THE

UNITED STATES PATENT OFFICE.

REVISED JANUARY 1, 1916

Since January 1, 1916, the Rules have been amended as
  follows:
Rule 12, June 9, 1916
Rule 93, June 5, 1917
Rule 77, June 19, 1917
Rule 17, July 31, 1918, part (*h*) added
Court Rule XXI, paragraph 4.

CORRESPONDENCE AND INTERVIEWS.

1. All business with the office should be transacted in
writing Unless by the consent of all parties, the action
of the office will be based exclusively on the written
record No attention will be paid to any alleged oral
promise, stipulation, or understanding in relation to
which there is a disagreement or doubt

2 All office letters must be sent in the name of the
"Commissioner of Patents " All letters and other communications intended for the office must be addressed to
him , if addressed to any of the other officers, they will
ordinarily be returned

3 Express charges, freight, postage, and all other
charges on matter sent to the Patent Office must be prepaid in full; otherwise it will not be received

4. The personal attendance of applicants at the Patent

Office is unnecessary. Their business can be transacted by correspondence.

5 The assignee of the entire interest of an invention is entitled to hold correspondence with the office to the exclusion of the inventor (See Rule 20)

6 When there has been an assignment of an undivided part of an invention, amendments and other actions requiring the signature of the inventor must also receive the written assent of the assignee; but official letters will only be sent to the post-office address of the inventor, unless he shall otherwise direct

7. When an attorney shall have filed his power of attorney, duly executed, the correspondence will be held with him

A double correspondence with the inventor and an assignee, or with a principal and his attorney, or with two attorneys, can not generally be allowed

8. A separate letter should in every case be written in relation to each distinct subject of inquiry or application. Assignments for record, final fees, and orders for copies or abstracts must be sent to the office in separate letters

Papers sent in violation of this rule will be returned

9 When a letter concerns an application, it should state the name of the applicant, the title of the invention, the serial number of the application (see Rule 31), and the date of filing the same (see Rule 32)

10 When the letter concerns a patent, it should state the name of the patentee, the title of the invention, and the number and date of the patent

11 No attention will be paid to unverified *ex parte* statements or protests of persons concerning pending applications to which they are not parties, unless information of the pendency of these applications shall have been voluntary communicated by the applicants

12 Mail reaching the post office at Washington, D C., up to 4 30 p m , on week days, excepting holidays, and

1 p m on half holidays, is entered as received in the Patent Office on the day it reaches the post office

Special-delivery letters and other papers may be deposited in a box provided at the watchman's desk at the F Street entrance of the Patent Office up to midnight *on week-days, including holidays*, and all papers deposited therein are entered as received in the Patent Office on the day of deposit

Letters received at the office will be answered, and orders for printed copies filled, without unnecessary delay Telegrams, if not received before 3 o'clock p m., can not ordinarily be answered until the following day.

13 Interviews with examiners concerning applications and other matters pending before the office must be had in the examiners' rooms at such times, within office hours, as the respective examiner may designate, in the absence of the primary examiners, with the assistant in charge Interviews will not be permitted at any other time or place without the written authority of the Commissioner Interviews for the discussion of pending applications will not be had prior to the first official action thereon

INFORMATION TO CORRESPONDENTS.

14 The office can not respond to inquiries as to the novelty of an alleged invention in advance of the filing of an application for a patent, nor to inquiries propounded with a view to ascertaining whether any alleged improvements have been patented, and, if so, to whom; nor can it act as an expounder of the patent law, nor as counsellor for individuals, except as to questions arising within the office.

Of the propriety of making an application for a patent the inventor must judge for himself The office is open to him, and its records and models pertaining to all patents granted may be inspected either by himself or by any attorney or expert he may call to his aid, and its re-

171

ports are widely distributed (See Rule 196) Further than this the office can render him no assistance until his case comes regularly before it in the manner prescribed by law A copy of the rules, with this section marked, sent to the individual making an inquiry of the character referred to, is intended as a respectful answer by the office

Examiners' digests are not open to public inspection

15 Pending applications are preserved in secrecy No information will be given, without authority, respecting the filing by any particular person of an application for a patent or for the reissue of a patent, the pendency of any particular case before the office or the subject matter of any particular application, unless it shall be necessary to the proper conduct of business before the office, as provided by Rules 97, 103, and 108, *except that authorized officers of the Army and Navy will be allowed during the war to inspect cases which in the opinion of the Commissioner disclose inventions that might be of value in the prosecution of the war, after having filed a duly executed oath with the Commissioner that no contents of any application will be divulged except as it may become necessary in the prosecution of the war*

16. After a patent has issued, the model, specification, drawings and all documents relating to the case are subject to general inspection, and copies, except of the model, will be furnished at the rates specified in Rule 191

ATTORNEYS.

17 An applicant or an assignee of the entire interest may prosecute his own case, but he is advised, unless familiar with such matters, to employ a competent patent attorney, as the value of patents depends largely upon the skillful preparation of the specification and claims. The office can not aid in the selection of an attorney.

A register of attorneys will be kept in this office, on which will be entered the names of all persons entitled to

172

represent applicants before the Patent Office in the presentation and prosecution of applications for patent. The names of persons in the following classes will, upon their written request, be entered upon this register

(*a*) Any attorney at law who is in good standing in any court of record in the United States or any of the States or Territories thereof and who shall furnish a certificate of the clerk of such United States, State, or Territorial court, duly authenticated under the seal of the court, that he is an attorney in good standing

(*b*) Any person not an attorney at law who is a citizen or resident of the United States and who shall file proof to the satisfaction of the Commissioner that he is of good moral character and of good repute and possessed of the necessary legal and technical qualifications to enable him to render applicants for patents valuable service and is otherwise competent to advise and assist them in the presentation and prosecution of their applications before the Patent Office

(*c*) Any foreign patent attorney not a resident of the United States, who shall file proof to the satisfaction of the Commissioner that he is registered and in good standing before the patent office of the country of which he is a citizen or subject, and is possessed of the qualifications stated in paragraph (*b*).

(*d*) Any firm will be registered which shall show that the individual members composing the firm are each and all registered under the provisions of the preceding sections.

(*e*) The Commissioner may require proof of qualifications other than those specified in paragraph (*a*) and reserves the right to decline to recognize any attorney, agent, or other person applying for registration under this rule

(*f*) Any person or firm not registered and not entitled to be recognized under this rule as an attorney or agent to represent applicants generally may, upon a showing

173

of circumstances which render it necessary or justifiable, be recognized by the Commissioner to prosecute as attorney or agent certain specified application or applications, but this limited recognition shall not extend further than the application or applications named

(g) No person not registered or entitled to recognition as above provided will be permitted to prosecute applications before the Patent Office

(h) Every attorney registered to practice before the United States Patent Office shall submit to the Commissioner of Patents for approval copies of all proposed advertising matter, circulars, letters, cards, etc, intended to solicit patent business, and if it be not disapproved by him and the attorney so notified within 10 days after submission, it may be considered approved.

Any registered attorney sending out or using any such matter, a copy of which has not been submitted to the Commissioner of Patents in accordance with this rule, or which has been disapproved by the Commissioner of Patents, shall be subject to suspension or disbarment, so that the rule as amended will read as follows.

18 Before any attorney, original or associate, will be allowed to inspect papers or take action of any kind, his power of attorney must be filed But general powers given by a principal to an associate can not be considered In each application the written authorization must be filed A power of attorney purporting to have been given to a firm or copartnership will not be recognized, either in favor of the firm or of any of its members, unless all its members be named in such power of attorney

19 Substitution or association can be made by an attorney upon the written authorization of his principal but such authorization will not empower the second agent to appoint a third

20 Powers of attorney may be revoked at any stage in the proceedings of a case upon application to and approval by the Commissioner, and when so revoked the

office will communicate directly with the applicant, or another attorney appointed by him An attorney will be promptly notified by the docket clerk of the revocation of his power of attorney An assignment will not operate as a revocation of the power previously given, but the assignee of the entire interest may be represented by an attorney of his own selection

21. Parties or their attorneys will be permitted to examine their cases in the attorneys' room, but not in the rooms of the examiners Personal interviews with examiners will be permitted only as hereinbefore provided (See Rule 13)

22 (a) Applicants and attorneys will be required to conduct their business with the office with decorum and courtesy. Papers presented in violation of this requirement will be submitted to the Commissioner, and returned by his direct order.

(b) Complaints against examiners and other officers must be made in communications separate from other papers, and will be promptly investigated.

(c) For gross misconduct the Commissioner may refuse to recognize any person as a patent agent, either generally or in any particular case; but the reasons for the refusal will be duly recorded and be subject to the approval of the Secretary of the Interior

(d) The Secretary of the Interior may, after notice and opportunity for a hearing, suspend or exclude from further practice before the Patent Office any person, firm, corporation, or association shown to be incompetent, disreputable, or refusing to comply with the rules and regulations thereof, or with intent to defraud, in any manner deceiving, misleading, or threatening any claimant or prospective claimant, by word, circular, letter, or by advertisement, or guaranteeing the successful prosecution of any application for patent or the procurement of any patent, or by word, circular, letter, or advertise-

175

ment making any false promise or misleading representation (See 5, act approved July 4, 1884.)

23. Inasmuch as applications can not be examined out of their regular order, except in accordance with the provisions of Rule 63, and Members of Congress can neither examine nor act in patent cases without written powers of attorney applicants are advised not to impose upon Senators or Representatives labor which will consume their time without any advantageous results

APPLICANTS

24 A patent may be obtained by any person who has invented or discovered any new and useful art, machine, manufacture, or composition of matter, or any new and useful improvement thereof, not known or used by others in this country before his invention or discovery thereof, and not patented or described in any printed publication in this or any foreign country before his invention or discovery thereof, or more than two years prior to his application, and not patented in a country foreign to the United States on an application filed by him or his legal representatives or assigns more than twelve months before his application, and not in public use or on sale in the United States for more than two years prior to his application, unless the same is proved to have been abandoned upon payment of the fees required by law and other due proceedings had (For designs, see Rule 79)

25 In case of the death of the inventor, the application will be made by and the patent will issue to his executor or administrator In that case the oath required by Rule 46 will be made by the executor or administrator. In case of the death of the inventor during the time intervening between the filing of his application and the granting of a patent thereon, the letters patent will issue to the executor or administrator upon proper intervention by him The executor or administrator duly authorized under the law of any foreign country to admin-

176

ister upon the estate of the deceased inventor shall, in case the said inventor was not domiciled in the United States at the time of his death, have the right to apply for and obtain the patent The authority of such foreign executor or administrator shall be proved by certificate of a diplomatic or consular officer of the United States

In case an inventor become insane, the application may be made by and the patent issued to his legally appointed guardian, conservator, or representative, who will make the oath required by Rule 46

26. In case of an assignment of the whole interest in the invention, or of the whole interest in the patent to be granted, the patent will, upon request of the applicant embodied in the assignment, issue to the assignee   and if the assignee hold an undivided part interest, the patent will, upon like request, issue jointly to the inventor and the assignee, but the assignment in either case must first have been entered of record, and at a day not later than the date of the payment of the final fee (see Rule 188) , and if it be dated subsequently to the execution of the application, it must give the date of execution of the application, or the date of filing, or the serial number, so that there can be no mistake as to the particular invention intended The application and oath must be signed by the actual inventor, if alive, even if the patent is to issue to an assignee (see Rules 30, 40) , if the inventor be dead, the application may be made by the executor or administrator.

27 If it appear that the inventor, at the time of making his application, believed himself to be the first inventor or discoverer, a patent will not be refused on account of the invention or discovery, or any part thereof, having been known or used in any foreign country before his invention or discovery thereof, if it had not been before patented or described in any printed publication

28. Joint inventors are entitled to a joint patent;

neither of them can obtain a patent for an invention jointly invented by them Independent inventors of distinct and independent improvements in the same machine can not obtain a joint patent for their separate inventions The fact that one person furnishes the capital and another makes the invention does not entitle them to make an application as joint inventors, but in such case they may become joint patentees, upon the conditions prescribed in Rule 26.

29 No person otherwise entitled thereto shall be debarred from receiving a patent for his invention or discovery by reason of its having been first patented or caused to be patented by the inventor or his legal representatives or assigns in a foreign country, unless the application for said foreign patent was filed more than twelve months prior to the filing of the application in this country, in which case no patent shall be granted in this country

An application for patent filed in this country by any person who has previously regularly filed an application for a patent for the same invention or discovery in a foreign country which, by treaty, convention, or law, affords similar privileges to citizens of the United States shall have the same force and effect as the same application would have if filed in this country on the date on which the application for patent for the same invention or discovery was first filed in such foreign country, provided the application in this country is filed within twelve months from the earliest date on which any such foreign application was filed; but no patent shall be granted upon such application if the invention or discovery has been patented or described in a printed publication in this or any foreign country, or has been in public use or on sale in this country, for more than two years prior to the date of filing in this country

THE APPLICATION.

30 Applications for letters patent of the United States must be made to the Commissioner of Patents, and must be signed by the inventor, or by one of the persons indicated in Rule 25 (See Rules 26, 33, 40, 46.) A complete application comprises the first fee of $15, a petition, specification, and oath; and drawings, when required. (See Rule 49) The petition, specification, and oath must be in the English language All papers which are to become a part of the permanent records of the office must be legibly written or printed in permanent ink

31 An application for a patent will not be placed upon the files for examination until all its parts as required by Rule 30 shall have been received

Every application signed or sworn to in blank, or without actual inspection by the applicant of the petition and specification, and every application altered or partly filled up after being signed or sworn to, will be stricken from the files.

Completed applications are numbered in regular order, the present series having been commenced on the 1st of January, 1915

The applicant will be informed of the serial number of his application

The application must be completed and prepared for examination within one year, as indicated above, and in default thereof, or upon failure of the applicant to prosecute the same within one year after any action thereon (Rule 77), of which notice shall have been duly mailed to him or his agent, the application will be regarded as abandoned, unless it shall be shown to the satisfaction of the Commissioner that such delay was unavoidable (See Rules 171 and 172)

32 It is desirable that all parts of the complete application be deposited in the office at the same time, and that all the papers embraced in the application be attached together , otherwise a letter must accompany each

179

part, accurately and clearly connecting it with the other parts of the application (See Rule 10.)

33 The petition must be addressed to the Commissioner of Patents, and must state the name, residence, and post-office address of the petitioner requesting the grant of a patent, designate by title the invention sought to be patented, contain a reference to the specification for a full disclosure of such invention, and must be signed by the inventor or one of the persons indicated in Rule 25.

34 The specification is a written description of the invention or discovery and of the manner and process of making, constructing, compounding, and using the same, and is required to be in such full, clear, concise, and exact terms as to enable any person skilled in the art or science to which the invention or discovery appertains, or with which it is most nearly connected, to make, construct, compound, and use the same

35 The specification must set forth the precise invention for which a patent is solicited, and explain the principle thereof, and the best mode in which the applicant has contemplated applying that principle in such manner as to distinguish it from other inventions

36 In case of a mere improvement, the specification must particularly point out the parts to which the improvement relates, and must by explicit language distinguish between what is old and what is claimed as new, and the description and the drawings, as well as the claims, should be confined to the specific improvement and such parts as necessarily cooperate with it

37. The specification must conclude with a specific and distinct claim or claims of the part, improvement, or combination which the applicant regards as his invention or discovery

38 When there are drawings the description shall refer to the different views by figures and to the different parts by letters or numerals (preferably the latter)

39. The following order of arrangement should be observed in framing the specification:

(a) Preamble stating the name and residence of the applicant and the title of the invention.

(b) General statement of the object and nature of the invention

(c) Brief description of the several views of the drawings (if the invention admit of such illustration).

(d) Detailed description

(e) Claim or claims

(f) Signature of applicant

40 The specification must be signed by the inventor or one of the persons indicated in Rule 25 Full names must be given, and all names must be legibly written

41 Two or more independent inventions can not be claimed in one application, but where several distinct inventions are dependent upon each other and mutually contribute to produce a single result they may be claimed in one application

42 If several inventions, claimed in a single application, be of such a nature that a single patent may not be issued to cover them, the inventor will be required to limit the description, drawing, and claim of the pending application to whichever invention he may elect. The other inventions may be made the subjects of separate applications, which must conform to the rules applicable to original applications. If the independence of the inventions be clear, such limitation will be made before any action upon the merits; otherwise it may be made at any time before final action thereon, in the discretion of the examiner A requirement of division will not be repeated without the written approval of a law examiner. After a final requirement of division, the applicant may elect to prosecute one group of claims, retaining the re-

181

maining claims in the case with the privilege of appealing from the requirement of division after final action by the examiner on the group of claims prosecuted.

43 When an applicant files two or more applications relating to the same subject matter of invention, all showing but only one claiming the same thing the applications not claiming it must contain references to the application claiming it.

44 A reservation for a future application of subject matter disclosed but not claimed in a pending application will not be permitted in the pending application.

45 The specification and claims must be plainly written or printed on but one side of the paper All interlineations and erasures must be clearly referred to in marginal or foot notes on the same sheet of paper Legal-cap paper with the lines numbered is deemed preferable, and a wide margin must always be reserved upon the left-hand side of the page.

THE OATH

46 The applicant, if the inventor, must make oath or affirmation that he does verily believe himself to be the original and first inventor or discoverer of the art, machine, manufacture, composition or improvement for which he solicits a patent; that he does not know and does not believe that the same was ever known or used before his invention or discovery thereof, and shall state of what country he is a citizen and where he resides, and whether he is a sole or joint inventor of the invention claimed in his application. In every original application the applicant must distinctly state under oath that to the best of his knowledge and belief the invention has not been in public use or on sale in the United States for more than two years prior to his application, or patented or described in any printed publication in any country before his invention or more than two years prior to his application, or patented in any foreign country on an

application filed by himself or his legal representatives or assigns more than twelve months prior to his application in this country If any application for patent has been filed in any foreign country by the applicant in this country, or by his legal representatives or assigns, prior to his application in this country, he shall state the country or countries in which such application has been filed, giving the date of such application, and shall also state that no application has been filed in any other country or countries than those mentioned, and if no application for patent has been filed in any foreign country, he shall so state This oath must be subscribed to by the affiant.

If the application be made by an executor or administrator of a deceased person or the guardian, conservator, or representative of an insane person, the oath shall allege the relationship of the affiant to the inventor and, upon information and belief, the facts which the inventor is required by this rule to make oath to

The Commissioner may require an additional oath in cases where the applications have not been filed in the Patent Office within a reasonable time after the execution of the original oath

47 The oath or affirmation may be made before any person within the United States authorized by law to administer oaths, or, when the applicant resides in a foreign country, before any minister, chargé d'affaires, consul, or commercial agent holding commission under the Government of the United States, or before any notary public, judge, or magistrate having an official seal and authorized to administer oaths in the foreign country in which the applicant may be, whose authority shall be proved by a certificate of a diplomatic or consular officer of the United States, the oath being attested in all cases in this and other countries, by the proper official seal of the officer before whom the oath or affirmation is made, except that no oath or affirmation may be administered by any attorney appearing in the case. When the person

183

before whom the oath or affirmation is made in this country is not provided with a seal, his official character shall be established by competent evidence, as by a certificate from a clerk of a court of record or other proper officer having a seal.

When the oath is taken before an officer in a country foreign to the United States all the application papers must be attached together and a ribbon passed one or more times through all the sheets of the application, and the ends of said ribbon brought together under the seal before the latter is affixed and impressed, or each sheet must be impressed with the official seal of the officer before whom the oath was taken

48 When an applicant presents a claim for matter originally shown or described but not substantially embraced in the statement of invention or claim originally presented, he shall file a supplemental oath to the effect that the subject matter of the proposed amendment was part of his invention, was invented before he filed his original application, was not known or used before his invention was not patented or described in a printed publication in any country more than two years before his application, was not patented in any foreign country on an application filed by himself or his legal representatives or assigns more than twelve months prior to his application, was not in public use or on sale in this country for more than two years before the date of his application, and has not been abandoned Such supplemental oath must be attached to and properly identify the proposed amendment

In proper cases the oath here required may be made by an executor or administrator of a deceased person or a guardian, conservator, or representative of an insane person (See Rule 46)

184

49 The applicant for a patent is required by law to furnish a drawing of his invention whenever the nature of the case admits of it

50 The drawing may be signed by the inventor or one of the persons indicated in Rule 25, or the name of the applicant may be signed on the drawing by his attorney in fact   The drawing must show every feature of the invention covered by the claims, and the figures should be consecutively numbered, if possible   When the invention consists of an improvement of an old machine the drawing must exhibit, in one or more views, the invention itself, disconnected from the old structure, and also in another view, so much only of the old structure as will suffice to show the connection of the invention therewith

51. Two editions of patent drawings are printed and published—one for office use, certified copies, etc., of the size and character of those attached to patents, the work being about 6 by 9½ inches; and one reduction of a selected portion of each drawing for the Official Gazette.

52 This work is done by the photolithographic process, and therefore the character of each original drawing must be brought as nearly as possible to a uniform standard of excellence, suited to the requirements of the process, to give the best results in the interests of inventors, of the office, and of the public   The following rules will therefore be rigidly enforced, and any departure from them will be certain to cause delay in the examination of an application for letters patent

(*a*) Drawings must be made upon pure white paper of a thickness corresponding to two-sheet or three-sheet Bristol board   The surface of the paper must be calendered and smooth   India ink alone must be used, to secure perfectly black and solid lines.

(*b*) The size of a sheet on which a drawing is made must be exactly 10 by 15 inches   One inch from its edges a single marginal line is to be drawn, leaving the "sight" precisely 8 by 13 inches Within this margin all work and signatures must be included One of the shorter sides of the sheet is regarded as its top, and measuring downwardly from the marginal line a space of not less than 1¼ inches is to be left blank for the heading of title, name, number and date

(c) All drawings must be made with the pen only Every line and letter (signatures included) must be absolutely black This direction applies to all lines, however fine, to shading and to lines representing cut surfaces in sectional views. All lines must be clean, sharp, and solid, and they must not be too fine or crowded Surface shading when used, should be open. Sectional shading should be made by oblique parallel lines, which may be about one-twentieth of an inch apart Solid black should not be used for sectional or surface shading Free-hand work should be avoided wherever it is possible to do so

(d) Drawings should be made with the fewest lines possible consistent with clearness By the observance of this rule the effectiveness of the work after reduction will be much increased Shading (except on sectional views) should be used only on convex and concave surfaces, where it should be used sparingly and may even there be dispensed with if the drawing be otherwise well executed The plane upon which a sectional view is taken should be indicated on the general view by a broken or dotted line, which should be designated by numerals corresponding to the number of the sectional view. Heavy lines on the shade sides of objects should be used, except where they tend to thicken the work and obscure letters of reference The light is always supposed to come from the upper left-hand corner at an angle of 45 degrees

(e) The scale to which a drawing is made ought to be large enough to show the mechanism without crowding, and two or more sheets should be used if one does not

186

give sufficient room to accomplish this end, but the number of sheets must never be more than is absolutely necessary

(*f*) The different views should be consecutively numbered Letters and figures of reference must be carefully formed They should, if possible, measure at least one-eighth of an inch in height, so that they may bear reduction to one twenty-fourth of an inch, and they may be much larger when there is sufficient room They must be so placed in the close and complex parts of drawings as not to interfere with a thorough comprehension of the same, and therefore, should rarely cross or mingle with the lines When necessarily grouped around a certain part they should be placed at a little distance, where there is available space, and connected by lines with the parts to which they refer They should not be placed upon shaded surfaces, but when it is difficult to avoid this, a blank space must be left in the shading where the letter occurs, so that it shall appear perfectly distinct and separate from the work If the same part of an invention appear in more than one view of the drawing it must always be represented by the same character, and the same character must never be used to designate different parts

(*g*) The signature of the applicant should be placed at the lower right-hand corner of each sheet, and the signatures of the witnesses, if any, at the lower left-hand corner, all within the marginal line, but in no instance should they trespass upon the drawings (See specimen drawing, appendix) The title should be written with pencil on the back of the sheet. The permanent names and title constituting the heading will be applied subsequently by the office in uniform style

(*h*) All views on the same sheet must stand in the same direction and must if possible stand so that they can be read with the sheet held in an upright position If views longer than the width of the sheet are necessary

187

for the proper illustration of the invention the sheet may be turned on its side. The space for heading must then be reserved at the right and the signatures placed at the left, occupying the same space and position as in the upright views and being horizontal when the sheet is held in an upright position. One figure must not be placed upon another or within the outline of another.

(*i*) As a rule, one view only of each invention can be shown in the Gazette illustrations. The selection of that portion of a drawing best calculated to explain the nature of the specific improvement would be facilitated and the final result improved by the judicious execution of a figure with express reference to the Gazette, but which must at the same time serve as one of the figures referred to in the specification. For this purpose the figure may be a plan, elevation, section, or perspective view, according to the judgment of the draftsman. All its parts should be especially open and distinct, with very little or no shading, and it must illustrate the invention claimed only, to the exclusion of all other details. (See specimen drawing.) When well executed, it will be used without curtailment or change, but any excessive fineness, or crowding, or unnecessary elaborateness of detail will necessitate its exclusion from the Gazette.

(*j*) Drawings transmitted to the office should be sent flat, protected by a sheet of heavy binder's board, or should be rolled for transmission in a suitable mailing tube, but should never be folded.

(*h*) An agent's or attorney's stamp, or advertisement, or written address will not be permitted upon the face of a drawing, within or without the marginal line.

53. All reissue applications must be accompanied by new drawings, of the character required in original applications, and the inventor's name must appear upon the same in all cases; and such drawings shall be made upon the same scale as the original drawing, or upon a

188

larger scale, unless a reduction of scale shall be authorized by the Commissioner.

54 The foregoing rules relating to drawings will be rigidly enforced. A drawing not executed in conformity thereto may be admitted for purposes of examination if it sufficiently illustrate the invention, but in such case the drawing must be corrected or a new one furnished before the application will be allowed. The necessary corrections will be made by the office, upon applicant's request and at his expense. (See Rule 72.)

55 Applicants are advised to employ competent draftsmen to make their drawings

The office will furnish the drawings at cost, as promptly as its draftsmen can make them, for applicants who can not otherwise conveniently procure them.

56 A model will be required or admitted as a part of the application only when on examination of the case in its regular order the primary examiner shall find it to be necessary or useful. In such case, if a model has not been furnished, the examiner shall notify the applicant of such requirement, which will constitute an official action in the case. When a model has been received in compliance with the official requirement, the date of its filing shall be entered on the file wrapper. Models not required nor admitted will be returned to the applicants. When a model is required, the examination may be suspended until it shall have been filed

57. The model must clearly exhibit every feature of the machine which forms the subject of a claim of invention, but should not include other matter than that covered by the actual invention or improvement, unless it be necessary to the exhibition of the invention in a working model

58 The model must be neatly and substantially made of durable material, metal being deemed preferable, but

189

when the material forms an essential feature of the invention, the model should be constructed of that material.

59 A working model may be required if necessary to enable the office fully and readily to understand the precise operation of the machine.

60 In all applications which have become abandoned, the model, unless it be deemed necessary that it be preserved in the office, may be returned to the applicant upon demand and at his expense, and the model in any pending case of less than one year's standing may be returned to the applicant upon the filing of a formal abandonment of the application, signed by the applicant in person and any assignee   (See Rule 171)

Models belonging to patented cases shall not be taken from the office except in the custody of some sworn employee of the office specially authorized by the Commissioner.

61 Models filed as exhibits in contested cases may be returned to the parties at their expense   If not claimed within a reasonable time, they may be disposed of at the discretion of the Commissioner.

SPECIMENS

62 When the invention or discovery is a composition of matter, the applicant if required by the Commissioner, shall furnish specimens of the composition, and of its ingredients, sufficient in quantity for the purpose of experiment   In all cases where the article is not perishable, a specimen of the composition claimed, put up in proper form to be preserved by the office, must be furnished   (Rules 56, 60, and 61 apply to specimens also)

THE EXAMINATION.

63 Applications filed in the Patent Office are classified according to the various arts, and are taken up for examination in regular order of filing, those in the same

class of invention being examined and disposed of, so far as practicable, in the order in which the respective applications have been completed

Applications which have been put into condition for further action by the examiner shall be entitled to precedence over new applications in the same class of invention

The following cases have preference over all other cases at every period of their examination in the order enumerated

(*a*) Applications wherein the inventions are deemed of peculiar importance to some branch of the public service, and when for that reason the head of some department of the Government requests immediate action and the Commissioner so orders, but in this case it shall be the duty of the head of that department to be represented before the Commissioner in order to prevent the improper issue of a patent

(*b*) Applications for reissues

(*c*) Cases remanded by an appellate tribunal for further action, and statements of grounds of decisions provided for in Rules 135 and 142

(*d*) Applications which appear to interfere with other applications previously considered and found to be allowable, or which it is demanded shall be placed in interference with an unexpired patent or patents

(*e*) Applications which have been renewed or revived, but the subject matter not changed

(*f*) Applications filed more than twelve months after the filing of an application for the same invention in a foreign country

Applications will not be advanced for examination excepting upon order of the Commissioner either to expedite the business of the office or upon a verified showing that delay will probably cause the applicant serious and irreparable injury

64 Where the specification and claims are such that

the invention may be readily understood, the examination of a complete application and the action thereon will be directed throughout to the merits; but in each letter the examiner shall state or refer to all his objections

Only in applications found by the examiner to present patentable subject matter and in applications on which appeal is taken to the examiners in chief will requirements in matters of form be insisted on (See Rules 95 and 134)

REJECTIONS AND REFERENCES.

65 Whenever, on examination, any claim of an application is rejected for any reason whatever, the applicant will be notified thereof   The reasons for the rejection will be fully and precisely stated, and such information and references will be given as may be useful in aiding the applicant to judge of the propriety of prosecuting his application or of altering his specification, and if, after receiving this notice he shall persist in his claim, with or without altering his specification, the application will be reexamined. If upon reexamination the claim shall be again rejected, the reasons therefor will be fully and precisely stated

66. Upon taking up an application for action on the merits the examiner shall make a thorough investigation of the prior art with respect to the invention sought to be protected in the application   Upon the rejection of an application for want of novelty, the examiner must cite the best references at his command   When the reference shows or describes inventions other than that claimed by the applicant, the particular part relied on must be designated as nearly as practicable The pertinence of the reference, if not obvious, must be clearly explained and the anticipated claim specified

If domestic patents be cited, then dates and numbers the names of the patentees, and the classes of invention

192

must be stated. If foreign patents be cited, their dates and numbers, the names of the patentees, and the classes of inventions must be stated, and such other data must be furnished as may be necessary to enable the applicant to identify the patents cited. In citing foreign patents the number of sheets of drawing involving the parts relied upon for anticipation must be specified, and in case part only of the patent be involved, the particular sheets of the drawing containing the parts relied upon must be identified by number, or by stating the numbers of the figures involved. If printed publications be cited, the title, date, page or plate, author, and place of publication, or place where a copy can be found, shall be given. When reference is made to facts within the personal knowledge of an employee of the office, the data shall be as specific as possible, and the reference must be supported, when called for, by the affidavit of such employee (Rule 76), such affidavit shall be subject to contradiction, explanation, or corroboration by the affidavits of the applicant and other persons. If the patent, printed matter, plates, or drawings so referred to are in the possession of the office, copies will be furnished at the rate specified in Rule 191, upon the order of the applicant.

67. Whenever, in the treatment of an *ex parte* application, an adverse decision is made upon any preliminary or intermediate question, without the rejection of any claim, notice thereof, together with the reasons therefor, will be given to the applicant, in order that he may judge of the propriety of the action. If, after receiving this notice, he traverse the propriety of the action, the matter will be reconsidered.

AMENDMENTS AND ACTIONS BY APPLICANTS.

68. The applicant has a right to amend before or after the first rejection or action, and he may amend as often as the examiner presents new references or reasons for rejection. In so amending the applicant must clearly

point out all the patentable novelty which he thinks the case presents in view of the state of the art disclosed by the references cited or the objections made. He must also show how the amendments avoid such references or objections.

After such action upon an application as will entitle the applicant to an appeal to the examiners in chief (Rule 134), or after appeal has been taken, amendments canceling claims or presenting those rejected in better form for consideration on appeal may be admitted, but the admission of such an amendment or its refusal, and any proceedings relative thereto, shall not operate to relieve the application from its condition as subject to appeal, or to save it from abandonment under Rule 171. If amendments touching the merits of the application be presented after the case is in condition for appeal, or after appeal has been taken, they may be admitted upon a showing, duly verified, of good and sufficient reasons why they were not earlier presented From the refusal of the primary examiner to admit an amendment a petition will lie to the Commissioner under Rule 142. No amendment can be made in appealed cases between the filing of the examiner's statement of the grounds of his decision (Rule 135) and the decision of the appellate tribunal After decision on appeal amendments can only be made as provided in Rule 140, or to carry into effect a recommendation under Rule 139

69 In order to be entitled to the reexamination or reconsideration provided for in Rules 65 and 67 the applicant must make request therefor in writing, and he must distinctly and specifically point out the supposed errors in the examiner's action. the applicant must respond to every ground of objection and rejection of the prior office action except as provided in Rule 64, and the applicant's action must appear throughout to be a *bona fide* attempt to advance the case to final action The mere allegation that the examiner has erred will not be received

as a proper reason for such reexamination or reconsideration.

70 In original applications all amendments of the drawings or specifications, and all additions thereto, must conform to at least one of them as it was at the time of the filing of the application Matter not found in either, involving a departure from the original invention, can not be added to the application even though supported by a supplemental oath, and can be shown or claimed only in a separate application

71. The specification and drawing must be amended and revised when required, to correct inaccuracies of description or unnecessary prolixity, and to secure correspondence between the claim, the specification, and the drawing But no change in the drawing may be made except by written permission of the office and after a photographic copy of the drawing as originally presented has been filed

72 After the completion of the application the office will not return the specification for any purpose whatever If applicants have not preserved copies of the papers which they wish to amend, the office will furnish them on the usual terms

The drawing may be withdrawn only for such corrections as can not be made by the office, but a drawing can not be withdrawn unless a photographic copy has been filed and accepted by the examiner as a part of the application Permissible changes in the construction shown in any drawing may be made only by the office and after an approved photographic copy has been filed Substitute drawings will not be admitted in any case unless required by the office.

73 In every amendment the exact word or words to be stricken out or inserted in the application must be specified and the precise point indicated where the erasure or insertion is to be made. All such amendments must be on sheets of paper separate from the papers previously

195

filed and written on but one side of the paper. Erasures, additions. insertions, or mutilations of the papers and records must not be made by the applicant

Amendments and papers requiring the signature of the applicant must also. in case of assignment of an undivided part of the invention, be signed by the assignee. (Rules 6, 107.)

74. When an amendatory clause is amended it must be wholly rewritten. so that no interlineation or erasure shall appear in the clause as finally amended, when the application is passed to issue. If the number or nature of the amendments shall render it otherwise difficult to consider the case. or to arrange the papers for printing or copying the examiner may require the entire specification to be rewritten.

75 When an original or reissue application is rejected on reference to an expired or unexpired domestic patent which substantially shows or describes but does not claim the rejected invention. or on reference to a foreign patent or to a printed publication, and the applicant shall make oath to facts showing a completion of the invention in this country before the filing of the application on which the domestic patent issued or before the date of the foreign patent or before the date of the printed publication, and shall also make oath that he does not know and does not believe that the invention has been in public use or on sale in this country, or patented or described in a printed publication in this or any foreign country for more than two years prior to his application, and that he has never abandoned the invention, then the patent or publication cited shall not bar the grant of a patent to the applicant, unless the date of such patent or printed publication be more than two years prior to the date on which application was filed in this country

76 When an application is rejected on reference to an expired or unexpired domestic patent which shows or describes but does not claim the invention, or on reference

196

to a foreign patent, or to a printed publication, or to facts within the personal knowledge of an employee of the office, set forth in an affidavit (when requested) of such employee (Rule 66), or when rejected on the ground of public use or sale, or upon a mode or capability of operation attributed to a reference or because the alleged invention is held to be inoperative or frivolous or injurious to public health or morals, affidavits or depositions supporting or traversing these references or objections may be received, but affidavits will not be received in other cases without special permission of the Commissioner (See Rule 138.)

77 If an applicant neglect to prosecute his application for one year after the date when the last official notice of any action by the office was mailed to him, the application will be held to be abandoned, as set forth in Rule 171.

Suspensions will only be granted for good and sufficient cause, and for a reasonable time specified. Only one suspension may be granted by the primary examiner, any further suspension must be approved by the Commissioner

Whenever action upon an application is suspended upon request of an applicant, and whenever an applicant has been called upon to put his application in condition for interference, the period of one year running against the application shall be considered as beginning at the date of the last official action preceding such actions

Whenever, during a time when the United States is at war, publication of an invention by the granting of a patent might, in the opinion of the Commissioner, be detrimental to the public safety or defense or might assist the enemy or endanger the successful prosecution of the war, he may suspend action on the application therefor

78 Amendments after the notice of allowance of an application will not be permitted as a matter of right, but may be made, if the specification has not been print-

197

ed, on the recommendation of the primary examiner, approved by the Commissioner, without withdrawing the case from issue (See Rule 165)

DESIGNS.

79. A design patent may be obtained by any person who has invented any new, original, and ornamental design for an article of manufacture, not known or used by others in this country before his invention thereof, and not patented or described in any printed publication in this or any foreign country before his invention thereof, or more than two years prior to his application, and not caused to be patented by him in a foreign country on an application filed more than four months before his application in this country, and not in public use or sale in this country for more than two years prior to his application, unless the same is proved to have been abandoned, upon payment of the fees required by law and other due proceedings had, the same as in cases of inventions or discoveries

80 Patents for designs are granted for the term of three and one-half years, or for seven years, or for fourteen years, as the applicant may, in his application, elect

Where the applicant requests that the patent issue for one of the shorter terms, he may, at any time before the allowance of the application, upon the payment of the additional fee amend his application by requesting that the patent be issued for a longer term

81 The proceedings in applications for patents for designs are substantially the same as in applications for other patents Since a design patent gives to the patentee the exclusive right to make, use, and vend articles having the appearance of that disclosed, and since the appearance can be disclosed only by a picture of the article, the claim should be in the broadest form for the article as shown

82 The following order of arrangement should be observed in framing design specifications

(*a*) Preamble, stating name and residence of the applicant, title of the design, and the name of the article for which the design has been invented

(*b*) Description of the figure or figures of the drawing

(*c*) Claim

(*d*) Signature of applicant.

83 When the design can be sufficiently represented by drawings a model will not be required

84 The design must be represented by a drawing made to conform to the rules laid down for drawings of mechanical inventions

(For forms to be used in applications for design patents, see appendix)

REISSUES

85 A reissue is granted when the original patent is inoperative or invalid by reason of a defective or insufficient specification or by reason of the patentee claiming as his invention or discovery more than he had a right to claim as new, provided the error has arisen through inadvertence, accident, or mistake, and without any fraudulent or deceptive intention

Reissue applications must be made and the specifications sworn to by the inventors if they be living

86 The petition for a reissue must be accompanied by an order for a certified copy of the abstract of title, to be placed in the file, giving the names of all assignees owning any undivided interest in the patent. In case the application be made by the inventor it must be accompanied by the written assent of such assignees

A reissue will be granted to the original patentee, his legal representatives or assigns, as the interest may appear

87. Applicants for reissue, in addition to the require-

199

ments of the first sentence of Rule 46, must also file with their petitions a statement on oath as follows·

(*a*) That applicant verily believes the original patent to be inoperative or invalid and the reason why

(*b*) When it is claimed that such patent is so inoperative or invalid "by reason of a defective or insufficient specification," particularly specifying such defects or insufficiencies.

(*c*) When it is claimed that such patent is inoperative or invalid "by reason of the patentee claiming as his own invention or discovery more than he had a right to claim as new," distinctly specifying the part or parts so alleged to have been improperly claimed as new.

(*d*) Particularly specifying the errors which it is claimed constitute the inadvertence, accident, or mistake relied upon, and how they arose or occurred.

(*e*) That said errors arose "without any fraudulent or deceptive intention" on the part of the applicant.

88 New matter shall not be allowed to be introduced into the reissue specification, nor in the case of a machine shall the model or drawings be amended except each by the other.

89 The Commissioner may, in his discretion, cause several patents to be issued for distinct and separate parts of the thing patented, upon demand of the applicant, and upon payment of the required fee for each division of such reissued letters patent Each division of a reissue constitutes the subject of a separate specification descriptive of the part or parts of the invention claimed in such division, and the drawing may represent only such part or parts, subject to the provisions of Rule 50 Unless otherwise ordered by the Commissioner, all the divisions of a reissue will issue simultaneously; if there be any controversy as to one division, the others will be withheld from issue until the controversy is ended, unless the Commissioner shall otherwise order.

90 An original claim, if reproduced in the reissue

specification, is subject to reexamination, and the entire application will be revised and restricted in the same manner as original applications, excepting that division will not be required

91. The application for a reissue must be accompanied by the original patent and an offer to surrender the same, or, if the original be lost, by an affidavit to that effect, and a certified copy of the patent If a reissue be refused, the original patent will be returned to applicant upon his request

92 Matter shown and described in an unexpired patent which is an indivisible part of the invention claimed therein, but which was not claimed by reason of a defect or insufficiency in the specification, arising from inadvertence, accident, or mistake, and without fraud or deceptive intent, can not be subsequently claimed by the patentee in a separate patent, but only in a reissue of the original patent

INTERFERENCES.

93. An interference is a proceeding instituted for the purpose of determining the question of priority of invention between two or more parties claiming substantially the same patentable invention. *In order to ascertain whether any question of priority arises the Commissioner may call upon any junior applicant to state in writing the date when he conceived the invention under consideration All statements filed in compliance with this rule will be returned to the parties filing them In case the applicant makes no reply within the time specified, not less than ten days, the Commissioner will proceed upon the assumption that the said date is the date of the oath attached to the application* The fact that one of the parties has already obtained a patent will not prevent an interference, for, although the Commissioner has no power to cancel a patent, he may grant another

201

patent for the same invention to a person who proves to be the prior inventor

94 Interferences will be declared between applications by different parties for patent or for reissue when such applications contain claims for substantially the same invention which are allowable in the application of each party, and interferences will also be declared between applications for patent, or for reissue, and unexpired original or reissued patents, of different parties, when such applications and patents contain claims for substantially the same invention which are allowable in all of the applications involved· *Provided*, That where the filing date of any applicant is subsequent to the filing date of any patentee, the applicant shall file an affidavit that he made the invention before the filing date of the patentee

Parties owning applications or patents which contain conflicting claims will be required before an interference is declared to show cause why these claims shall not be eliminated from all but one of the applications or patents of common ownership

95 Before the declaration of interference all preliminary questions must be settled by the primary examiner, and the issue must be clearly defined, the invention which is to form the subject of the controversy must have been patented to one of the parties or have been decided to be patentable, and the claims of the respective parties must be put in such condition that they will not require alteration after the interference shall have been finally decided, unless the evidence adduced upon the trial shall necessitate or justify such change

In case the subject matter in controversy has been patented to one of the parties but is deemed by the examiner not to be patentable, he shall call the case to the attention of the Commissioner, who may direct the declaration of the interference

96 Whenever the claims of two or more applications differ in phraseology, but relate to substantially the

202

same patentable subject matter, the examiner, when one of the applications is ready for allowance, shall suggest to the parties such claims as are necessary to cover the common invention in substantially the same language The examiner shall send copies of the letter suggesting claims to the applicant and to the assignees, as well as to the attorney of record in each case. The parties to whom the claims are suggested will be required to make those claims and put the applications in condition for allowance within a specified time in order that an inter- ence may be declared Upon the failure of any appli- cant to make the claim suggested within the time speci- fied, such failure or refusal shall be taken without fur- ther action as a disclaimer of the invention covered by the claim, and the issue of the patent to the applicant whose application is in condition for allowance will not be delayed unless the time for making the claim and put- ting the application in condition for allowance be ex- tended upon a proper showing If a party make the claim without putting his application in condition for allowance, the declaration of the interference will not be delayed, but after judgment of priority the application of that party will be held for revision and restriction, subject to interference with other applications

Whenever it shall be found that two or more parties whose interests are in conflict are represented by the same attorney, the examiner shall notify each of said principal parties and also the attorney of this fact.

97 When an interference is found to exist and the applications are prepared therefor, the primary exam- iner shall forward to the examiner of interferences the files and drawings, notices of interference for all the parties (as specified in Rule 103) disclosing the name and residence of each party and those of his attorney, and of any assignee, and, if any party be a patentee, the date and number of the patent, the ordinals of the con- flicting claims and the title of the invention claimed; and

203

the issue, which shall be clearly and concisely defined in so many counts or branches as may be necessary in order to include all interfering claims. Where the issue is stated in more than one count the respective claims involved in each count shall be specified The primary examiner shall also forward to the examiner of interferences for his use a statement disclosing the applications involved in interference fully identified, arranged in the inverse chronological order of the filing of the completed applications, and also disclosing the issue or issues and the ordinals of the conflicting claims. the name and residence of any assignee, and the names and residences of all attorneys, both principal and associate.

98 Upon receipt of the notices of interference, the examiner of interferences shall make an examination thereof, in order to ascertain whether the issues between the parties have been clearly defined, and whether they are otherwise correct If he be of the opinion that the notices are ambiguous or are defective in any material point, he shall transmit his objections to the primary examiner, who shall promptly notify the examiner of interferences of his decision to amend or not to amend them

99 In case of a material disagreement between the examiner of interferences and the primary examiner, the points of difference shall be referred to the Commissioner for decision

100 The primary examiner will retain jurisdiction of the case until the declaration of interference is made

101 Upon the institution and declaration of the interference, as provided in Rule 102, the examiner of interferences will take jurisdiction of the same, which will then become a contested case; but the law examiner will determine the motions mentioned in Rule 122, as therein provided

102 When the notices of interference are in proper form, the examiner of interferences shall add thereto a

designation of the time within which the preliminary statements required by Rule 110 must be filed, and shall, *pro forma*, institute and declare the interference by forwarding the notices to the several parties to the proceeding

103 The notices of interference shall be forwarded by the examiner of interferences to all the parties, in care of their attorneys, if they have attorneys, and, if the application or patent in interference has been assigned, to the assignee When one of the parties has received a patent, a notice shall be sent to the patentee and to his attorney of record

When the notices sent in the interest of a patent are returned to the office undelivered, or when one of the parties resides abroad and his agent in the United States is unknown, additional notice may be given by publication in the Official Gazette for such period of time as the Commissioner may direct

104 If either party require a postponement of the time for filing his preliminary statement, he shall present his motion, duly served on the other parties, with his reasons therefor, supported by affidavit, and such motion should be made, if possible, prior to the day previously set But the examiner of interferences may, in his discretion, extend the time on *ex parte* request or upon his own motion

105. When an application is involved in an interference in which a part only of the invention is included in the issue, the applicant may file certified copies of the part or parts of the specification, claims, and drawings which cover the interfering matter, and such copies may be used in the proceeding in place of the original application

106 When a part only of an application is involved in an interference, the applicant may withdraw from his application the subject matter adjudged not to interfere, and file a new application therefor, or he may file a divi-

205

sional application for the subject matter involved, if the invention can be legitimately divided. *Provided,* That no claim shall be made in the application not involved in the interference broad enough to include matter claimed in the application involved therein.

107 An applicant involved in an interference may, with the written consent of the assignee, when there has been an assignment, before the date fixed for the filing of his preliminary statement (see Rule 110), in order to avoid the continuance of the interference, disclaim under his own signature the invention of the particular matter in issue, and upon such disclaimer judgment shall be rendered against him

108 When applications are declared to be in interference, the interfering parties will be permitted to see or obtain copies of each other's file wrappers, and so much of their contents as relates to the interference, after the preliminary statements referred to in Rule 110 have been received and approved, but information of an application will not be furnished by the office to an opposing party, except as provided in Rules 97 and 103, until after the approval of such statements.

109. An applicant involved in an interference may, at any time within thirty days after the preliminary statements (referred to in Rule 110) of the parties have been received and approved, on motion duly made, as provided by Rule 153, file an amendment to his application containing any claims which in his opinion should be made the basis of interference between himself and any of the other parties. Such motion must be accompanied by the proposed amendment, and when in proper form will be set for hearing before the law examiner Where a party opposes the admission of such an amendment in view of prior patents or publications, full notice of such patents or publications must be given at least five days prior to the date of hearing. On the admission of such amendment, and the adoption of the claims by the other

206

parties within a time specified by the law examiner, the primary examiner shall redeclare the interference, or shall declare such other interferences as may be necessary to include the said claims New preliminary statements will be received as to the added claims, but motions for dissolution with regard thereto will not be considered where the questions raised could have been disposed of in connection with the admission of the•claims. Amendments to the specification will not be received during the pendency of the interference, without the consent of the Commissioner, except as provided herein, and in Rule 106.

Any party to an interference may bring a motion to put in interference any claims already in his application or patent, which in his opinion should be made the basis of interference between himself and any of the other parties Such motions are subject to the same conditions, and the procedure in connection therewith is the same, so far as applicable, as hereinabove set forth for motions to amend.

110 Each party to the interference will be required to file a concise preliminary statement, under oath, on or before a date to be fixed by the office, showing the following facts

(*a*) The date of original conception of the invention set forth in the declaration of interference.

(*b*) The date upon which the first drawing of the invention and the date upon which the first written description of the invention were made.

(*c*) The date upon which the invention was first disclosed to others

(*d*) The date of the reduction to practice of the invention

(*e*) A statement showing the extent of use of the invention.

(*f*) The applicant shall state the date and number of any application for the same invention filed within twelve

207

months before the filing date in the United States in any foreign country adhering to the International Convention for the Protection of Industrial Property or having similar treaty relations with the United States

If a drawing has not been made, or if a written description of the invention has not been made or if the invention has not been reduced to practice or disclosed to others or used to any extent, the statement must specifically disclose these facts

When the invention was made abroad the statement should set forth.

(*a*) That the applicant made the invention set forth in the declaration of interference

(*b*) Whether or not the invention was ever patented, if so, when and where, giving the date and number of each patent, the date of publication, and the date of sealing thereof

(*c*) Whether or not the invention was ever described in a printed publication, if so, when and where, giving the title, place, and date of such publication

(*d*) When the invention was introduced into this country, giving the circumstances with the dates connected therewith which are relied upon to establish the fact

The preliminary statements should be carefully prepared, as the parties will be strictly held in their proofs to the dates set up therein

If a party prove any date earlier than alleged in his preliminary statement, such proof will be held to establish the date alleged and none other

The statement must be sealed up before filing (to be opened only by the examiner of interferences, see Rule 111), and the name of the party filing it, the title of the case, and the subject of the invention indicated on the envelop The envelop should contain nothing but this statement

(For forms, see 36 and 37, appendix)

208

111 The preliminary statements shall not be opened to the inspection of the opposing parties until each one shall have been filed, or the time for such filing, with any extension thereof, shall have expired, and not then unless they have been examined by the proper officer and found to be satisfactory.

Any party in default in filing his preliminary statement shall not have access to the preliminary statement or statements of his opponent or opponents until he has either filed his statement or waived his right thereto, and agreed to stand upon his record date

A party who alleges no date in his preliminary statement earlier than the filing date of the application or applications of the other party or parties shall not have access to the preliminary statement of said party or parties

112 If, on examination, a statement is found to be defective in any particular, the party shall be notified of the defect and wherein it consists, and a time assigned within which he must cure the same by an amended statement, but in no case will the original or amended statement be returned to the party after it has been filed Unopened statements will be removed from interference files and preserved by the office, and in no case will such statements be open to the inspection of the opposing party without authority from the Commissioner If a party shall refuse to file an amended statement he may be restricted to his record date in the further proceedings in the interference

113 In case of material error arising through inadvertence or mistake, the statement may be corrected on motion (see Rule 153), upon a satisfactory showing that the correction is essential to the ends of justice The motion to correct the statement must be made, if possible, before the taking of any testimony, and as soon as practicable after the discovery of the error.

114 If the junior party to an interference, or if any

party thereto other than the senior party, fail to file a statement, or if his statement fail to overcome the *prima facie* case made by the respective dates of application, such party shall be notified by the examiner of interferences that judgment upon the record will be rendered against him at the expiration of thirty days, unless cause be shown why such action should not be taken Within this period any of the motions permitted by the rules may be brought Motions brought after judgment on the record has been rendered will not be entertained unless sufficient reasons appear for the delay

115 If a party to an interference fail to file a statement, testimony will not be received subsequently from him to prove that he made the invention at a date prior to his application.

116. The parties to an interference will be presumed to have made the invention in the chronological order in which they filed their completed applications for patents clearly disclosing the invention, and the burden of proof will rest upon the party who shall seek to establish a different state of facts

117. The preliminary statement can in no case be used as evidence in behalf of the party making it

118 Times will be assigned in which the junior applicant shall complete his testimony in chief, and in which the other party shall complete the testimony on his side, and a further time in which the junior applicant may take rebutting testimony; but he shall take no other testimony If there be more than two parties to the interference, the times for taking testimony will be so arranged that each shall have an opportunity to prove his case against prior applicants and to rebut their evidence, and also to meet the evidence of junior applicants.

119 Upon the filing of an affidavit by any senior party to an interference that the time for taking testimony on behalf of any junior party has expired and that no testimony has been taken by him, an order shall be entered

210

that the junior party show cause within a time set therein, not less than ten days, why judgment should not be rendered against him, and in the absence of a showing of good and sufficient cause judgment shall be so rendered If any showing be made in response to the order, it must be served upon the opposing party and noticed for hearing by the party filing it.

120 If either party desire to have the hearing continued, he shall make application for such postponement by motion (see Rule 153), and shall show sufficient reason therefor by affidavit.

121 If either party desire an extension of the time assigned to him for taking testimony, he shall make application therefor, as provided in Rule 154 (d)

122 Motions to dissolve an interference (1) alleging that there has been such informality in declaring the same as will preclude the proper determination of the question of priority of invention, or (2) denying the patentability of an applicant's claim, or (3) denying his right to make the claim, should contain a full statement of the grounds relied upon and should, if possible, be made not later than the thirtieth day after the statements of the parties have been received and approved Such motions and all motions of a similar character, if in the opinion of the Commissioner they be in proper form, will be heard and determined by the law examiner, due notice of the day of hearing being given by the office to all parties If in the opinion of the Commissioner the motion be not in proper form, or if it be not brought within the time specified and no satisfactory reason be given for the delay, it will not be considered and the parties will be so notified.

When the motion has been decided by the law examiner the files and papers, with his decision, will be sent at once to the docket clerk

Motions to shift the burden of proof should be made before, and will be determined by, the examiner of in-

211

terferences No appeal from the decision on such motions will be entertained, but the matter may be reviewed on appeal from the final decision upon the question of priority of invention

123 Setting a motion brought under the provisions of Rule 109 or of Rule 122 for hearing by the law examiner will act as a stay of proceedings pending the determination of the motion To effect a stay of proceedings in other cases, motion should be made before the tribunal having jurisdiction of the interference, who will, sufficient grounds appearing therefor, order a suspension of the interference pending the determination of such motion

124 Where, on motion for dissolution, the law examiner renders an adverse decision upon the merits of a party's case, as when he holds that the issue is not patentable or that a party has no right to make a claim, he shall fix a limit of appeal not less than twenty days from the date of his decision Appeal lies to the examiners in chief in the first instance and will be heard *inter partes* If the appeal be not taken within the time fixed, it will not be entertained except by permission of the Commissioner

No appeal will be permitted from a decision rendered upon motion for dissolution affirming the patentability of a claim or the applicant's right to make the same

Appeals may be taken directly to the Commissioner, except in the cases provided for in the preceding portions of this rule from decisions on such motions as, in his judgment, should be appealable

125 After an interference is finally declared it will not, except as herein otherwise provided, be determined without judgment of priority founded either upon the evidence, or upon a written concession of priority, or upon a written disclaimer of the invention, or upon a written declaration of abandonment of the invention,

212

signed by the inventor himself (and by the assignee, if any)

126 The examiner of interferences or the examiners in chief may, either before or in their decision on the question of priority, direct the attention of the Commissioner to any matter not relating to priority which may have come to their notice, and which, in their opinion, establishes the fact that no interference exists, or that there has been irregularity in declaring the same (Rule 122), or which amounts to a statutory bar to the grant of a patent to either of the parties for the claim or claims in interference The Commissioner may suspend the interference and remand the case to the primary examiner for his consideration of the matters to which attention has been directed. From the decision of the examiner appeal may be taken as in other cases If the case shall not be so remanded, the primary examiner will, after judgment, consider any matter affecting the rights of either party to a patent which may have been called to his attention, unless the same shall have been previously disposed of by the Commissioner

127 A second interference will not be declared upon a new application for the same invention filed by either party

128 If, during the pendency of an interference, a reference be found, the primary examiner shall call the attention of the law examiner thereto, and the latter may request the suspension of the interference until the final determination of the pertinency and effect of the reference, and the interference shall then be dissolved or continued as the result of such determination The consideration of such reference shall be *inter partes* and before the law examiner

129 If, during the pendency of an interference, another case appear, claiming substantially the subject matter in issue, the primary examiner shall request the suspension of the interference for the purpose of adding

213

said case Such suspension will be granted as a matter of course by the examiner of interferences if no testimony has been taken If, however, any testimony has been taken, a notice for the proposed new party, disclosing the issue in interference and the names and addresses of the interferants and of their attorneys, and notices for the interferants disclosing the name and address of the said party and his attorney, shall be prepared by the primary examiner and forwarded to the examiner of interferences, who shall mail said notices and set a time of hearing on the question of the admission of the new party. If the examiner of interferences be of the opinion that the interference should be suspended and the new party added, he shall prescribe the terms for such suspension The decision of the examiner of interferences as to the addition of a party shall be final.

130 Where the patentability of a claim to an opponent is material to the right of a party to a patent, said party may urge the nonpatentability of the claim to his opponent as a basis for the decision upon priority of invention A party shall not be entitled to raise this question, however, unless he has duly presented and prosecuted a motion under Rule 122 for dissolution upon this ground or shows good reason why such a motion was not presented and prosecuted. When the law examiner has denied such a motion for dissolution the question shall not be reinvestigated by the examiner of interferences except in view of evidence which was not before the law examiner, but it may be raised before the appellate tribunals on appeal from award of priority by the examiner of interferences

131 When, on motion duly made and upon satisfactory proof, it shall be shown that, by reason of the inability or refusal of the inventor to prosecute or defend an interference, or from other cause, the ends of justice require that an assignee of an undivided interest in the

214

invention be permitted to prosecute or defend the same, it may be so ordered

132 Whenever an award of priority has been rendered in an interference proceeding by any tribunal and the limit of appeal from such decision has expired, and whenever an interference has been terminated by reason of the written concession, signed by the applicant in person, of priority of invention in favor of his opponent or opponents, the primary examiner shall advise the defeated or unsuccessful party or parties to the interference that their claim or claims which were so involved in the issue stand finally rejected.

APPEALS TO THE EXAMINERS IN CHIEF AND TO THE COMMISSIONER AND PETITIONS TO THE COMMISSIONER IN THE EX PARTE PROSECUTION OF APPLICATIONS

133. Every applicant for a patent, any of the claims of whose application have been twice rejected for the same reasons, upon grounds involving the merits of the invention, such as lack of invention, novelty, or utility, or on the ground of abandonment, public use or sale, inoperativeness of invention, aggregation of elements, incomplete combination of elements, or, when amended, for want of identity with the invention originally disclosed, or because the amendment involves a departure from the invention originally presented, and every applicant who has been twice required to divide his application, and every applicant for the reissue of a patent whose claims have been twice rejected for any of the reasons above enumerated, or on the ground that the original patent is not inoperative or invalid, or if so inoperative or invalid that the errors which rendered it so did not arise from inadvertence, accident, or mistake, may, upon payment of a fee of $10, appeal from the decision of the primary examiner to the examiners in chief   The appeal must set forth in writing the points of the decision upon which

215

it is taken, and must be signed by the applicant or his duly authorized attorney or agent.

134 There must have been two rejections of the claims as originally filed, or, if amended in matter of substance, of the amended claims, and all the claims must have been passed upon, and except in cases of division all preliminary and intermediate questions relating to matters not affecting the merits of the invention settled, before the case can be appealed to the examiners in chief

135 Upon the filing of the appeal the same shall be submitted to the primary examiner, who, if he find it to be regular in form and to relate to an appealable action, shall within ten days from the filing thereof furnish the examiners in chief with a written statement of the grounds of his decision on all the points involved in the appeal with copies of the rejected claims and with the references applicable thereto, giving a concise explanation of the invention claimed and of the subject matter of the references so far as pertinent to the appealed claims The examiner shall at the time of making such statement furnish a copy of the same to the appellant. If the primary examiner shall decide that the appeal is not regular in form or does not relate to an appealable action, a petition from such decision may be taken directly to the Commissioner as provided in Rule 142

136 From the adverse decision of the board of examiners in chief appeal may be taken to the Commissioner in person upon payment of the fee of $20 required by law

137 The appellant shall on or before the day of hearing file a brief of the authorities and arguments on which he will rely to maintain his appeal

If the appellant desire to be heard orally, he will so indicate when he files his appeal; a day of hearing will then be fixed, and due notice thereof given him

138 Affidavits received after the case has been appealed will not be admitted without remanding the ap-

216

plication to the primary examiner for reconsideration, but the appellate tribunals may in their discretion refuse to remand the case and proceed with the same without consideration of the affidavits

139 The examiners in chief in their decision shall affirm or reverse the decision of the primary examiner only on the points on which appeal shall have been taken. (See Rule 133) Should they discover any apparent grounds not involved in the appeal for granting or refusing letters patent in the form claimed, or any other form, they shall annex to their decision a statement to that effect with such recommendation as they shall deem proper

Should the examiners in chief recommend the refusal of letters patent in the form claimed, then recommendation will stand as a rejection and will reopen the case for amendment or showing of fact, or both, before the primary examiner, responsive to that rejection The recommendation of the examiners in chief is binding upon the primary examiner unless an amendment or showing of facts not previously of record be made which, in the opinion of the primary examiner, overcomes the recommendation. The applicant may waive the right to prosecution before the primary examiner and have the case reconsidered by the examiners in chief upon the same record, and from an adverse decision of the examiners in chief on reconsideration, appeal will lie to the Commissioner, as in other cases The applicant may also waive reconsideration by the examiners in chief and appeal directly to the Commissioner

Should the examiners in chief recommend the granting of letters patent in an amended form, the applicant shall have the right to amend in conformity with such recommendation, which shall be binding upon the primary examiner in the absence of new references or grounds for rejection

If the Commissioner, in reviewing the decision of the

217

examiners in chief, discovers any apparent grounds for refusing letters patent not involved in the appeal, he will, before or after decision on the appeal, give reasonable notice thereof to the applicant; and if any amendment or action based thereon be proposed, he will remand the case to the primary examiner for consideration.

140 Cases which have been heard and decided by the Commissioner on appeal will not be reopened except by his order, cases which have been decided by the examiners in chief will not be reheard by them, when no longer pending before them, without the written authority of the Commissioner, and cases which have been decided by either the Commissioner or the examiners in chief will not be reopened by the primary examiner without like authority, and then only for the consideration of matters not already adjudicated upon, sufficient cause being shown   (See Rule 68)

141 After decision by an appellate tribunal the case shall be remanded at once to the primary examiner, subject to the applicant's right of appeal, for such action as will carry into effect the decision, or for such further action as the applicant is entitled to demand

142. Upon receiving a petition stating concisely and clearly any proper question which has been twice acted upon by the examiner, and which does not involve the merits of the invention claimed, the rejection of a claim or a requirement for division and also stating the facts involved and the point or points to be reviewed, an order will be made directing the examiner to furnish a written statement of the grounds of his decision upon the matters averred within five days. The examiner shall at the time of making such statement furnish a copy thereof to the petitioner   No fee is required for such a petition. Hearing will be granted in the discretion of the Commissioner

APPEALS TO THE EXAMINERS IN CHIEF AND TO THE COMMISSIONER IN CONTESTED CASES

143 In interference cases parties have the same remedy by appeal to the examiners in chief and to the Commissioner as in *ex parte* cases.

144 Appeals in interference cases must be accompanied by brief statements of the reasons therefor Parties will be required to file six copies of printed briefs of their arguments, the appellant ten days before the hearing and the appellee three days (See Rule 163)

145 The appellant shall have the right to make the opening and closing arguments, unless it shall be otherwise ordered by the tribunal having jurisdiction of the case

146 Contested cases will be regarded as pending before a tribunal until the limit of appeal, which must be fixed, has expired, or until some action has been had which waives the appeal or carries into effect the decision from which appeal might have been taken

RECONSIDERATION OF CASES DECIDED BY FORMER COMMISSIONER.

147 Cases which have been decided by one Commissioner will not be reconsidered by his successor except in accordance with the principles which govern the granting of new trials

APPEALS TO THE COURT OF APPEALS OF THE DISTRICT OF COLUMBIA.

148 From the adverse decision of the Commissioner upon the claims of an application and in interference cases. an appeal may be taken to the Court of Appeals of the District of Columbia in the manner prescribed by the rules of that court. (See Appendix, pp 95-102)

149 When an appeal is taken to the Court of Appeals of the District of Columbia, the appellant shall give notice thereof to the Commissioner, and file in the Patent

219

Office, within forty days, exclusive of Sundays and holidays but including Saturday half holidays, from the date of the decision appealed from, his reasons of appeal specifically set forth in writing

150 *Pro forma* proceedings will not be had in the Patent Office for the purpose of securing to applicants an appeal to the Court of Appeals of the District of Columbia   .

(For forms of appeals and rules of the Court of Appeals of the District of Columbia respecting appeals, see Appendix, pp 95-102.)

HEARINGS.

151 Hearings will be had by the Commissioner at 10 o'clock a m , and by the board of examiners in chief at 1 o'clock p m , and by the examiner of interferences upon interlocutory matters at 10 o'clock a m , and upon final hearings at 11 o'clock a m , on the day appointed unless some other hour be specifically designated   If either party in a contested case, or the appellant in an *ex parte* case, appear at the proper time, he will be heard   After the day of hearing, a contested case will not be taken up for oral argument except by consent of all parties   If the engagements of the tribunal having jurisdiction be such as to prevent the case from being taken up on the day of hearing, a new assignment will be made, or the case will be continued from day to day until heard   Unless it shall be otherwise ordered before the hearing begins, oral arguments will be limited to one hour for each party in contested cases, and to one-half hour in other cases   After a contested case has been argued, nothing further relating thereto will be heard unless upon request of the tribunal having jurisdiction of the case   and all interviews for this purpose with parties in interest or their attorneys will be invariably denied

152 Hearings in *ex parte* and contested cases will, as far as is convenient and proper, be set, advanced, and

220

adjourned to meet the wishes of the parties and their attorneys

MOTIONS

153 In contested cases reasonable notice of all motions, and copies of motion papers and affidavits, must be served as provided in Rule 154 (*b*) Proof of such service must be made before the motion will be entertained by the office Motions will not be heard in the absence of either party except upon default after due notice Motions will be heard in the first instance by the officer or tribunal before whom the particular case may be pending In original hearings on motions the moving parties shall have the right to make the opening and closing arguments In contested cases the practice on points to which the rules are not applicable shall conform as nearly as possible, to that of the United States courts in equity proceedings

TESTIMONY IN INTERFERENCES AND OTHER CONTESTED CASES.

154 The following rules have been established for taking and transmitting testimony in interferences and other contested cases ·

(*a*) Before the depositions of witnesses shall be taken by either party due notice shall be given to the opposing party, as hereinafter provided, of the time when and place where the depositions will be taken, of the cause or matter in which they are to be used, and of the names and residences of the witnesses to be examined, and the opposing party shall have full opportunity, either in person or by attorney, to cross-examine the witnesses. If the opposing party shall attend the examination of witnesses not named in the notice, and shall either cross-examine such witnesses or fail to object to their examination, he shall be deemed to have waived his right to object to such examination for want of notice. Neither party shall take testimony in more than one place at the same

221

time, nor so nearly at the same time that reasonable opportunity for travel from one place of examination to the other can not be had.

(*b*) The notice for taking testimony or for motions must be served (unless otherwise stipulated in an instrument in writing filed in the case) upon the attorney of record, if there be one, or, if there be no attorney of record, upon the adverse party Reasonable time must be given therein for such adverse party to reach the place of examination. Service of such notice may be made in either of the following ways (1) By delivering a copy of the notice to the adverse party or his attorney; (2) by leaving a copy at the usual place of business of the adverse party or his attorney with some one in his employment, (3) when such adverse party or his attorney has no usual place of business, by leaving a copy at his residence, with a member of his family over 14 years of age and of discretion; (4) transmission by registered letter, (5) by express Whenever it shall be satisfactorily shown to the Commissioner that neither of the above modes of obtaining or reserving notice is practicable, the notice may be published in the Official Gazette. Such notice shall, with sworn proof of the fact, time, and mode of service thereof, be attached to the deposition or depositions, whether the opposing party shall have cross-examined or not

(*c*) Each witness before testifying shall be duly sworn according to law by the officer before whom his deposition shall be taken The deposition shall be carefully read over by the witness, or by the officer to him, and shall then be subscribed by the witness in the presence of the officer The officer shall annex to the deposition his certificate showing (1) the due administration of the oath by the officer to the witness before the commencement of his testimony, (2) the name of the person by whom the testimony was written out, and the fact that, if not written by the officer, it was written in his pres-

222

ence, (3) the presence or absence of the adverse party, (4) the place, day, and hour of commencing and taking the deposition (5) the reading by, or to, each witness of his deposition before he signs the same, and (6) the fact that the officer was not connected by blood or marriage with either of the parties, nor interested, directly or indirectly, in the matter in controversy. The officer shall sign the certificate and affix thereto his seal of office, if he have such seal. He shall then, without delay, securely seal up all the evidence, notices, and paper exhibits, inscribe upon the envelop a certificate giving the title of the case, the name of each witness, and the date of sealing, address the package, and forward the same to the Commissioner of Patents. If the weight or bulk of an exhibit shall exclude it from the envelop, it shall be authenticated by the officer and transmitted in a separate package, marked and addressed as above provided.

(d) If a party shall be unable to take any testimony within the time limited and desire an extension for such purpose, he must file a motion, accompanied by a statement under oath setting forth specifically the reason why such testimony has not been taken, and distinctly averring that such motion is made in good faith, and not for the purpose of delay. If either party shall be unable to procure the testimony of a witness or witnesses within the time limited, and desire an extension for such purpose, he must file a motion, accompanied by a statement under oath setting forth the cause of such inability, the name or names of such witness or witnesses, the facts expected to be proved by such witness or witnesses, the steps which have been taken to procure such testimony, and the dates on which efforts have been made to procure it. (See Rule 153.)

(e) Upon notice given to the opposite party before the closing of the testimony, any official record, and any special matter contained in a printed publication, if com-

223

petent evidence and pertinent to the issue, may be used as evidence at the hearing

(*f*) All depositions which are taken must be duly filed in the Patent Office On refusal to file, the office at its discretion will not further hear or consider the contestant with whom the refusal lies, and the office may, at its discretion, receive and consider a copy of the withheld deposition, attested by such evidence as is procurable

155 The pages of each deposition must be numbered consecutively, and the name of the witness plainly and conspicuously written at the top of each page The testimony must be written upon legal cap or foolscap paper, with a wide margin on the left-hand side of the page, and with the writing on one side only of the sheet

156 The testimony will be taken in answer to interrogatories, with the questions and answers committed to writing in their regular order by the officer, or, in his presence, by some person not interested in the case either as a party thereto or as attorney. But with the written consent of the parties the testimony may be taken stenographically, and the deposition may be written out by other persons in the presence of the officer.

Where testimony is taken stenographically, a longhand or typewritten copy shall be read to the witness, or read over by him, as soon as it can be made, and shall be signed by him as provided in paragraph 3 of Rule 154 No officer who is connected by blood or marriage with either of the parties, or interested, directly or indirectly, in the matter in controversy, either as counsel, attorney, agent, or otherwise, is competent to take depositions, unless with the written consent of all the parties

157 Upon motion duly made and granted (see Rule 153) testimony taken in an interference proceeding may be used in any other or subsequent interference proceeding, so far as relevant and material, subject, however, to the right of any contesting party to recall witnesses

whose depositions have been taken, and to take other testimony in rebuttal of the depositions

158 Upon motion duly made and granted (see Rule 153) testimony may be taken in foreign countries, upon complying with the following requirements·

(a) The motion must designate a place for the examination of the witnesses at which an officer duly qualified to take testimony under the laws of the United States in a foreign country shall reside, and it must be accompanied by a statement under oath that the motion is made in good faith, and not for purposes of delay or of vexing or harassing any party to the case; it must also set forth the names of the witnesses, the particular facts to which it is expected each will testify, and the grounds on which is based the belief that each will so testify.

(b) It must appear that the testimony desired is material and competent, and that it can not be taken in this country at all, or can not be taken here without hardship and injury to the moving party greatly exceeding that to which the opposite party will be exposed by the taking of such testimony abroad

(c) Upon the granting of such motion, a time will be set within which the moving party shall file in duplicate the interrogatories to be propounded to each witness, and serve a copy of the same upon each adverse party, who may, within a designated time, file, in duplicate, cross-interrogatories Objections to any of the interrogatories or cross-interrogatories may be filed at any time before the depositions are taken, and such objections will be considered and determined upon the hearing of the case

(d) As soon as the interrogatories and cross-interrogatories are decided to be in proper form, the Commissioner will cause them to be forwarded to the proper officer, with the request that, upon payment of, or satisfactory security for, his official fees, he notify the witnesses named to appear before him within a designated time and make answer thereto under oath. and that he reduce their answers to writing, and transmit the same, under his official seal and signature, to the Commissioner of Patents, with the certificate prescribed in Rule 154 (c)

(e) By stipulation of the parties the requirements of paragraph (c) as to written interrogatories and cross-interrogatories may be dispensed with, and the testimony may be taken before the proper officer upon oral interrogatories by the parties or their agents.

(f) Unless false swearing in the giving of such testimony before the officer taking it shall be punishable as perjury under the laws of the foreign state where it shall be taken, it will not stand on the same footing in the Patent Office as testimony duly taken in the United States, but its weight in each case will be determined by the tribunal having jurisdiction of such case.

159 Evidence touching the matter at issue will not be considered on the hearing which shall not have been taken and filed in compliance with these rules But notice will not be taken of merely formal or technical objections which shall not appear to have wrought a substantial injury to the party raising them · and in case of such injury it must be made to appear that, as soon as the party became aware of the ground of objection, he gave notice thereof to the office, and also to the opposite party, informing him at the same time that, unless it be removed, he (the objector) will urge his objection at the hearing This rule is not to be so construed as to modify established rules of evidence, which will be applied strictly in all practice before the office

160 The law requires the clerks of the various courts of the United States to issue subpœnas to secure the attendance of witnesses whose depositions are desired as evidence in contested cases in the Patent Office

161 After testimony is filed in the office it may be inspected by any party to the case, but it can not be withdrawn for the purpose of printing It may be print-

226

ed by some one specially designated by the office for that purpose, under proper restrictions

162. Thirty-one or more printed copies of the testimony must be furnished—five for the use of the office, one for each of the opposing parties, and twenty-five for the Court of Appeals of the District of Columbia, should appeal be taken If no appeal be taken, the twenty-five copies will be returned to the party filing them. The preliminary statement required by Rule 110 must be printed as a part of the record These copies of the record of the junior party's testimony must be filed not less than forty days before the day of final hearing, and in the case of the senior party not less than twenty days. They will be of the same size, both page and print, as the Rules of Practice, with the names of the witnesses at the top of the pages over their testimony, and will contain indexes with the names of all witnesses and reference to the pages where copies of papers and documents introduced as exhibits are shown.

When it shall appear, on motion duly made and by satisfactory proof, that a party, by reason of poverty, is unable to print his testimony, the printing may be dispensed with, but in such case typewritten copies must be furnished—one for the office and one for each adverse party Printing of the testimony can not be dispensed with upon the stipulation of the parties without the approval of the Commissioner.

BRIEFS.

163 Briefs at final hearing and on appeals from final decisions in contested cases shall be submitted in printed form and shall be of the same size and the same as to page and print as the printed copies of testimony But in case satisfactory reason therefor is shown, typewritten briefs may be submitted Six copies of the briefs at final hearing shall be filed three days before the hearing. Briefs on appeals shall be filed as provided in Rule 144

At interlocutory hearings and on appeal from interlocutory decisions typewritten briefs may be used, and such
briefs may be filed at or before the hearing. By stipulation of the parties or by order of the tribunal before
whom the hearing is had briefs may be filed otherwise
than as here prescribed.

ISSUE.

164 If, on examination, it shall appear that the applicant is justly entitled to a patent under the law, a notice
of allowance will be sent him or his attorney, calling for
the payment of the final fee within six months from the
date of such notice of allowance, upon the receipt of
which within the time fixed by law the patent will be
prepared for issue (See Rules 167, 194)

165 After notice of the allowance of an application is
given, the case will not be withdrawn from issue except
by approval of the Commissioner, and if withdrawn for
further action on the part of the office a new notice of
allowance will be given When the final fee has been
paid upon an application for letters patent, and the case
has received its date and number, it will not be withdrawn from issue on account of any mistake or change
of purpose of the applicant or his attorney, nor for the
purpose of enabling the inventor to procure a foreign
patent, nor for any other reasons except mistake on the
part of the office, or because of fraud, or illegality in the
application, or for interference (See Rule 78)

166 Whenever the Commissioner shall direct the with-
drawal of an application from issue on request of an applicant for reasons not prohibited by Rule 165, this with-
drawal will not operate to stay the period of one year
running against the application, which begins to attach
from the date of the notice of allowance

DATE, DURATION, AND FORM OF PATENTS.

167 Every patent shall issue within a period of three
months from the date of the payment of the final fee,

228

which fee shall be paid not later than six months from the time at which the application was passed and allowed and notice thereof was sent to the applicant or his agent; and if the final fee be not paid within that period the patent shall be withheld (See Rule 175.) In the absence of request to suspend issue the patent will issue in regular course. The issue closes weekly on Thursday, and the patents bear date as of the fourth Tuesday thereafter.

A patent will not be antedated.

168. Every patent will contain a short title of the invention or discovery indicating its nature and object, and a grant to the patentee, his heirs and assigns, for the term of seventeen years, of the exclusive right to make, use, and vend the invention or discovery throughout the United States and the Territories thereof. The duration of a design patent may be for the term of three and one-half, seven, or fourteen years, as provided in Rule 80. A copy of the specifications and drawings will be annexed to the patent and form part thereof.

DELIVERY.

169. The patent will be delivered or mailed on the day of its date to the attorney of record, if there be one, or, if the attorney so request, to the patentee or assignee of an interest therein, or, if there be no attorney, to the patentee or to the assignee of the entire interest, if he so request.

CORRECTION OF ERRORS IN LETTERS PATENT.

170. Whenever a mistake, incurred through the fault of the office, is clearly disclosed by the records or files of the office, a certificate, stating the fact and nature of such mistake, signed by the Commissioner of Patents, and sealed with the seal of the Patent Office, will, at the request of the patentee or his assignee, be indorsed without charge upon the letters patent, and recorded in the rec-

229

oids of patents, and a printed copy thereof attached to each printed copy of the specification and drawing

Whenever a mistake, incurred through the fault of the office, constitutes a sufficient legal ground for a reissue, the reissue will be made, for the correction of such mistake only, without charge of office fees, at the request of the patentee.

Mistakes not incurred through the fault of the office, and not affording legal grounds for reissues, will not be corrected after the delivery of the letters patent to the patentee or his agent

Changes or corrections will not be made in letters patent after the delivery thereof to the patentee or his attorney, except as above provided

ABANDONED, FORFEITED, REVIVED, AND RENEWED APPLICATIONS.

171 An abandoned application is one in which all the essential parts have not been filed so that it is completed and prepared for examination within a period of one year, or which the applicant has failed to prosecute within one year after any action therein of which notice has been duly given (see Rules 31 and 77), or which the applicant has expressly abandoned by filing in the office a written declaration of abandonment, signed by himself and assignee, if any, identifying his application by title of invention, serial number, and date of filing. (See Rule 60.)

Prosecution of an application to save it from abandonment must include such proper action as the condition of the case may require The admission of an amendment not responsive to the last official action, or refusal to admit the same, and any proceedings relative thereto, shall not operate to save the application from abandonment under section 4894 of the Revised Statutes.

172 Before an application abandoned by failure to complete or prosecute can be revived as a pending appli-

cation it must be shown to the satisfaction of the Commissioner that the delay was unavoidable

173 When a new application is filed in place of an abandoned or rejected application, a new petition, specification, oath, and fee will be required, but the old drawing, if suitable, may be used upon the filing of suitable permanent photographic copies thereof.

174 A forfeited application is one upon which a patent has been withheld for failure to pay the final fee within the prescribed time (See Rule 167)

175 When the patent has been withheld by reason of nonpayment of the final fee, any person, whether inventor or assignee, who has an interest in the invention for which the patent was ordered to issue may file a renewal of the application for the same invention; but any renewal application must be made within two years after the allowance of the original application Upon the hearing of the new application abandonment will be considered as a question of fact

176 In a renewal the oath, petition, specification, drawing, and model of the original application may be used, but a new fee will be required The renewal application will not be regarded for all purposes as a continuation of the original one, but must bear date from the time of renewal and be subject to examination like an original application

177 Forfeited and abandoned applications will not be cited as references

178 Notice of the filing of subsequent applications will not be given to applicants while their cases remain forfeited

179 Copies of the files of forfeited and abandoned applications may be furnished when ordered by the Commissioner The requests for such copies must be presented in the form of a petition properly verified as to all matters not appearing of record in the Patent Office (See Form 35)

231

EXTENSIONS.

180 Patents can not be extended except by act of Congress

DISCLAIMERS.

181 Whenever, through inadvertence, accident, or mistake, and without any fraudulent or deceptive intention, a patentee has claimed as his invention or discovery more than he had a right to claim as new, his patent will be valid for all that part which is truly and justly his own, provided the same is a material or substantial part of the thing patented; and any such patentee, his heirs or assigns, whether of the whole or any sectional interest therein, may, on payment of the fee required by law ($10), make disclaimer of such parts of the thing patented as he or they shall not choose to claim or to hold by virtue of the patent or assignment, stating therein the extent of his interest in such patent Such disclaimer shall be in writing, attested by one or more witnesses, and recorded in the Patent Office; and it shall thereafter be considered as part of the original specification to the extent of the interest possessed by the claimant and by those claiming under him after the record thereof But no such disclaimer shall affect any action pending at the time of filing the same, except as to the question of unreasonable neglect or delay in filing it

182. The statutory disclaimers treated of in Rule 181 are to be distinguished from those which are embodied in original or reissue applications, as first filed or subsequently amended, referring to matter shown or described, but to which the disclaimant does not choose to claim title and also from those made to avoid the continuance of an interference The disclaimers falling within this present rule must be signed by the applicant in person and require no fee (See Rule 107 For forms of disclaimers see Appendix, Forms 28 and 29.)

ASSIGNMENTS.

183 Every patent or any interest therein is assignable in law by an instrument in writing, and the patentee or his assigns or legal representatives may, in like manner, grant and convey an exclusive right under the patent to the whole or any specified part of the United States

184 Interest in patents may be vested in assignees, in grantees of exclusive territorial rights, in mortgagees, and in licensees.

(*a*) An assignee is a transferee of the whole interest of the original patent or of an undivided part of such whole interest, extending to every portion of the United States The assignment must be written or printed and duly signed.

(*b*) A grantee acquires by the grant the exclusive right, under the patent, to make, use, and vend, and to grant to others the right to make, use, and vend, the thing patented within and throughout some specified part of the United States, excluding the patentee therefrom The grant must be written or printed and be duly signed

(*c*) A mortgage must be written or printed and be duly signed

(*d*) A licensee takes an interest less than or different from either of the others A license may be oral, written, or printed, and if written or printed, must be duly signed

185 An assignment, grant, or conveyance of a patent will be void as against any subsequent purchaser or mortgagee for a valuable consideration without notice unless recorded in the Patent Office within three months from the date thereof

If any assignment, grant, or conveyance of any patent shall be acknowledged before any notary public of the several States or Territories or the District of Columbia, or any commissioner of the United States circuit court, or before any secretary of legation or consular officer authorized to administer oaths or perform notarial acts

233

under section 1750 of the Revised Statutes, the certificate of such acknowledgment, under the hand and official seal of such notary or other officer, shall be *prima facie* evidence of the execution of such assignment or conveyance.

186 No instrument will be recorded which is not in the English language and which does not, in the judgment of the Commissioner, amount to an assignment, grant, mortgage, lien, incumbrance, or license, or which does not affect the title of the patent or invention to which it relates Such instrument should identify the patent by date and number; or, if the invention be unpatented, the name of the inventor, the serial number, and date of the application should be stated

187 Assignments which are made conditional on the performance of certain stipulations, as the payment of money, if recorded in the office are regarded as absolute assignments until canceled with the written consent of both parties or by the decree of a competent court The office has no means for determining whether such conditions have been fulfilled.

188 In every case where it is desired that the patent issue to an assignee, the assignment must be recorded in the Patent Office at a date not later than the day on which the final fee is paid (See Rule 26) The date of the record is the date of the receipt of the assignment at the office

189 The receipt of assignments is generally acknowledged by the office They are recorded in regular order as promptly as possible, and then transmitted to the persons entitled to them. (For form of assignment, see Appendix, forms 38-43)

OFFICE FEES.

190 Nearly all the fees payable to the Patent Office are positively required by law to be paid in advance—that is, upon making application for any action by the office for which a fee is payable For the sake of uni-

formity and convenience, the remaining fees will be required to be paid in the same manner

191 The following is the schedule of fees and of prices of publications of the Patent Office

On filing each original application for a patent, except in design cases	$15 00
On issuing each original patent, except in design cases	20 00
In design cases	
For 3 years and 6 months	10 00
For 7 years	15 00
For 14 years	30 00
On every application for the reissue of a patent	30 00
On filing each disclaimer	10 00
On an appeal for the first time from the Primary Examiner to the Examiners in Chief	10 00
On every appeal from the Examiners in Chief to the Commissioner	20 00
For certified copies of patents if in print	
For specification and drawing, per copy	05
For the certificate	25
For the grant	50
For certifying to a duplicate of a model	50
For manuscript copies of records, for every 100 words or fraction thereof	10
If certified, for the certificate additional	25
For 20-coupon orders, each coupon good for one copy of a printed specification and drawing, and receivable in payment for photographic prints	1 00
For 100 coupons in stub book	5 00
For uncertified copies of the specifications and accompanying drawings of patents, if in print, each,	10
For the drawings if in print	05
For copies of drawings not in print, the reasonable cost of making them	
For photo prints of drawings, for each sheet of drawings	
Size 10 by 15 inches, per copy	25
Size 8 by 12½ inches, per copy	15
For recording every assignment, agreement, power of attorney, or other paper, of 300 words or under	1 00
Of over 300 and under 1,000 words	2 00
For each additional 1,000 words or fraction thereof	1 00
For abstracts of title to patents or inventions	
For the search, one hour or less, and certificate	1 00

Each additional hour or fraction thereof . 50
For each brief from the digest of assignments of 200
    words or less . . . 20
Each additional 100 words or fraction thereof 10
For searching titles or records, one hour or less . 50
Each additional hour or fraction thereof . 50
For assistance to attorneys in the examination of publica-
    tions in the Scientific Library, one hour or less . . 1 00
    Each additional hour or fraction thereof 1 00
For copies of matter in any foreign language, for every 100
    words or a fraction thereof 10
For translation, for every 100 words or fraction thereof 50
The Official Gazette
    Annual subscriptions . $5 00
        For postage upon foreign subscriptions, except those
        from Canada and Mexico, $5 or more as required
        Moneys received from foreign subscribers in ex-
        cess of the subscription price of $5 will be depos-
        ited to the credit of the subscriber and applied to
        postage upon the subscription as incurred *All
        communications respecting the Gazette and all sub-
        scriptions should be addressed to the Superintend-
        ent of Documents Government Printing Office*
    Single numbers . 10
    Decision leaflets 05
    Trade mark supplements . 05
For bound volumes of the Official Gazette
    Semi-annual volumes, from Jan. 1 1872, to June 30,
        1883, full sheep binding, per volume . 4 00
    In half sheep binding, per volume . . . 3 50
    Quarterly volumes, from July 1, 1883, to Dec. 31, 1902,
        full sheep binding, per volume 2 75
    Bi-monthly volumes, from Jan 1, 1903, to Mar. 1 1906,
        full sheep binding, per volume . . . 2 50
    Bi monthly volumes from Mar 1, 1906, to Jan 1, 1909,
        tan duck binding . . . 2 50
    Monthly volumes, from Jan 1 1909, tan duck binding,
        per volume . . . 2 50
Monthly volumes, unbound with title page, digest and
    index, per volume 50
For the annual index, from Jan, 1872, to Jan 1, 1906, full
    law binding, per volume 2 00
    In paper covers, per volume . 1 00
For the annual index from Jan. 1, 1906, buckram binding 2 00
    In paper covers, per volume 1.00

236

For the general index—a list of inventions patented from
 1790 to 1873—three volumes, full law binding, per set   10 00
For the index from 1790 to 1836—one volume, full law binding   . .   5 00
For the library edition, monthly volumes to Jan 1, 1906,
 containing the specifications and photolithographed copies
 of the drawings of all patents issued during the month,
 certified, bound in full sheep, per volume   .   5 00
     In half sheet, to Jan 1, 1906, per volume   3 00
For the library edition, monthly volumes from Jan 1, 1906,
 to June 30, 1912, tan duck binding   .   ..   5 00
For the index to patents relating to electricity, granted by
 the United States prior to June 30, 1882, one volume, 250
 pages, bound 5 00
     In paper covers 3 00
Annual appendixes for each fiscal year subsequent to June
 30, 1882, paper covers 1.50
For Commissioner's decisions·
     For 1869, 1870, and 1871, one volume, full law binding   2 00
     For 1872, 1873, and 1874, one volume, full law binding   2 00
For 1875 and 1876, one volume, with decisions of United
     States courts in patent cases, full law binding   2 00
     In paper covers   1 00
Annual volumes with decisions of United States courts, for
 1877 to 1906, full law binding, per volume   2 00
     In paper covers   1 00
Subsequent annual volumes, buckram binding   2 00
     In paper covers   .   1 00

192 An order for a copy of an assignment must give
the liber and page of the record, as well as the name of
the inventor, otherwise an extra charge will be made
for the time consumed in making any search for such assignment

193 Persons will not be allowed to make copies or
tracings from the files or records of the office   Such
copies will be furnished, when ordered, at the rates already specified.

194 All payments of money required for office fees
must be made in specie, Treasury notes, national-bank
notes, certificates of deposit, post-office money orders, or
certified checks   Money orders and checks should be

237

made payable to the "Commissioner of Patents " Payment may also be made to the Treasurer, or to any of the assistant treasurers of the United States, or to any of the depositaries, national banks, or receivers of public money, designated by the Secretary of the Treasury for that purpose, who will issue a certificate of deposit in triplicate and will forward the original and the duplicate certificates to the Secretary of the Treasury and the Commissioner of Patents, respectively, and will give the triplicate certificate to the depositor. Money sent by mail to the Patent Office will be at the risk of the sender Letters containing money should be registered. In no case should money be sent with models

REPAYMENT OF MONEY.

195 Money paid by actual mistake, such as a payment in excess, or when not required by law, or by neglect or misinformation on the part of the office, will be refunded, but a mere change of purpose after the payment of money, as when a party desires to withdraw his application for a patent or for the registration of a trade-mark, or to withdraw an appeal, will not entitle a party to demand such a return

PUBLICATIONS.

196 The Official Gazette, a weekly publication which has been issued since 1872, takes the place of the old Patent Office Report. It contains claims of all patents issued, including reissues and designs, with portions of the drawings selected to illustrate the inventions claimed, illustrations of trade-marks published, and lists of trade-marks, prints, and labels registered It also contains decisions rendered by the courts in patent cases and by the Commissioner of Patents, and other special matters of interest to inventors

The Gazette is furnished to subscribers at the rate of $5 per annum When sent abroad, an additional charge is made for the payment of postage Single copies are furnished for ten cents All orders and remittances for the Gazette should be sent to the Superintendent of Documents, Government Printing Office, Washington, D C The Gazette is issued in monthly volumes, with a title page and index to each volume. An index is published annually, which is sent to all subscribers without additional cost.

On June 30, 1912 the publication of the monthly library edition, issued since 1872, containing the full specifications and drawings of all patents granted during the previous month, was suspended

LIBRARY REGULATIONS.

197 Officers of the bureau and members of the examining corps only are allowed to enter the alcoves or take books from the scientific library

Books taken from this library must be entered in a register kept for the purpose, and returned on the call of the librarian They must not be taken from the building except by permission of the Commissioner.

Any book lost or defaced must be replaced by a new copy

Patentees and others doing business with the office can examine the books only in the library hall

Translations will be made only for official use.

Copies or tracings from works in the library will be furnished by the office at the usual rates.

AMENDMENTS OF THE RULES.

198 All amendments of the foregoing rules will be published in the Official Gazette.

QUESTIONS NOT SPECIFICALLY PROVIDED FOR.

199 All cases not specifically defined and provided for in these rules will be decided in accordance with the merits of each case under the authority of the Commis-

239

sioner, and such decision will be communicated to the interested parties in writing

200 Questions arising in applications filed prior to January 1, 1898, where these rules do not apply, shall be governed by the rules of June 18, 1897.

THOMAS EWING,
Commissioner of Patents.

DEPARTMENT OF THE INTERIOR,
December 22, 1915

Approved to take effect January 1, 1916

BO SWEENEY,
Assistant Secretary

APPENDIX OF FORMS.

PETITIONS.

1. By a Sole Inventor.

To the Commissioner of Patents:

Your petitioner, ... , a citizen of the United States and a resident of . . , in the county of .
and State of . . (or subject, etc), whose post office address is . , prays that letters patent may be granted to him for the improvement in . . , set forth in the annexed specification

Signed at . ., in the county of .. . and State of . , this day of . . , 19

. . ..

2. By Joint Inventors.

To the Commissioner of Patents:

Your petitioners, . . and . . . ,
citizens of the United States and residents, respectively, of . , in the county of and State of . . ,
and of . , in the county of . and State of .. ... (or subjects, etc), whose post office addresses are, respectively, ... and ... , pray that letters patent may be granted to them, as joint inventors, for the improvement in , set forth in the annexed specification.

Signed at , in the county of . .. and State of ......, this .... day of ......, 19..

....

....

3. By An Inventor, for Himself and Assignee.

To the Commissioner of Patents.

Your petitioner, . , a citizen of the United States and a resident of , in the county of . . and State of (or subject, etc), whose post office address is . , prays that letters patent may be granted to himself and . , a citizen of the United States and a resident of . , in the county of . . . . . and State of . . , whose post office address is . . . . ., as his assignee, for the improvement in . . . . , set forth in the annexed specification

Signed at . . ., in the county of . . and State of . . . . . ., this . . day of . . . , 19 .

4 Petition With Power of Attorney.

To the Commissioner of Patents:

Your petitioner, . . , a citizen of the United States and a resident of . , in the county of . . . . and State of . (or subject, etc), whose post office address is . . . . . ., prays that letters patent may be granted to him for the improvement in , set forth in the annexed specification, and he hereby appoints . . . . . of . , State of , his attorney, with full power of substitution and revocation, to prosecute this application, to make alterations and amendments therein, to receive the patent, and to transact all business in the Patent Office connected therewith

Signed at , in the county of and State of . . ., this . day of . . , 19. .

5. By An Administrator.

To the Commissioner of Patents.

Your petitioner. . . . ., a citizen of the United States and a resident of . . . . . in the county of . . . . and State of . . . (or subject, etc), whose post office

address is ... , administrator of the estate of .   .,
late a citizen of .   . , deceased (as by reference to the
duly certified copy of letters of administration, hereto
annexed, will more fully appear), prays that letters patent may be granted to him for the invention of the said
.. .. (improvement in .   .   ), set forth in the annexed specification

Signed at   .. , in the county of   and State
of   , this   .   day of   , 19

. . . .

Administrator, etc.

6 By An Executor.

To the Commissioner of Patents:

Your petitioner,   , a citizen of the United
States and a resident of ....., in the county of ...
and State of   .   .   (or subject, etc), whose post office
address is . . . , executor of the last will and testament
of   , late a citizen of   , deceased (as by reference to the duly certified copy of letters testamentary,
hereto annexed, will more fully appear), prays that letters patent may be granted to him for the invention of
the said   (improvement in   ), set forth in
the annexed specification

Signed at   in the county of .   .   and State
of .   , this   day of . . , 19

.   .   .,

Executor, etc

7. By a Guardian of An Insane Person.

To the Commissioner of Patents:

Your petitioner,   . . . , a citizen of the United
States and a resident of . .. , in the county of
and State of .   (or subject, etc), whose post office
address is .   . and who has been appointed guardian (or conservator or representative) of   .   (as by
reference to the duly certified copy of the order of court,

243

hereto annexed, will more fully appear), prays that letters patent may be granted to him for the invention of the said (improvement in . ....), set forth in the annexed specification

Signed at . , in the county of . and State of .. , this . day of . , 19

. . .. ,

Guardian, etc.

8. For a Reissue (By the Inventor).

To the Commissioner of Patents·

Your petitioner, ..., a citizen of the United States and a resident of , in the county of . and State of . (or subject, etc), whose post office address is , prays that he may be allowed to surrender the letters patent for an improvement in . ..., granted to him . , 19 ., whereof he is now sole owner (or whereof , on whose behalf and with whose assent this application is made, is now sole owner, by assignment), and that letters patent may be reissued to him (or the said .) for the same invention upon the annexed amended specification With this petition is filed an abstract of title, duly certified, as required in such cases

Signed at .. ..., in the county of ...... and State of ......, this .. . day of ... , 19..

. . . .

[Assent of assignee to reissue]

The undersigned, assignee of the entire (or of an undivided) interest in the above-mentioned letters patent, hereby assents to the accompanying application

, , , , , ...

9. For a Reissue (By the Assignee).

[To be used only when the inventor is dead]

To the Commissioner of Patents:

Your petitioner, ... , a citizen of the United States and a resident of ......, in the county of . . . and State of   (or subject, etc), whose post office address is .   , prays that he may be allowed to surrender the letters patent for an improvement in . . , No. ... ., granted ... . , 19 , to . ...   ., now deceased, whereof he is now owner, by assignment of the entire interest, and that the letters patent may be reissued to him for the same invention, upon the annexed amended specification With this petition is filed an abstract of title (or an order for making and filing the same, etc.).

Signed at   , in the county of   and State of   ., this .   day of   .   , 19

. . . .

10. For Letters Patent for a Design.

To the Commissioner of Patents.

Your petitioner,   .   . , a citizen of the United States and a resident of . .. ., in the county of ....   and State of .   (or subject, etc), whose post office address is ......, prays that letters patent may be granted to him for the term of three and one-half years (or seven years or fourteen years) for the new and original design for   , set forth in the annexed specification

Signed at .   , in the county of ..... and State of   , this .   . day of . . , 19

.   . ..

11. For a Caveat.

This form is obsolete, law relating to caveats repealed by the Act of July 1, 1910

245

12. For the Renewal of a Forfeited Application.

To the Commissioner of Patents:

Your petitioner, ..., a citizen of the United States and a resident of ......, in the county of ...... and State of ...... (or subject, etc.), whose post office address is ......, represents that on ......, 19.., he filed an application for letters patent for an improvement in ......, serial number ......, which application was allowed ......, 19.., but that he failed to make payment of the final fee within the time allowed by law. He now makes renewed application for letters patent for said invention, and prays that the original specification, oath. drawings, and model may be used as a part of this application.

Signed at ......, in the county of ...... and State of ......, this .... day of ......, 19..

....

SPECIFICATIONS.

13. For an Art or Process.

To all whom it may concern:

Be it known that I, ..., a citizen of the United States, residing at ......, in the county of ...... and State of ...... (or subject, etc.), have invented new and useful improvements in processes of extracting gold from its ores. of which the following is a specification:

This invention relates to the process of extracting gold from its ores by means of a solution of cyanide of an alkali or alkaline earth, and has for its object to render the process more expeditious and considerably cheaper.

In extracting gold from its ores by means of a solution of cyanide of potassium, sodium, barium, etc.. the simultaneous oxidation of the gold is necessary, and this has hitherto been effected by the action of the air upon the gold which is rendered oxidizable thereby by the action of the cyanide solution.

246

Instead of depending solely upon the agency of the air for the oxidizing action I employ, to assist the oxidation of the gold, ferricyanide of potassium or another ferricyanogen salt of an alkali or of an earth alkali in an alkaline solution By this means the oxidation, being rendered very much more energetic, is effected with a considerably smaller quantity of the solvent Thus, by the addition of ferricyanide of potassium or other ferricyanides to the cyanide of potassium solution, as much as eighty per cent. of potassium cyanide may be saved

It may be remarked that the ferricyanide of potassium alone will not dissolve the gold and does not therefore come under the category of a solvent hitherto employed in processes of extraction. It does not therefore render unnecessary the employment of the simple cyanide as a solvent, but only reduces the amount required owing to the capacity of the ferricyanide to assist the air to rapidly oxidize the gold in the presence of the simple salt Consequently the cyanogen of the latter is not used to form the gold cyanide compound

I claim.

The process of extracting gold from its ores consisting in subjecting the ores to the dissolving action of cyanide of potassium in the presence of ferricyanide of potassium, substantially as herein described

. . . .,

14 For a Machine

To all whom it may concern:

Be it known that I, ..., a citizen of the United States, residing at   , in the county of .. . and State of . . . . . (or subject, etc), have invented a new and useful meat-chopping machine, of which the following is a specification :

My invention relates to improvements in meat-chopping machines in which vertically reciprocating knives operate in conjunction with a rotating chopping block

247

and the objects of my improvement are, first, to provide a continuously lubricated bearing for the block, second, to afford facilities for the proper adjustment of the knives independently of each other in respect to the face of the block, and, third, to reduce the friction of the reciprocating rod which carries the knives

I attain these objects by the mechanism illustrated in the accompanying drawing, in which—

Figure 1 is a vertical section of the entire machine, Fig 2, a plan view of the machine as it appears after the removal of the chopping block and knives; Fig. 3, a vertical section of a part of the machine on the line 3 3, Fig 2, and Fig 4, a detailed view in perspective of the reciprocating crosshead and its knives.

Similar numerals refer to similar parts throughout the several views.

The table or plate 1, its legs or standards 2 2, and the hanger 3, secured to the underside of the table, constitute the framework of the machine In the hanger 3 turns the shaft 4, carrying a fly-wheel 5, to the hub of which is attached a crank 6, and a crank-pin 7 connected by a link 8, to a pin passing through a crosshead 9, and to the latter is secured a rod 10, having at its upper end a crosshead 11, carrying the adjustable chopping knives, 12 12, referred to hereinafter

The crosshead 9, reciprocated by the shaft 4, is provided with anti-friction rollers 13 13, adapted to guides 14 14, secured to the underside of the table 1, so that the reciprocation of this crosshead may be accompanied with as little friction as possible

To the underside of a wooden chopping block 15 is secured an annular rib 16, adapted to and bearing in an annular groove 17 in the table 1   (See Figs 1 and 2) This annular groove or channel is not of the same depth throughout, but communicates at one or more points (two in the present instance) with pockets or receptacles 18, 18 wider than the groove and containing supplies of

248

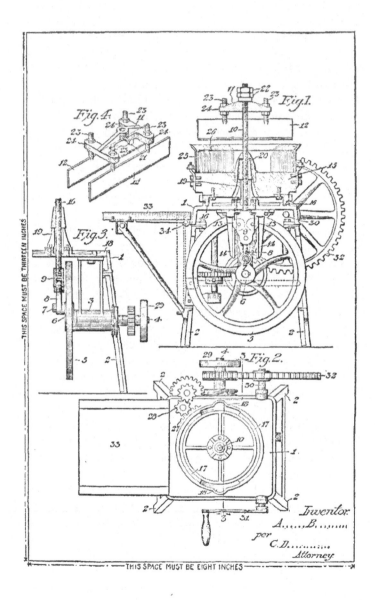

Fig.4.

Fig.3.

Fig.1.

Fig.2.

Inventor.

A......B........

per

C.D...........

Attorney

oil, in contact with which the rib 16 rotates, so that the continuous lubrication of the groove and rib is assured. The rod 10 passes through and is guided by a central stand 19, secured to the table 1, and projecting through a central opening in the chopping block without being in contact therewith the upper portion of the said stand being contained within a cover 20, which is secured to the block and which prevents particles of meat from escaping through the central opening of the same

The crosshead 11, previously referred to and shown in perspective in Fig 4, is vertically adjustable on the rod 10 and can be retained after adjustment by a set-screw 21 the upper end of the rod being threaded for the reception of nuts 22, which resist the shocks imparted to the crosshead when the knives are brought into violent contact with the meat or the chopping block

The knives 12, 12 are adjustable independently of each other and of the said crosshead, so that the coincidence of the cutting-edge of each knife with the face of the chopping-block may always be assured

I prefer to carry out this feature of my invention in the manner shown in Fig 4, where it will be seen that two screw-rods 23, 23 rise vertically from the back of each knife and pass through lugs 24, 24 on the cross-head, each rod being furnished with two nuts, one above and the other below the lug through which it passes The most accurate adjustment of the knives can be effected by the manipulation of these nuts

A circular casing 25 is secured to the chopping-block, so as to form on the same a trough 26 for keeping the meat within proper bounds; and on the edge of the annular rib 16, secured to the bottom of the block, are teeth 27, for receiving those of a pinion 28, which may be driven by the shaft 4 through the medium of any suitable system of gearing, that shown in the drawing forming no part of my present invention

This shaft 4 may be driven by a belt passing round the

pulleys 29, or it may be driven by hand from a shaft 30, furnished at one end with a handle 31, and at the other with a cog-wheel 32, gearing into a pinion on the said shaft 4

A platform 33 may be hinged, as at 34, to one edge of the table 1, to support a vessel in which the chopped meat can be deposited The means by which it may be supported are shown in full lines, and the most convenient method of disposing of it when not in use is shown in dotted lines, in Fig 1

I am aware that prior to my invention meat-chopping machines have been made with vertically-reciprocating knives operating in conjunction with rotating chopping-blocks I therefore do not claim such a combination broadly, but

I claim.

1. The combination, in a meat-chopping machine, of a rotary chopping-block having an annular rib, with a table having an annular recess to receive said rib, and a pocket communicating with the said recess, all substantially as set forth

2 In a meat-chopping machine, the combination of a rotary chopping-block with a reciprocating cross-head carrying knives, each of which is vertically adjustable on the said cross-head independently of the other, substantially as described.

3. A chopping knife having two screw rods projecting perpendicularly from its back and parallel with the sides of the knife

4 A meat chopping machine provided with a rod carrying chopping knives and adapted to be reciprocated. a cross-head secured to said rod, anti-friction rollers mounted on the cross-head, and guides with which the rollers cooperate, substantially as described.

. . . .

251

15 For a Composition of Matter.

To all whom it may concern

Be it known that I, .   .   . , a citizen of

[Full name of applicant]

., residing at   . .. . in the county of

. .. . and State of   . . (or subject of, etc), have invented a new and useful Non-Conducting Plastic Composition, of which the following is a specification

The object of my invention is the pioduction of a plastic non-conducting composition or cement to be applied to the surfaces of steam-boilers and steam-pipes and other receptacles and conduits as a lagging foi preventing radiation of heat and the permeation of water, and rendering them fireproof

My composition consists of a mixture of paper-pulp or other vegetable fibrous material, a powdered mineral filler. such as soapstone or Portland cement, a mineral fibrous material, such as asbestos, and a mineral cementing material, such as silicate of sodium or potassium (soluble glass)

In preparing the composition I prefer to use the ingredients in about the following proportions, viz fifty pounds of paper-pulp, fifty pounds of soapstone, twenty-five pounds of asbestos, and three quarts of a 33° Baumé solution of soluble glass. Good results may be obtained, however, when the ingredients are varied within the following limits vegetable fibrous material, foity to sixty pounds; powdered mineral filler, forty-five to fifty-five pounds, mineral fibrous material, twenty to thirty pounds, soluble glass, two to foui quarts of a 30° Baumé to 35° Baumé solution

The asbestos may in some cases be omitted when a cheaper pioduct is desired, though the composition is not then so efficient for the lagging of surfaces subjected to high temperatures

These ingredients are mixed with a quantity of water

252

sufficient to form a paste or mortar of such consistency as to enable it to be plastered over the surface to be protected It may be applied in one or more coats or layers, in the ordinary manner, according to the nature of the article and the amount of protection required

My composition is light, is fireproof, is a very efficient non-conductor of heat, is impervious to water, adheres without cracking when it dries to the surface to which it is applied, and, as a whole, possesses in a high degree all the desired properties of a lagging for steam heated surfaces

I claim ·

1 A plastic composition adapted to form a light weight, fireproof, and waterproof lagging for steam heated surfaces, comprising a vegetable fibrous material, a mineral filler in powdered form and a mineral cementing substance

2. A plastic composition adapted to form a lagging for steam pipes and the like comprising forty to sixty pounds of paper-pulp, forty-five to fifty-five pounds of powdered soapstone, and two to four quarts of a 30° Baumé to 35° Baumé solution of soluble glass.

3 A plastic composition consisting of a vegetable fibrous material, a powdered mineral filler, a mineral fibrous material and a mineral cementing substance substantially as described

4 A plastic composition consisting of fifty pounds of paper pulp, fifty pounds of powdered soapstone, twenty-five pounds of asbestos fiber and three quarts of a 33° Baumé solution of soluble glass.

16 For a Design.

To all whom it may concern·

Be it known that I,   , a citizen of the United States, residing at   , in the county of .   .   , and State of ...   (or subject, etc.), have invented a new, original, and ornamental Design for Watch-

Cases, of which the following is a specification, reference being had to the accompanying drawing, forming part thereof

The figure is a plan view of a watch case, showing my new design

I claim

The ornamental design for a watch case, as shown.

. . . .

17. For a Caveat.

This form is obsolete, law relating to caveats repealed by Act of July 1, 1910

OATHS

18. Oath to Accompany an Application for United States Patent.

. . . . } *ss:*
. . . .

. . . . ,[1] the above-named petitioner.., being sworn (or affirmed), depose and say that . . . .
. . . . citizen.. of[2] . . . and resident . of[3] . ,
that . . . . verily believe . to be the original, first, and[4] . inventor. of the improvement in[5] . . described and claimed in the annexed specification, that . . do not know and do not believe that the same was ever known or used before . . . .
invention or discovery thereof, or patented or described in any printed publication in any country before . invention or discovery thereof, or more than two years

[1] If the inventor be dead the oath will be made by the administrator, if insane, by the guardian conservator, or legal representative In either case the affiant will declare his belief that the party named as inventor was the original and first inventor

[2] If the applicant be an alien, state of what foreign country he is a citizen or subject

[3] Give residence address in full, as "a resident of in the county of , and State of ," or 'of No Street, in the city of , county of , and State (Kingdom, Republic, or Empire) of . . . . .

[4] "Sole" or "joint"

[5] Insert title of invention

254

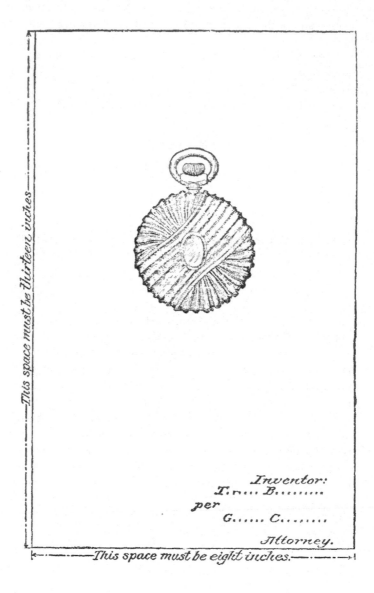

This space must be thirteen inches

Inventor:
I. r.... B..........
per
G...... C..........

Attorney.

This space must be eight inches.

255

prior to this application, or in public use or on sale in the United States for more than two years prior to this application; that said invention has not been patented in any country foreign to the United States on an application filed by   or . . . . legal representatives or assigns more than twelve months prior to this application, and that no application for patent on said improvement has been filed by ..... or . . representatives or assigns in any country foreign to the United States, except as follows.[6] . . . . .

Inventor's full name [7] $\left\{\begin{array}{l}\text{. . . \quad . . .\quad . . \quad. . . . . .}\\ \text{. \quad . \quad . . .}\end{array}\right.$

Sworn to and subscribed before me this .   . day of
.   , 19..

[SEAL]
           . . . .
           [Signature of justice or notary]
           [8]
         . . .   .
           [Official character]

19. Oath to Accompany an Application for United States Patent for Design.

. . . . $\left.\begin{array}{l}\\ \\ \end{array}\right\}$ ss.
. . . .

. . . ,[1] the above-named petitioner ., being sworn (or affirmed), depose. and say.. that . . . ...,
. citizen.. of[2] ...... and resident.. of[3] ......,

6Name each country in which an application has been filed, and in each case give date of filing the same If no application has been filed, erase the words "except as follows "

7All oaths must bear the signature of the affiant

8* * * "When the person before whom the oath or affirmation is made is not provided with a seal his official character shall be established by competent evidence as by a certificate from a clerk of a court of record or other proper officer having a seal '

A certificate of the official character of a magistrate, stating date of appointment and term of office may be filed in the Patent Office, which will obviate the necessity of separate certificates in individual cases

When the oath is taken abroad before a notary public, judge, or magistrate, his authority should in each instance be proved by a certificate of a diplomatic or consular officer of the United States

1If the inventor be dead, the oath will be made by the administrator, if insane, by the guardian, conservator, or legal representative In either case the affiant will declare his belief that the party named as inventor was the original and first inventor

2If the applicant be an alien, state of what foreign country he is a citizen or subject.

3Give residence address in full. as "a resident of ...., in the

that   verily believe   to be the original, first, and [4]... .. inventor of the design for [5]   .

. . described and claimed in the annexed specification, that . .. do.. not know and do not believe
that the same was ever known or used before   . invention thereof, of patented or described in any printed
publication in any country before   . invention thereof, or more than two years prior to this application, or
in public use or on sale in the United States for more
than two years prior to this application, that said design has not been patented in any country foreign to the
United States on an application filed by .   or   .
legal representatives or assigns more than four months
prior to this application, and that no application for
patent on said design has been filed by ..... or ......
representatives or assigns in any country foreign to the
United States, except as follows.[6] .. ...

Inventor's full name [7] $\left\{ \right.$.   .. .

                                                    .

Sworn to and subscribed before me this   . day of
  . ., 19 .

[SEAL]   [8]   .

[Signature of justice or notary]

.. ..

[Official character]

---

county of   . , and State of   ,' or "of No
Street, in the city of   , county of   and State (Kingdom, Republic, or Empire) of   "
   4"Sole" or "joint "
   5Insert title of invention
   6Name each country in which an application has been filed, and in
each case give date of filing the same If no application has been filed,
erase the words "except as follows "
   7All oaths must bear the signature of the affiant
   8* * * 'When the person before whom the oath or affirmation is
made is not provided with a seal his official character shall be established by competent evidence as by a certificate from a clerk of a court
of record or other proper officer having a seal "
   A certificate of the official character of a magistrate, stating date of
appointment and term of office, may be filed in the Patent Office, which
will obviate the necessity of separate certificates in individual cases
   When the oath is taken abroad before a notary public, judge, or magistrate his authority should in each instance be proved by a certificate
of a diplomatic or consular officer of the United States

20 By an Applicant for a Reissue (Inventor).

[When the original patent is claimed to be inoperative or invalid "by reason of the patentee claiming as his own invention or discovery more than he had a right to claim as new," this form can be modified accordingly.]

. . . . } *ss:*

. . . . , the above-named petitioner, being duly sworn (or affirmed), deposes and says that he does verily believe himself to be the original, first, and[1] . inventor of the improvement set forth and claimed in the foregoing specification and for which improvement he solicits a patent, that deponent does not know and does not believe that said improvement was ever before known or used, that deponent is a citizen of the United States of America, and resides at .   , in the county of . . . and State of . . . . . ;[2] that deponent verily believes that the letters patent referred to in the foregoing petition and specification and herewith surrendered are inoperative (or invalid), for the reason that the specification thereof is defective (or insufficient), and that such defect (or insufficiency) consists particularly in[3] . . . . , and deponent further says that the errors which render such patent so inoperative (or invalid) arose from inadvertence (or accident, or mistake), and without any fraudulent or deceptive intention on the part of deponent,[4] that the following is a true specification of the errors which it is claimed constitute such inadvertence (or accident, or mistake) relied upon[3] . . . ; that such errors so particularly specified arose (or occurred) as follows:[3]   .. . .

Inventor's full name { . . .   .
                       { . . . .

Subscribed and sworn to before me this ..   day of , 19

[SEAL.]

. . . .
[Signature of Justice or Notary]

.   . . .
[Official character]

---

1 "Solo" or "joint"   2 Rule 46   3 Rule 87   4 Rule 87 (5)

258

21. By an Applicant for a Reissue (Assignee)

. . . . } ss·

. . . . , the above-named petitioner, being duly sworn (or affirmed), deposes and says that he verily believes that the aforesaid letters patent granted to   .
are (here follows Form 20, the necessary changes being made) , that the entire title to said letters patent is vested in him, and that he verily believes the said   . .   to be the first and original inventor of the invention set forth and claimed in the foregoing amended specification, and that the said   .   is now deceased

. . . .
Sworn to and subscribed before me this . . . . . . day of . . . ., 19 . .

[SEAL]

. . . .
[Signature of justice or notary]

. .   . .
[Official character]

22. Supplemental Oath to Accompany a Claim for Matter Disclosed But Not Claimed in an Original Application.

. . . . } ss:
. . . .

. . . ., whose application for letters patent for an improvement in   . . , serial No. . . . . , was filed in the United States Patent Office on or about the . . . day of . . . . , 19 , being duly sworn (or affirmed), deposes and says that the subject matter of the foregoing amendment was part of his invention, was invented before he filed his original application, above identified, for such invention, was not known or used before his invention, was not patented or described in a printed publication in any country more than two years before his application, was not patented in a foreign

259

country on an application filed by himself or his legal representatives or assigns more than twelve months before his application, was not in public use or on sale in this country for more than two years before the date of his application, and has not been abandoned

Sworn to and subscribed before me this . . day of 19

[SEAL]

[Signature of justice or notary]

[Official character]

23. Oath as to the Loss of Letters Patent.

⎱ ss:

.. .. ., being duly sworn (or affirmed), depose and say. that the letters patent No ... ., granted to him, and bearing date on the ..... day of .. ., 19. , have been either lost or destroyed, that he has made diligent search for the said letters patent in all places where the same would probably be found, if existing, and that he has not been able to find them.

Subscribed and sworn to before me this . day of . .: , 19.

[SEAL]

[Signature of justice or notary]

[Official character]

24 Oath of Adminsitartor as to the Loss of Letters Patent

⎱ ss:

. . , being duly sworn, depose. and say.. that he is administrator of the estate of . . . . ., deceased, late of . .. in said county. that the letters patent No ......, granted to said . .. ., and

bearing date of the   day of .   , 19 , have been
lost or destroyed as he verily believes; that he has made
diligent search for the said letters patent in all places
where the same would probably be found, if existing, and
especially among the papers of the decedent, and that he
has not been able to find said letters patent

                                        .   .   . ,
                                    Administrator, etc
Subscribed and sworn to before me this   day of
.. ..., 19..

                              .   . .   .   .
                              [Signature of justice or notary]
                                .   .   . . .
                                    [Official character]

25 Power of Attorney After Application Filed

[If the power of attorney be given at any time other than that of
making application for letters patent, it will be in substantially the following form]

To the Commissioner of Patents

The undersigned having, on or about the   .   day
of . ., 19—, made application for letters patent for
an improvement in   .   (serial number   . .),
hereby appoints ....,[1] of   .   , in the county
of .   . and State of   ...   his attorney, with full
power of substitution and revocation, to prosecute said
application, to make alterations and amendments therein to receive the patent, and to transact all business in
the Patent Office connected therewith.

Signed at   , in the county of   , State of
. ., this . . . day of . . ., 19 .

26. Revocation of Power of Attorney

To the Commissioner of Patents:

The undersigned having, on or about the   . day
of . ., 19 ., appointed . . . . . , of .   , in
the county of   and State of   . , his attorney to

───────────────

1If the power of attorney be to a firm, the name of each member of
the firm must be given in full

261

prosecute an application for letters patent, which application was filed on or about the . . . day of . . . ., 19. , for an improvement in . (serial number .), hereby revokes the power of attorney then given

Signed at . ., in the county of and State of , this . . day of . . ., 19. .

. . . .

27. Amendment.[1]

To the Commissioner of Patents

In the matter of my application for letters patent for an improvement in . ., filed . . , 19 (serial number .), I hereby amend my specification as follows

By striking out all between the and . . . . lines, inclusive, of page ;

By inserting the words ". .. ... ," after the word ". ," in the . line of the . claim: and

By striking out the . claim and substituting therefor the following:

. . ..

Signed at , in the county of . ... . and State of . ....

. . . . ,

By .. . .,
His Attorney in Fact

DISCLAIMERS

28. Disclaimer After Patent

To the Commissioner of Patents

Your petitioner, ... , a citizen of the United States, residing at .. . in the county of and State of ... (or subject, etc), represents that in the

---

[1] In the preparation of all amendments a separate paragraph should be devoted to each distinct erasure or insertion, in order to aid the office in making the entry of the amendment into the case to which it pertains

262

matter of a certain improvement in .   , for which
letters patent of the United States No.   .   were granted
to   . .. .., on the . .. .day of . .. ., 19 , he is
(here state the exact interest of the disclaimant, if assignee, set out liber and page where assignment is recorded), and that he has reason to believe that through
inadvertence (accident or mistake) the specification and
claim of said letters patent are too broad, including that
of which said patentee was not the first inventor Your
petitioner, therefore, hereby enters this disclaimer to that
part of the claim in said specification which is in the following words, to wit:

. ...
Signed at ...   ., in the county of   ...., and State
of   ..., this .. . day of ......, 19..
                                   . .   .   . ..
Witnesses ·

. .   .. .

.   .   .

29. Disclaimer During Interference.

Interference

. .   . .⎫
              vs   ⎬ Before the examiner of interfer-
.   . ..   ..⎭   ences

Subject matter .... .
To the Commissioner of Patents:
SIR: In the matter of the interference above noted,
under the provisions of and for the purpose set forth
in Rule 107, I disclaim (set forth the matter as given in
declaration of interference), as I am not the first inventor thereof
Signed at   , in the county of   .., and State
of . .. , this   . day of   . , 19 .
                                . .. .
Witnesses.

.. ..

.. ..

APPEALS AND PETITIONS.

30. From a Principal Examiner to the Examiners in Chief

To the Commissioner of Patents.

SIR: I hereby appeal to the Examiners in Chief from the decision of the Principal Examiner in the matter of my application for letters patent for an improvement in . . . . . , filed . . , 19 , serial number , which on the . day of . . , 19 , was rejected the second time The following are the points of the decision on which the appeal is taken (Here follows a statement of the points on which the appeal is taken)

Signed at , in the county of . , and State of . ., this day of . . ., 19.

. . . .

31. From the Examiner in Charge of Interferences to the Examiners in Chief.

To the Commissioner of Patents·

SIR I hereby appeal to the Examiners in Chief from the decision of the Examiner of Interferences in the matter of the interference between my applications for letters patent for improvement in . . . and the letters patent of , in which priority of invention was awarded to said . The following are assigned as reasons of appeal· (Here should follow an explicit statement of alleged errors in the decision of the Examiner of Interferences.)

Signed at . . . , in the county of ., and State of ., this day of . . ., 19..

32. From the Examiners in Chief to the Commissioner in Ex Parte Cases.

To the Commissioner of Patents·

SIR I hereby appeal to the Commissioner in person from the decision of the Examiners in Chief in the matter of my application for letters patent for an improve

ment in   . , filed   , 19 ., serial number   .   The following are assigned as reasons of
appeal   (Here follow the reason as in Form 30.)
     Signed at   . , in the county of   .   . , and State
of   . ., this   day of   ...., 19 .

                                   . . .   .

33. From the Examiners in Chief to the Commissioner in Interference Cases.

To the Commissioner of Patents

     SIR I hereby appeal to you in person from the deci-
sion of the Examiners in Chief, made .. .., 19. , in the
interference between my application for letters patent for
improvement in .   .   ..   and the letters patent of
.. .., in which priority of invention was awarded to said .   The following are assigned
as reasons of appeal· (Here should follow an explicit
statement of the alleged errors in the decision of the
Examiners in Chief.)
     Signed at .   .   ., in the county of . ... , and State
of ....., this .. .. day of ..   , 19 .

                                  .   .   .   .

34. Petition From a Principal Examiner to the Commissioner

     Application of . . ..
     Serial number ...   .
     Subject of invention   ..   ..

To the Commissioner of Patents:

     Your petitioner avers—
     First That he is the applicant above named
     Second. That said application was filed on the .....
day of .   .   , 19.
     Third. That when so filed said application contained.
     .. claims
     Fourth. That your petitioner was informed by office

letter of the   , 19 ., (1) that his   .
claim was rendered vague and indefinite by the employment of the words "   .   ," which words should
be erased, (2) that his   . claim was met by certain
references which were given, and (3) that the ...
claim was mere surplusage and should be eliminated.

    Fifth   That on the   ⁀ day of . . ... your peti-
tioner filed an amendment so eliminating his .
claim, and accompanied such amendment with a communication in which he declined to amend such   . .
claim, and asked for another action thereon

    Sixth   That your petitioner was then informed by of-
fice letter of the .. ... day of .. . that the former
requirement relating to claim ..   would be adhered
to, and that no action would be had on the merits of
either claim until said amendment so required had been
made

    Wherefore your petitioner requests that the Examiner
in charge of such application be advised that such amendment so required by him to said   claim be not insisted upon and directed to proceed to examine both said
remaining claims upon their merits

    A hearing of this petition is desired on the .   day
of   , 19.

.   ,
Applicant.

. ... ⁀ · · ,
    Attorney for Applicant

35. Petition for Copies of Rejected and Abandoned Appli-cations.

To the Commissioner of Patents·

    The petition of .... , a resident of ..   , in
the county of   and State of .   , respectfully
shows·

    First   That on the ..   day of   .. 19   , pat-
ent No   .., issued to one . ..   . .

Second That your petitioner is informed and believes that on the   day of .. ..., 19 , said patentee filed in the United States Patent Office an application for patent for improvement in .   ..

Third. That your petitioner verily believes that said application has not been prosecuted during the past two years and upward, and he also verily believes that the last action had therein was on or about the   . day of   , 19...

Fourth That said application has therefore become and now stands abandoned

Fifth That on the ... .. day of ...   , 19 , said patentee began suit, in the Circuit Court of the United States for the . ..   district of   . , against your petitioner, which suit is based upon said patent, and the same is now pending and undetermined

Sixth Your petitioner is informed and believes that to enable him to prepare and conduct his defense in such suit it is material and necessary that he be allowed access to and copies of the files of such abandoned case.

Seventh Your petitioner therefore requests that he or   .. , in his behalf and as his attorney, be permitted to inspect and be furnished copies of all or any portion of such case

....,
Petitioner

By .. ..,
His Attorney

. . . .⎫
....⎭ *ss*·

On this ....   day of .   , 19 , before me, a notary public in and for said county and State, personally appeared   , the above-named attorney, who, being by me duly sworn, deposes and says that he has read the foregoing petition and knows its contents, and that the same is true, except as to the matters therein stated on in-

267

formation or belief, and as to those matters he believes it to be true

⟋ . . .,

Notary Public

36 Preliminary Statement of Domestic Inventor.

. . . . . ⎧Interference in the United States
  vs ⎨ Patent Office
. . . . . . ⎩Preliminary statement of . . . . . .

. . .   . , of   . , in the county of   . , and State of   . , being duly sworn (or affirmed), doth depose and say that he is a party to the interference declared by the Commissioner of Patents   , 19 ., between   . .   's application for letters patent, filed   . , 19 , serial number .   , and the patent to .   . , granted . .   . , 19 , numbered .   , for a   .   ., that he conceived the invention set forth in the declaration of interference[1] on or about the   . day of   . , 19. ; that on or about the   . . day of   , 19 , he first made drawings of the invention (if he has not made a drawing, then he should say that no drawing of the invention in issue has been made) . that on the . . . . day of . . .   ., 19 ., he made the first written description of the invention (if he has not made a written description of the invention, he should so state) . that on or about the . . .   . day of . . . . . ., 19 . , he first explained the invention to others , that he first embodied his invention in a full-size machine, which was completed about the   day of   , 19 , and that on the

[1] If the party has doubts as to whether the matter of his application is properly involved in the issue as declared, then in lieu of the term "the invention set forth in the declaration of interference," he may say "the invention contained in the claims of my application (or patent) declared to be involved in this interference," and should specify such claims by number

. day of   , 19 , the said machine was first successfully operated, in the town of .. . , county of .. , and State of   , and that he has since continued to use the same, and that he has manufactured others for use and sale to the following extent, viz (if he has not embodied the invention in a full-size machine, he should so state, and if he has embodied it but has not used it, he should so state)

. .   . .
[Signature of inventor]

Subscribed and sworn to before me this   .   day of . . ., 19 .

. . . .
[Signature of justice or notary]

.. .   .
[Official character]

37 Preliminary Statement of Foreign Inventor

.   .. .   .   . ⎧Interference in United States
        vs   ⎨   Patent Office.
. . . . ⎩Preliminary statement of .. .

.. . . , of London, in the county of Middlesex, England, being duly sworn, doth depose and say that he is a party to the interference declared by the Commissioner of Patents,   , 19 , between his application for patent, filed   , 19 , serial number ': , and the patent of ..   ., granted   . , 19 , No   , for an improvement in   .   ., that he made the invention set forth in the declaration of interference,[1] being at that time in England; that patents for such invention were applied for and obtained as follows·

Application filed in Great Britain, .. . , 19 , patent dated . . , 19 ., No   .. . , published the . day of .. . , 19.., and sealed the . . . . . day of .. . . ,

---

[1] If the party has doubts as to whether the matter of his application is properly involved in the issue as declared then in lieu of the terms "the invention set forth in the declaration of interference," he may say 'the invention contained in the claims of my application (or patent) declared to be involved in this interference," and should specify such claims by number

269

19 , application filed in France . , 19 , patent dated . , 19 , No . , published the . day of .. . , 19 , and sealed the . . day of . , 19.. (If a patent has not been obtained in any country it should be so stated)

That such invention was fully described in a magazine published at ... ., on the . day of . .., 19 , by .. . . .., entitled .. . . . (see page . . of such magazine), and in the following newspapers. . . ... , of . , 19 ., . . , published at . , on . , 19.. (If the invention was never described in a printed publication it should be so stated)

The knowledge of such invention was introduced into the United States under the following circumstances. On . . , 19 ., the said .. .. .. wrote a letter to . .. , residing at .., State of .. , describing such invention and soliciting his services in procuring a patent therefor in the United States   This letter, he is informed and believes, was received by the said . . .. . . on , 19 . Also on .. .. 19 , he wrote a letter to the firm of . . ., of . . , State of . . , describing such invention and requesting their assistance in manufacturing and putting it on the market, which letter, he is informed and believes, was received by them on , 19 Such invention was manufactured by such firm and described in their trade circulars, as he is informed and verily believes, on or about the . ... day of .... , 19 (If the invention has not been introduced into the United States otherwise than by the application papers, it should be so stated, and the date at which such papers were received in the United States alleged)

. . . . . .

[Signature of inventor]

270

Subscribed and sworn to before me this . . day of
. . , 19...

. . . .
. . . .

ASSIGNMENTS.

38 Of an Entire Interest in an Invention Before the Issue of Letters Patent.

Whereas I,   . 　　　　, of   . . , county of . . .
and State of 　　　, have invented a certain improvement in 　　　, for which I am about to make application for letters patent of the United States, and whereas
.. .. .. , of 　 . , county of   . . , and State
of . . , is desirous of acquiring an interest therein.

Now, therefore, in consideration of .   dollars, the
receipt of which is hereby acknowledged, I,   . .
   . , by these presents do sell, assign, and transfer
unto .   . . .   the full and exclusive right to the
said invention, as described in the specification executed
by me on the .   day of   . , 19 , preparatory to
obtaining letters patent of the United States therefor,
and I hereby request the Commissioner of Patents to
issue said letters patent to .... 　 . ... as the assignee,
for his interest, for the sole use and behoof of said
 . .   . . and his legal representatives

Executed 　 . day of 　 .., 19 .

 ..   . . . [SEAL.]

In presence of—

 .. ... .

 .   ..

(If assignment, grant, or conveyance be acknowledged as provided for
by Rule 185, the certificate will be *prima facie* evidence of the execution
of such assignment, grant, or conveyance)

271

39 Of the Entire Interest in Letters Patent.

Whereas I, ..., of . . . ., county of . . . . . ,
State of .   ., did obtain letters patent of the United
States for an improvement in   . , which letters patent are numbered . . . , and bear date the .   . . . day
of . . ., 19. , and whereas I am now the sole owner
of said patent, and whereas . .   . , of . . . . . ., county
of   ., and State of   . ., is desirous of acquiring
the entire interest in the same

Now, therefore, in consideration of the sum of
dollars, the receipt of which is hereby acknowledged, I,
           . .   , by these presents do sell, assign, and
transfer unto the said   . .   , the whole right,
title, and interest in and to the said letters patent therefor aforesaid, the same to be held and enjoyed by the
said . . . . , for his own use and behoof, and for
his legal representatives, to the full end of the term for
which said letters patent are granted, as fully and entirely as the same would have been held by me had this
assignment and sale not been made

Executed . . . . . day of . . . . , 19. .

                                  . . . .   [L s]

In presence of

     . . . .

     . . . .
(See note under Form 38)

40. Of an Undivided Interest in Letters Patent.

Whereas I, ... , of . . . . . ., county of
.   ., State of   . . ., did obtain letters patent of the
United States for an improvement in . . . , which letters patent are numbered   . . , and bear date the
. . . day of . . .,   . ; and whereas . . . . ,
of .   , county of   , State of   , is desirous
of acquiring an interest in the same·

Now, therefore, in consideration of the sum of .
dollars, the receipt of which is hereby acknowledged, I

.   .   , by these presents do sell, assign, and transfer unto the said   .   .   , the undivided one-half part of the whole right, title, and interest in and to the said invention and in and to the letters patent therefor aforesaid, the said undivided one-half part to be held by ...., for his own use and behoof, and his legal representatives, to the full end of the term for which said letters patent are granted, as fully and entirely as the same would have been held by me had this assignment and sale not been made

Executed   .   day of   .   ., 19

.   .   [L s]

In presence of—

.

.   .

(See note under Form 38)

41. Territorial Interest After Grant of Patent.

Whereas I,   .   , of   .   ., county of   .   .,
State of .   ., did obtain letters patent of the United States for an improvement in   .   . ...., which letters patent are numbered   .   . and bear date the   .   .   .
day of   ., in the year 19   , and whereas I am now the sole owner of the said patent and of all rights under the same in the below-recited territory, and whereas   .   .   , of   , county of .   .   , State of   .   , is desirous of acquiring an interest in the same :

Now, therefore for and in consideration of the sum of .   .   .. dollars to me in hand paid, the receipt of which is hereby acknowledged, I   .   .   , by these presents do sell, assign, and transfer unto the said ......

all the right, title, and interest in and to the said invention, as secured to me by said letters patent, for, to, and in the State of   .. . and for, to, or in no other place or places, the same to be held by ....
within and throughout the above-specified territory, but not elsewhere, for his own use and behoof, and of his

legal representatives, to the full end of the term for which said letters patent are granted, as fully and entirely as the same would have been held by me had this assignment and sale not been made

Executed ...... day of ......, 19..

.... [L s]

In presence of—

. . .

. . . .

(See note under Form 38.)

42. License—Shop-Right.

In consideration of the sum of dollars, to be paid by the firm of . .. .. , of ., in the county of . , State of , I do hereby license and empower the said . .. to manufacture in said (or other place agreed upon) the improvement in . , for which letters patent of the United States No .. were granted to me the day of . . in the year 19 , and to sell the machines so manufactured throughout the United States to the full end of the term for which said letters patent are granted.

Signed at ...., in the county of ... ... and State of . ... , this .. .. day of . ..., 19...

....

In presence of—

.. ... .

... .

43 License—Not Exclusive—With Royalty.

This agreement, made this . day of . , 19 , between . . , of . ....., in the county of . and State of .. ., party of the first part, and . . . .. , of , in the county of .. . . and State of .... , party of the second part, witnesseth, that whereas letters patent of the United States No . ., for improvement in . . , were granted

274

to the party of the first part in the   day of   ,
19   , and whereas the party of the second part is desirous of manufacturing   .   .   . containing said patented improvements: Now, therefore, the parties have
agreed as follows.

I   The party of the first part hereby licenses and
empowers the party of the second part to manufacture
subject to the conditions hereinafter named, at their fac-
tory in   , and in no other place or places, to the
end of the term for which said letters patent were granted, ... containing the patented improvements,
and to sell the same within the United States

II   The party of the second part agrees to make full
and true returns to the party of the first part, under
oath, upon the first days of   and .   . in each
year, of all   .   containing the patented improvements manufactured by them

III   The party of the second part agrees to pay to
the party of the first part   .   dollars as a license fee
upon every   manufactured by said party of the
second part containing the patented improvements,
provided, that if the said fee be paid upon the days provided herein for semi-annual returns, or within ..
days thereafter, a discount of   .   per cent shall be
made from said fee for prompt payment

IV   Upon a failure of the party of the second part to
make returns or to make payment of license fees, as
herein provided, for .   .   days after the days herein
named, the party to the first part may terminate this license by serving a written notice upon the party of the
second part, but the party of the second part shall not
thereby be discharged from any liability to the party of
the first part for any license fees due at the time of the
service of said notice

In witness whereof the parties above named have here-

unto set their hands the day and year first above written
at . . . , in the county of   and State of   .

                              .. ..
                              . . ..

    In the presence of—

        ....
        . .. .

DEPOSITIONS.

44. Notice of Taking Testimony.

                      . .. , .   ., . . , 19
In the matter of the interference between the application
    of . .... for a .. . . machine and the patent
    No .   ., granted .. .., 19. , to .... ,
    now pending before the Commissioner of Patents

    Sir. You are hereby notified that on Wednesday,
        ., 19 ., at the office of . . . . . . , Esq , No
        . Street,   ,   . at   .   o'clock in the
    forenoon, I shall proceed to take the testimony of   ..
        . , residing at   . .   , and . .   . , resid-
    ing at   . . , all of   .. , as witnesses in my be-
    half

    The examination will continue from day to day until
    completed   You are invited to attend and cross-examine.

                          ....,
                    By .   .   . ,
                          His Attorney
    Signed at .   . , in the county of .   and State
    of   , this   . day of .   , 19 .
    Witnesses·

        .   .

        .   .   .

            Proof of Service

    ...... ⎫
    .. .. ⎬ *ss:*
            ⎭
                      276

Personally appeared before me, a . (or other officer), the above-named . , who, being duly sworn, deposes and says that he served the above notice upon . . . . ., the attorney of the said .. ., at o'clock . .. of the . . day of . . . , 19. , by leaving a copy at his office in . ., in the county of . . and State of .. . , in charge of

. . . .

. . . .

Sworn to and subscribed before me at . . , in the county of and State of .. , this day of .. , 19 ..

[SEAL]

. . . . . .

[Signature of justice or notary]

. . .

[Official character]

(Service may be acknowledged by the party upon whom it is made as follows

Service of the above notice acknowledged this . of . . . . . ., 19...

. . . .,

By . . . . . .,

His Attorney

45. Form of Deposition.

Before the Commissioner of Patents, in the matter of the interference between the application of . . for a . . . . and Letters Patent No . . . granted . . .. , 19 , to . . .

Depositions of witnesses examined on behalf of . . , pursuant to the annexed notice, at the office of . . ., No .. .. Street, . ,

on .. , ... , 19 Present, . , Esq, on behalf of . . . , and . . . . , Esq , on behalf of .

. . . ., being duly sworn (or affirmed), doth depose and say, in answer to interrogatories proposed to

277

him by . . , Esq , counsel for . . ,
as follows, to wit .

Question 1 What is your name, age, occupation, and residence?

Answer 1 My name is . . . , I am . years of age; I am a manufacturer of . and reside at , in the State of . . .

Question 2, etc ....

....

And in answer to cross-interrogatories proposed to him by . , Esq , counsel for ...., he saith .

Cross-question 1 How long have you known .
..... ?

Answer 1 . . ..

....

46. Certificate of Officer

[To follow deposition]

. . .. ⎫
             ⎬ ss:
. . .. ⎭

I, .. , a notary public within and for the county of and State of .. (or other officer, as the case may be), do hereby certify that the foregoing deposition of .... was taken on behalf of .... in pursuance of the notice hereto annexed, before me, at .. , in the city of .. , in said county, on the .. day (or days) of ., 19 , that said witness was by me duly sworn before the commencement of his testimony, that the testimony of said witness was written out by myself (or by .. . . in my presence), that the opposing party, ..., was present (or absent or represented by counsel) during the taking of said testimony; that said testimony was taken at . , and was commenced at o'clock . on the . of . ., 19 . , was continued pursuant to adjournment on the . , . .

278

(etc), and was concluded on the .. of said month; that the deposition was read by, or to, each witness before the witness signed the same, that I am not connected by blood or marriage with either of said parties, nor interested directly or indirectly in the matter in controversy.

In testimony whereof I have hereunto set my hand and affixed by seal of office at ......, in said county, this . . day of , 19. .

[SEAL]

.. . ..
[Signature of justice or notary]

. . . .
[Official character]

(The magistrate will then append to the deposition the notice under which it was taken, and will seal up the testimony and direct it to the Commissioner of Patents, placing upon the envelope a certificate in substance as follows.)

I hereby certify that the within deposition of ... .
(if the package contains more than one deposition give all the names), relating to the matter of interference between .... and ...., was taken, sealed up, and addressed to the Commissioner of Patents by me this .. day of .... ., 19...

[SEAL]

. . . . . .
[Signature of justice or notary]

. . . . . .
[Official character]

APPEALS FROM THE COMMISSIONER OF PATENTS TO THE COURT OF APPEALS OF THE DISTRICT OF COLUMBIA.

Court Rules.

No. XXI.

APPEALS FROM THE COMMISSIONER OF PATENTS

1 All certified copies of papers and evidence on appeal from the decision of the Commissioner of Patents, authorized by Section 9 of the Act of Congress approved February 9, 1893, shall be received by the clerk of this court, and the cases, by titling and number as they appear on the record in the Patent Office, shall be placed on a separate docket from the docket of the cases brought into this court by appeal from the Supreme Court of the District of Columbia, to be designated as the "Patent Appeal Docket", and upon filing such copies the party appellant shall deposit with the clerk, or secure to be paid as demanded, an amount of money sufficient to cover all legal costs and expenses of said appeal; and upon failure to do so his appeal shall be dismissed The clerk shall under this titling of the case on the docket. make brief entries of all papers filed and of all proceedings had in the case

2 The appellant, upon complying with the preceding section of this rule, shall file in the case a petition addressed to the court, in which he shall briefly set forth and show that he has complied with the requirements of sections 4912 and 4913 of the Revised Statutes of the United States to entitle him to an appeal, and praying that his appeal may be heard upon and for the reasons

assigned therefor to the Commissioner; and said appeal shall be taken within forty days from the date of the ruling or order appealed from and not afterwards

If the petition for an appeal and the certified copies of papers and evidence on appeal mentioned in this and the preceding section of this rule shall not be filed and the case duly docketed in this court within forty days (exclusive of Sundays and legal holidays) from the day upon which notice of appeal is given to the Commissioner of Patents, the commissioner, upon such facts being brought to his attention by motion of the appellee, duly served upon the appellant or his attorney, may take such further proceedings in the case as may be necessary to dispose of the same, as though no notice of appeal had ever been given

3 The clerks shall provide a minute book of his office, in which he shall record every order, rule, judgment, or decree of the court in each case, in the order of time in which said proceedings shall occur, and of this book the index shall be so kept as to show the name of the party applying for the patent, the invention by subject matter or name, and, in the cases of interference, the name of the party with whose pending application or unexpired patent the subsequent application is supposed to interfere

4 The cases on this docket shall be called for argument on the second Monday of January, March, May, and November in each year, and the cases shall be called in regular order as they may stand on the docket   A copy of these rules shall be furnished to the Commissioner of Patents, and it shall be the duty of the clerk of this court to give special notice to the said Commissioner at least fifteen days immediately preceding the times thus respectively fixed for the hearing of said cases; the said notice to name the place of the sitting of the court, the titling of the cases on the docket of this court, the respective numbers thereof, and the number

281

of each case as it appears of record in the Patent Office, and thereupon the Commissioner shall give notice to the parties interested or concerned by notice addressed to them severally by mail

5 The clerk shall furnish to any applicant a copy of any paper in any of said appeals on payment of the legal fees therefor.

6 The appeals from the Commissioner of Patents shall be subject to all the rules of this court provided for other cases therein, except where such rules, from the nature of the case, or by reason of special provisions inconsistent therewith, are not applicable

7 *Models, diagrams, and exhibits of material forming part of the evidence taken in the court below or in the Patent Office in any case pending in this court on writ of error or appeal shall be placed in the custody of the clerk of this court at least three days before the case is heard or submitted.*

8 *All models, diagrams, and exhibits of material placed in the custody of the clerk for the inspection of the court on the hearing of the case must be taken away by the parties within twenty days after the case is decided. When this is not done, it shall be the duty of the clerk to notify the counsel in the case and the Commissioner of Patents, by mail or otherwise, of the requirements of this rule, and if the articles are not removed within ten days after the notice is given, he shall destroy them or make such other disposition of them as to him may seem best*

No. XXII

OPINIONS OF LOWER COURT AND COMMISSIONER OF PATENTS MADE PART OF RECORD

Whenever the judgment, decree, or order appealed from is based upon or has reference to a written opinion filed in the case by the court below, such opinion shall constitute a part of the transcript to be sent to this court, and such opinion, and also the written reasons or grounds assigned by the Commissioner of Patenst in appeals from the Patent Office, shall be printed as part of the record to be printed under Rule 6

* * * * *

No XXVII

SUNDAYS AND LEGAL HOLIDAYS.

That wherever days are mentioned in the foregoing rules as limitations of time, they shall be construed to exclude Sundays and legal holidays, *but to include Saturday half holidays*

Instructions to Appellants.

The Act of Congress creating the Court of Appeals of the District of Columbia, approved February 9, 1893, gives to that court jurisdiction of appeals from final decisions of the Commissioner of Patents both in *ex parte* cases and in interference cases.

Where an appeal of either class is to be prosecuted to the Court of Appeals of the District of Columbia, the first step is to file with the Commissioner of Patents a notice of appeal, together with an assignment of reasons of appeal   This step must be taken within forty days, exclusive of Sundays and legal holidays, *but including Saturday half holidays*, from the date of the decision of the Commissioner of Patents sought to be reviewed

The next step in the prosecution of such an appeal is to file with the clerk of the Court of Appeals of the District of Columbia a certified transcript of the record and proceedings in the Patent Office relating to the case in question, together with a petition for appeal, addressed to the Court of Appeals of the District of Columbia, make a deposit of $15, and have the appearance of a member of the bar of that court entered for the appellant.

The notice of appeal and reasons of appeal required to be served upon the Commissioner of Patents may be

283

signed by the appellant or by his attorney of record in the Patent Office, but the petition for an appeal that is filed in the Court of Appeals of the District of Columbia must be signed by a member of the bar of the Court of Appeals of the District of Columbia, who should enter a regular appearance in the case in the clerk's office.

After the petition for the appeal, the certified transcript, and the docket fee of $15 have been lodged in the office of the clerk of the Court of Appeals of the District of Columbia, the clerk will send to the solicitor of record an estimate of the cost of printing the petition, transcript, etc.

When the amount called for is deposited, the clerk will cause the printing to be done under his supervision, and when the printing is completed the case will be put on the calendar for hearing at the next term at which patent appeals are heard

In interference cases the clerk is authorized to receive printed copies of the evidence, such as have been used in the Patent Office, thus saving to the appellant the cost of reprinting such evidence When such printed copies are supplied, twenty-five copies must be furnished

As above stated, the notice of appeal and the reasons of appeal are required to be filed with the Commissioner of Patents within forty days, exclusive of Sundays and legal holidays, *but including Saturday half holidays*, of the date of the decision appealed from, but the petition for appeal and the certified transcript which are to be filed in the Court of Appeals of the District of Columbia are required to be filed in that court within forty days, exclusive of Sundays and legal holidays, *but including Saturday half holidays*, from the time of the giving of the notice of appeal, that is to say, if the decision complained of was rendered, for instance, on the 1st day of July, 1906, the party aggrieved might file his notice of appeal, with the reasons of appeal, at any time within forty days, exclusive of Sundays and legal holidays, *but*

284

including Saturday half holidays, thereafter; but if he filed his notice of appeal and reasons therefor on the 10th day of July, 1906, he would be required to file his petition for appeal and the certified transcript in the Court of Appeals of the District of Columbia within forty days, exclusive of Sundays and legal holidays, *but including Saturday half holidays,* of the 10th day of July, 1906

For convenience of appellants and to secure uniformity in practice the following forms are suggested as guides in the prosecution of patent appeals·

Forms.

1 FORM OF NOTICE OF APPEAL TO THE COURT OF APPEALS OF THE DISTRICT OF COLUMBIA IN AN EX PARTE CASE, WITH REASONS OF APPEAL AND REQUEST FOR TRANSCRIPT.

In the United States Patent Office

In re application of

. . . .

Serial No . . . . .

Filed . . . . .

Improvements in . . . .

To the Commissioner of Patents:

SIR You are hereby notified of my appeal to the Court of Appeals of the District of Columbia from your decision, rendered on or about the .. day of . . . . . 19 ., rejecting my above-entitled application and refusing me a patent for the invention set forth therein.

The following are assigned as reasons of appeal·

[Here insert in separate counts the specific errors complained of]

. . . . ,

By . . . . ,

· *His Attorney.*

285

2 FORM OF PETITION FOR AN APPEAL TO THE COURT OF APPEALS OF THE DISTRICT OF COLUMBIA IN AN EX PARTE CASE

In the Court of Appeals of the District of Columbia

In re application of

. . . .

Serial No. . . . . .

Filed   .

Improvements in . . . . .

To the Court of Appeals of the District of Columbia:

Your petitioner, . .   , of   , in the county of   .. . and State of .. ., respectfully represents:

That he is the original and first inventor of certain new and useful improvements in . . . .

That on the   .   day of   , 19 , in the manner prescribed by law he presented his application to the Patent Office, praying that a patent be issued to him for the said invention

That such proceedings were had in said office upon said application; that on the .. . day of . . .,19. , it was rejected by the Commissioner of Patents and a patent for said invention was refused him.

That on the . . . . day of . . .., 19.., your petitioner, pursuant to Sections 4912 and 4913, Revised Statutes, United States, gave notice to the Commissioner of Patents of his appeal to this honorable court from his refusal to issue a patent to him for said invention upon said application as aforesaid, and filed with him, in writing, the following reasons of appeal:

[Here recite the reasons of appeal assigned in the notice to the Commissioner]

That the Commissioner of Patents has furnished him a certified transcript of the record and proceedings relating to said application for patent, which transcript is filed herewith and is to be deemed and taken as a part hereof

Wherefore your petitioner prays that his said appeal may be heard upon and for the reasons assigned therefor to the Commissioner as aforesaid, and that said appeal may be determined and the decision of the Commissioner be revised and reversed, that justice may be done in the premises

. . . . . . ,

By .. . .. ,

His Attorney

[To be signed here by a member of the bar of the Court of Appeals of D C]

. . . . . .,

Solicitor and of Counsel

3   FORM OF NOTICE OF APPEAL TO THE COURT OF APPEALS OF THE DISTRICT OF COLUMBIA IN AN INTERFERENCE CASE, WITH REASONS OF APPEAL AND REQUEST FOR TRANSCRIPT

In the United States Patent Office

Before the Commissioner of Patents

. . . .⎱
    vs ⎰ Interference No . Subject-matter ·
. . . .⎰ Improvements in . ..

And now comes ... .. , by . .. ., his attorney, and gives notice to the Commissioner of Patents of his appeal to the Court of Appeals of the District of Columbia from the decision of the said Commissioner, rendered on or about the .. . day of . , 19 , awarding priority of invention to ... . .. in the above-entitled case, and assigns as his reasons of appeal the following:

[Here set out in separate counts the specific errors in the Commissioner s decision complained of]

$$\ldots\ldots\ldots\ldots,$$
By . . . . ,
His Attorney

4. FORM OF PETITION FOR AN APPEAL TO THE COURT OF APPEALS OF THE DISTRICT OF COLUMBIA IN AN INTERFERENCE CASE

In the Court of Appeals of the District of Columbia

In re Interference No. . . . .

$$\ldots\ldots\ldots,$$
Appellant,
vs
. . . .

To the Court of Appeals of the District of Columbia·

Your petitioner, ..., of . . . ., in the county of . . . ., and State of . . . . , respectfully represents.

That he is the original and first inventor of certain new and useful improvements in . . . .

That on the . . day of . . . . , 19. ., in the manner prescribed by law, he presented his application to the Patent Office, praying that a patent be issued to him for the said invention.

That thereafter, to wit, on the . day of , 19 . ., an interference proceeding was instituted and declared between his said application, and a pending application of one , serial No . ., filed . . , for a similar invention

That the subject matter of said interference as set forth in the official declaration was as follows:

[Here state the issues of the interference]

288

That thereafter, to wit, on the . day of ,
19 , the case having been submitted upon the preliminary statements and evidence presented by the parties
thereto, the Examiner of Interferences rendered a decision awarding priority of invention to . .

That, pursuant to the statutes and the rules of practice
in the Patent Office in such case made and provided,
. . . . . appealed from the said adverse decision
of the Examiner of Interferences to the Board of Examiners in Chief, and the case having been argued and submitted to said board, a decision was rendered by said
board on the . day of . ., 19 , affirming (or
reversing) the decision of the Examiner of Interferences

That thereafter, pursuant to said statutes and rules,
. . . . appealed from the said adverse decision
of the Board of Examiners in Chief to the Commissioner
of Patents, and the same coming on to be heard and having been argued and submitted, a decision was, on the
. . day of . . ., 19 , rendered by the Commissioner adverse to your petitioner, affirming (or reversing) the decision of the Board of Examiners in Chief and
awarding priority of invention to the said

That on the . . day of . . . . . . , 19. ., your petitioner, pursuant to Sections 4912 and 4913, Revised Statutes, United States, gave notice to the Commissioner of
Patents of his appeal to this honorable court from his
decision awarding priority of invention to said . .
. . . ., as aforesaid, and filed with him, in writing, the
following reasons of appeal

[Here insert reasons of appeal assigned in notice to Commissioner]

That the Commissioner of Patents has furnished your
petitioner a certified transcript of the record and proceedings relating to said interference case, which transcript is filed herewith and is to be deemed and taken as
a part hereof

Wherefore your petitioner prays that his said appeal

may be heard upon and for the reasons assigned theretor to the Commissioner, as aforesaid, and that said appeal may be determined and the decision of the commissioner be revised and reversed, that justice may be done in the premises.

. ...,

By ....,

His Attorney

[To be signed here by a member of the bar of the Court of Appeals of D C]

. ..,

Solicitor and of Counsel.

INDEX TO RULES.

291

293

301

304

INDEX TO FORMS.

INDEX TO RULES, INSTRUCTIONS, AND FORMS IN APPEALS TO COURT OF APPEALS OF THE DISTRICT OF COLUMBIA

GENERAL INDEX.

314

315

317

318

323

CPSIA information can be obtained
at www.ICGtesting.com
Printed in the USA
BVOW06*0616090118
504816BV00008BA/36/P